Tradition in Creative Writing

"Adrian May argues passionately for innovating through tradition, from ancient myths and stories, legends, ghost stories, and ballads; he draws on a wonderfully rich array of sources and quotations, old and new, and emphasises the writing of place, its memories, customs, and rituals. Combining humour and seriousness, this manual will prove a stimulus to much creative energy—and enjoyment—in the classroom."

—Dame Marina Warner, *Professor of English and Creative Writing, Birkbeck College, University of London; Distinguished Fellow, All Souls College, Oxford; and President of the Royal Society of Literature, UK*

"Very wise and exciting. May suggests how writing, informed by a sense of tradition, can be revolutionary (as opposed to the narcissistic and merely rebellious gesture which would devalue and discard knowledge and forms discovered, by others, in and from the past). This book provides a series of lively and approachable practical examples of imaginative alchemy: how engaging actively with tradition can generate a liberatingly prismatic sense of time and place: where the supposedly immediate linear priorities of 'here and now' can be examined more widely, in artful three-dimensional ways, to generate compelling new questions and initiatives; and thus make spaces (both personal and communal) for renewal."

—David Ian Rabey, *Professor of Theatre and Theatre Practice, Aberystwyth University, UK*

"This is a book I will use to reconnect myself and my Creative Writing students with the layered histories and communal spirit of storytelling. Full of original insight and useful writing inspiration for all writers at all stages of their careers, celebrating the richly entangled roots of storytelling and the pleasures of writing. A glorious and enduring way of looking at writing."

—Amanda Hodgkinson, *award winning novelist and Course Leader for MA Creative and Critical Writing, University of Suffolk, UK*

"Tradition is not a set of rules, archaic and out of touch, says Adrian May, but a living, breathing thing, with deep roots waiting to sustain us. Where are *your* roots? he asks the writer, and his new book—wise, human, and persuasive—is an excellent guide to help you find them."

—Norman Schwenk, *poet and formerly Convenor of Creative Writing, Cardiff University, UK*

Adrian May

Tradition in Creative Writing

Finding Inspiration Through Your Roots

Adrian May
University of Essex
Colchester, UK

ISBN 978-3-030-74775-6   ISBN 978-3-030-74776-3 (eBook)
https://doi.org/10.1007/978-3-030-74776-3

© The Editor(s) (if applicable) and The Author(s), under exclusive license to Springer Nature Switzerland AG 2021
This work is subject to copyright. All rights are solely and exclusively licensed by the Publisher, whether the whole or part of the material is concerned, specifically the rights of translation, reprinting, reuse of illustrations, recitation, broadcasting, reproduction on microfilms or in any other physical way, and transmission or information storage and retrieval, electronic adaptation, computer software, or by similar or dissimilar methodology now known or hereafter developed.
The use of general descriptive names, registered names, trademarks, service marks, etc. in this publication does not imply, even in the absence of a specific statement, that such names are exempt from the relevant protective laws and regulations and therefore free for general use.
The publisher, the authors and the editors are safe to assume that the advice and information in this book are believed to be true and accurate at the date of publication. Neither the publisher nor the authors or the editors give a warranty, expressed or implied, with respect to the material contained herein or for any errors or omissions that may have been made. The publisher remains neutral with regard to jurisdictional claims in published maps and institutional affiliations.

Cover design by eStudio Calamar & Illustration by gaga.vastard

This Palgrave Macmillan imprint is published by the registered company Springer Nature Switzerland AG
The registered company address is: Gewerbestrasse 11, 6330 Cham, Switzerland

*From everyone who passed it on I learn—
To everyone I pass it on in turn.*

Preface

Who is *Tradition in Creative Writing* for?

All writers can benefit from the tradition of writing and writers continually return to the roots of literature, storytelling and song for rekindling their imagination. Working with the idea of tradition can also light up all aspects of our lives and writings. Students and teachers of creative writing at all adult levels can learn from this linked-up share in their own traditional connections and actually take them into their practice as a way of looking at their present world, as well as at the past. Anyone who wants to explore their writing world through the connective ideas here will learn to see these hidden aspects of life in a useful way, to provide them with insight, inspiration and practicality.

When a folksinger sings a traditional song, she feels the strength of the past singers with her and likewise that the communication is being passed along into future singers, back into the community. This communal inspiration allows singers, as it allows any artist, to feel their work is wider in appeal and not about the isolation, or glorification of the self but the celebration of mankind. The four sections of the book move from reclaiming the known aspects of tradition (I: Literary and Historical Traditions) to the experiential (II: Folk and Song Traditions); thence to the personal and natural (III: Tradition, Self and Nature) and back to the universal and communal (IV: Tradition and Community). Chapter 14: Conclusions and Occlusions, where critiques are addressed, deals with the way tradition takes into account the relation of the self to the wider whole and to the other and how this has the most powerful implications. Tradition can then be seen in cross-cultural respectfulness for time-honoured aspects of all arts, a kind of universal language, where locality is universal, where we have all things in common.

For a brief summary of each chapter, see 'How to use the book', below.

The book is designed to be accessible and is written in a personal, relaxed style by a writer/teacher who has a lifetime of interest in tradition as an active force to communicate. The book aims to enable you to go deeper and wider in your writing and connect your writing to the world.

What is the Book Saying?

From Chapter 1, the Introduction, active tradition is treated as a positive, even radical force and reclaimed from its deniers and critics, who might see the world as inexorably commercial, personal and bound by technological and industrial advance. The book says that taking tradition seriously is a creative and enabling force for potential good and that it offers an alternative to the competitive world of literary and commercial success. It says that by paying attention to the worlds of, for example, work, history and nature, seen in a traditional light, creative work can be more engaged and engaging.

Tradition in Creative Writing is not aimed at any particular genre of writer. While the author's creative examples are given in song lyric and poem form, the writing exercises are there for any and all genres and cross-fertilisation and experimentation is encouraged.

When writers begin writing, the best way to explore genres is to try different ones and indeed to see what can be learned from one, which is useful to another. Likewise, when writers are developing their work, experiencing different genres is useful in stretching and developing their creative muscles. Please use the writing exercises here as starters for any genre.

In a way, genres are properly for bookshops, libraries and promoters in publishing. Writers may invent new ones, mixtures or even rediscover old ones, in the traditional way: 'Look up Miracle Books,' reads a note in my workbook, for example.

Traditional forms demand variation and the making of old things new. They have the possibility of innovation and experimentation built in as part of traditional thinking. Active tradition is somewhere to start from and the answer to the question, 'Where do you get your ideas from?'

The book is written in a personal way, as it tries to demonstrate that one's own culture is a wide space to be explored. Here it seeks to lead by example, so the student/reader might create their own 'root-map', tapping into the powerful energies of tradition. *Tradition in Creative Writing* seeks itself to pass on an attitude of openness where tradition, used creatively, is not a mere link to the past, but a kind of organic time-machine that widens the present vision and sees into the future.

How to Use the Book

Each chapter of the four sections contains an essayistic discussion of its topic, with literary and critical readings from a variety of sources, examples of creative work on the topic by the author, a selection of writing exercises and a reading, listening and watching list.

Many songs and poems, etc., mentioned are difficult to obtain permission to quote directly, so it is suggested that readers use the internet to read there readily available material mentioned in the book.

Tradition in Creative Writing can easily be used as the basis for a class or writing group's session, or individually by a writer seeking to find new ways to think about and practice writing. Reading Chapter 1, the introduction, might be a good start, to become familiar with the thinking behind what is an attempt to reclaim an unusual way of looking at writing and at life. Thereafter, chapters might be used to complement the reader/writer/teacher's own preferences, although the sequence of the book is intended to show a process of regaining a sense of tradition from the known into the self and back to the world.

Here is a brief summary of the chapters:

Chapter 1: Introduction: The Hidden Wealth: the positive, creative uses of tradition.

Part I: Literary and Historical Traditions: Chapter 2: Modern Traditionalists: How writers have always used tradition and examples of dealing with past classics for new inspirations.

Chapter 3: Not Just History and Ancient Inspirations: How history and natural history can be used by writers to make the past alive and related to now.

Chapter 4: Storytelling, Myth, Folklore and Magic: Oral literature and story, folklore and myth as omnipresent inspiring tales.

Part II: Folk and Song Traditions: Chapter 5: Folksong and Creativity: Bob Dylan and his hero Robert Burns provide evidence of the liveliness of artists steeped in traditional material.

Chapter 6: A Songwriter in the Tradition: A Creative Folk Life: The author's journey into songwriting, with many traditional influences.

Chapter 7: Protest Songs and the Comic Connection: The comedy and protest which makes tradition truly of the moment.

Part III: Tradition, Self and Nature: Chapter 8: Tradition and Locality: Belonging somewhere is a way to be deep-rooted in a creative way.

Chapter 9: Self and Family Trees: Exploring the self and family are seen as rewarding. The return journey as motif.

Chapter 10: Nature and Tradition: An Essex Apple: Nature close to the human world explained in the richly symbolic apple, in myth, tradition and life.

Part IV: Tradition and Community: Chapter 11: Work, Craft and Creativity: Tradition—It's Better Than Working: Work can be more positive if seen as part of a craft-based tradition. How are we to do this?

Chapter 12: Church Going? Religion and Community: There are many writing positives about seeing religion as a shared, rich potential for us.

Chapter 13: The Radical Tradition Today: Tradition is full of world-shaking characters and counterbalances to convention. From Dionysus to 'Authenticity Syndrome'.

Chapter 14: Conclusions and Occlusions: Narrowing views of tradition and how to counter them and accept the mocked Trickster role and keep tradition active and positive.

As the book draws on many sources and has a unique perspective, general background reading is difficult to recommend, as there is no one book on the subject that covers the ground. Tradition is a huge but diffuse topic, so the book does not try to be comprehensive but is aimed to be most useful for writers. Aain, Chapter 1, the Introduction provides some general readings and useful references which might help in using the rest of the book.

In writing *Tradition in Creative Writing*, my own creative work has flourished, while I have also rediscovered thoughts and aspects of work of my own from the past. So the writing of this book has been like a harvest: a gathering in of nourishment and a storing and restoring of future food for creative thought against the winters where the world seeks its new birth. So the book has been worked on itself in a traditional and processive way. It is my great hope that it clarifies, collects and inspires you towards a new value and nourishment in your writing world. I see the book as the final work of a trilogy of books for writers. It is my most personal of these books, but its subject is what we have in common.

Tradition is active participation and the traditional process is becoming aware of this and using it as a way to go forward. The book is dedicated to everyone who has inspired me and whom I have tried to inspire, past, present and future: tradition is the renewed now.

Colchester, UK   Adrian May

Contents

1	Introduction: The Hidden Wealth	1
Part I	Literary and Historical Traditions	
2	Modern Traditionalists	13
3	Not Just History and Ancient Inspirations	29
4	Storytelling, Myth, Folklore and Magic	39
Part II	Folk and Song Traditions	
5	Folksong and Creativity	59
6	A Songwriter in the Tradition: A Creative Folk Life	71
7	Protest Songs and the Comic Connection	83
Part III	Tradition, Self and Nature	
8	Tradition and Locality	95
9	Self and Family Trees	107
10	Nature and Tradition: An Essex Apple	117
Part IV	Tradition and Community	
11	Work, Craft and Creativity: Tradition—It's Better Than Working	131
12	Church Going? Religion and Community	141
13	The Radical Tradition Today	153

14   Conclusions and Occlusions 165

Index 177

CHAPTER 1

Introduction: The Hidden Wealth

> Not in Utopia …
> Or some secreted island, Heaven knows where!
> But in the very world which is the world
> Of all of us, - the place in which, in the end,
> We find our happiness, or not at all!
> (Wordsworth, *The Prelude*, 1805, 724–8)

One of the wonderful things about Dorothea Brande's still hugely influential book on writing, *Becoming A Writer* (1983), is that she tells us from the start that she has tried everything. This includes all the writing methods going, which still proliferate now, nearly eighty-five years later, as I write. When she came herself to teach creative writing, after a career as a publishers' reader as well as a writer herself, she began to realise why she still felt a great 'discontent', as she says in her introduction. 'The difficulties of the average student or amateur writer begin long before' coming to where they 'could benefit' from any 'technical instruction'. Her book goes on to outline the psychology of creativity, with practical methods of how to tap into it. I would advise you to read it, as I agree with Malcolm Bradbury, one of the founders of creative writing teaching in the UK, that it is still 'the great exception' to the rule that most books on writing are not worth reading, as he said in his Foreword to Brande's book (1983).

As a devotee of 'the divine Dorothea', as I call her, I believe that there is another related, fundamental thing that any writer needs to know before any other issue about writing makes sense. This is how to see your writing connected to your life, which is why this book is called *Tradition in Creative Writing: finding inspiration through your roots*. It is no coincidence that writers themselves often write about tradition as a force in their writing. Writers like Bob Dylan and Ted Hughes and perhaps most notably T.S. Eliot, have continued to emphasise the centrality of tradition to their practice. When writing about the composition of *Crow* to his brother, Hughes wrote about 'the vital and unchangeable tradition' which he saw himself part of, adding 'it will be invisible to those who hardly know that tradition exists (almost all litterateurs) and whose brains have been constructed by the aberrations of recent civilisations' (*Letters of Ted* Hughes, 2007, p. 196).

Hughes here makes the point that tradition can challenge the contemporary world and can stand apart from the fashions and inhibitions of the times. Tradition is not then a mere adherence to orthodox modes of thinking, but a kind of hidden wealth. All writing depends on a long continuum of the creative and the old Muses are still with us. It is an open secret how useful old writing is to new.

What I want to suggest in this book is that tradition can offer much more. It can be an access point to a huge amount of wealth that we already possess. It can be a shift of how we view our life as having an innate value and that this offers a real alternative to a merely commercial, or merely literary view of artistic value. We all have ways in which we act and think traditionally, usually without realising it. Often these are simple things that we already enjoy in life but perhaps do not normally examine for their value and their implications.

Some hint of this is given in W.B. Yeats' *Mythologies* (1959), in a section from the end of *The Celtic Twilight* (1893) called 'By The Roadside'. Here 'an old man sang about that country beauty that died so many years ago, and spoke of a singer he had known who sang so beautifully that no horse would pass him, but turn its head and cock it ears to listen'. After Yeats has listened to more songs 'the voices melted' and 'the roads they too melted away and were mixed with the generations of men'. The sense of the past being present in the sense of beauty in both the subject, the sound and the sense is for Yeats, not an escape but what amounts to a kind of experienced justification of the art of the singers he has come to the roadside to hear. The singers celebrate their art as a connection of now to the timeless, so that the experience was a kind of celebration or even a manifesto of the power of art. What he also celebrates is the power of art to reflect on and return art to the self. This is tradition in action.

I was lucky myself to have likewise come to my own thinking about writing through song. The folk scene from the late 1960s onwards, where I was involved both personally and professionally was full of people who were interested in tradition. As a songwriter, I now believe it was no coincidence that the people I found most interesting, even most creative, were those most devoted to tradition. Although some thought of songwriters and singers of traditional songs as being on opposite sides of the folk scene, I instinctively felt more at home with the 'traddies', perhaps for the same reasons as Yeats was when he went to hear the songs by the roadside. Having this sense of a hidden wealth in tradition has led me to thinking that much that is good in creativity comes from tradition.

T.S. Eliot always writes well about writing and his short essay on tradition has become one that many read but I feel that few actually take notice of in any practical way. It was thought at the time of writing 'Tradition and the individual talent' (1952) that a modernist poet like Eliot himself needed to be new and that novelty was the key to originality. Eliot was pointing out how absurd this position was and yet the conflict between these two points of view is arguably still around. Eliot also says that the word is only mentioned positively as a reference to something lost to 'archaeology'. Tradition is not a matter of repeating the past, he insists, which would be pointless. It is more a question of widening our scope. It is 'a sense of the timeless as well as the temporal and of the timeless and the temporal together' which 'makes a writer traditional'. Therefore being traditional can make us more aware of our 'place in time' and of our own 'contemporaneity', as he calls it. If we are not aware of what has been handed on to us, we cannot really be here.

Eliot himself embodied in his poetry an acutely sensitive intelligence, coupled with a width of knowledge, which amounts to a still great example of someone both traditional and contemporary. This shows that, as he said, you cannot have one without the other. His own reflections on the limits of writing seem to show his traditional newness to great effect. His discussion of these limits in *Four Quartets* (1935–1942) seem to make awareness of limits part of his sensibility as a modern writer, as well as part of a traditional creativity of engaging with the Muses.

One of the things Eliot can answer is the limits of self-expression, which I know from my own experience as a teacher is something young writers will eventually encounter. Seeing yourself as part of something bigger can enable the young or new writer to think with a wider sensibility which is just as sensitive. Writing as therapy or mere self-expression can take you so far, but, as the popularity of storytelling now shows, we need the narrative of the journey out from the self, in order to make the self a stronger part of the world, with something to report, something of value to bring home. Thus tradition can also be a barrier against the crassness of the commercial world and its tendency towards triviality.

Traditional ways of thinking are not about complexity, however. Returning to the roots of language is to turn to the word in the street. Again, the liveliness of the past is in its honesty and directness. The great traditional ballads are folk poems and songs which have a simple directness in their use of words. The traditional way is therefore often one of humility and simplicity.

The Anxiety of Influence (1973) by Harold Bloom describes, not as the title might suggest, the impossibility of writing with the weight of the past upon you, but rather a description of a number of ways in which you can respond to the past rather than merely imitate it in a diminished way. The radical simplicities of the traditional, the rooted basic work which Hughes alludes to are then available to be in conversation with. A popular idea from folksingers is that of older singers standing behind you, supporting you in your living version of what they sang long ago. It is true to the spirit of the song to be in conversation, even in conflict with it, as a way of honouring its extraordinary quality of resilience and self-transformation. In some ways then, the most radical experiments, like T.S. Eliot's *The Waste Land* (1922) for instance, are deeply traditional, as he would have argued. The radical move is then linked to tradition, as is somehow also suggested in the way Bloom ends his book with a poem, 'Reflections upon the Path', that suggests to travel is better than to arrive, or another way of arriving. The traditional writer is then the traveller, between past, present and future, where the path is more important than any fixity. Tradition must then be what is still useful, still available to be in contention with, still nourishing. It is anything but fixed.

Just as tradition offers radicalism rather than nostalgia, it offers complexity, or depth, in its apparent simplicity. Lewis Hyde, in his book *The Gift* (1983, Chapter 1), tells the story of an Englishman being offered a pipe of peace by Native American Indians, which he then takes home to the museum, not realising that the whole point of the gift is that you pass it on to someone else you meet, another stranger, as a token of trust. This is an example of that subtle gift culture, to which all art belongs, where the point is not possession but of continuation and sharing. The Native Americans were taken as simplistic, when in fact the Englishman, having lost his tradition, is the unsophisticated one in the story.

In my experience, this is how anyone who expresses an interest in tradition is still treated. You are accused of a kind of simple-mindedness and naivety by careerists and materialists who mistake their insecurity for truth. Margaret Atwood's favourite book about creativity, Hyde's work retains a radical view of a tradition of art, where 'a live tradition extends in both directions in time', as he says in Chapter 9.

Probably the most influential current thinker who directly tackles tradition is the politics and sociology writer Anthony Giddens. In his book *Runaway World* (2002), based on his Reith lectures on globalisation (1999), he devotes a chapter to tradition and had already written influentially on the subject in previous publications. At the start of his chapter he seems to be repeating the hollow attacks of the past about tradition as a kind of selling tool and conveyor of fakery, but quickly goes on to say something more useful to us here. The idea of tradition has been neglected, he indicates, from the Enlightenment, as 'the shadow side of modernity … that can be easily brushed aside' as nonsense. He then points out that the definition of tradition is rooted in Roman law and meant that which is passed or transmitted to you from previous generations, 'given in trust … to protect and nurture'. We can see here the connection to Hyde's concept of the gift. Before the Enlightenment, Giddens suggests, there was no need for the word, as tradition was all around.

Echoing Eliot, Giddens says that 'it is a myth to think of traditions as impervious to change', traditions are, positively, 'invented and reinvented'. The historian, the sociologist and the modernist have usually used the term as one of easy dismissal, if they used it at all, of 'archaeology', as Eliot says. Tradition, in its connection to religions, is social rather than personal and 'it defines a kind of truth' and has a kind of ritual element and the belief that it 'contains stored-up wisdom.' In parts of life like family, tradition persists and is probably the most easily accessible to us. Writing about your family could even be a first move to becoming a new traditional writer, as we shall see in Chapter 9.

Like nature, Giddens suggests, tradition has been under threat. The rise of recent 'new nature' writers and 'eco-criticism' seeks to redress this tide of modernisation in terms of the world, but I am suggesting a more natural and subtle, but potentially radical view of human culture is also needed in the rooted artist and especially the rooted writer.

Like others, he talks of the 'end' of nature and tradition while drawing attention to their persistence, even in the face of becoming the unreal comodification of 'heritage or kitsch'. He says that 'traditions are needed and will always persist, because they give continuity and form to life'. This is exactly what writers are attempting to do, in more ways than one. In addition there are the 'ritual, ceremonial and repetition' elements, in its religious context, to be discussed here in later chapters. Tradition can then be seen as a way of adapting to change, of even testing change for its usefulness to be passed forward, which is what tradition means.

Towards the end of his chapter, Giddens gets to an interesting and even crucial point about addiction, which he sees as a feature of modernisation. In some ways he seems to be saying that addiction is a kind of traditionalism reversed, or that it imitates aspects of traditional behaviour in a negative direction. Addiction is the need for tradition turned from a public, useful element of life into a damaging, personal form of isolated behaviour. The absence of tradition also leads to another extreme, which is a shutting down, an urge towards a closed, excessive forms of uncreative traditionalism. Teenage gangs might be a symptom of this.

In his short chapter on the subject, Giddens covers much that is useful in order to reflect on the use of tradition in the present day. He and Lewis Hyde answer somewhat the problems raised by W.H. Auden in his essay questioning the role of the writer in the modern world, 'The Poet and the City' (*The Dyer's Hand*, 1963). Writers 'have lost the social utility they once had' and the world is suspicious of 'the gratuitous' but Hyde addresses the continuing need for the latter, while the role of tradition for connection and continuity is addressed by Giddens.

What Giddens encouraged in my thinking is that in a very real sense we are all traditional already in much of what we do and that only its absence makes us notice it in an intellectual way. How liberating, then, I feel, if we were more aware of its hidden wealth, which is already ours—and how creative.

Raymond Williams, the influential writer on culture and society, in his alphabetical book *Keywords* (1976) talks of 'Tradition' as 'an active process' which tends towards being devalued into something static, implying that this must be guarded against. In his short entry on the topic, he concludes by saying, in relation to the devaluing of tradition, that 'considering only how much has been handed down to us, and how various it actually is, this [devaluing] ... is both a betrayal and a surrender.'

These various and hard-to find defenders of tradition can connect with two writers more specifically about literature. Joseph Campbell's *The Hero with a Thousand Faces* (1993) and Robert Graves' *The White Goddess* (1948) both seem to be post-World War attempts to reconnect the world through the mythology of creativity. This was then an active attempt from each to reactivate the traditions which make us human and the poetic and mythic elements which carry them to us. They turn human life into recurring, renewing narratives against the tide of materialism.

Campbell, especially, is at pains to show the specificity of myth in *Primitive Mythology* (1969, p. 462; 1976 edition), in a paragraph from 'The Functioning of Myth', in the 'Conclusion'. Here he says that the 'way' of myth is a ritual to take us from the local and from our own history into the universal. This local universal he calls an 'antimony', but emphasises that this process is '*to render an experience of the ineffable through the local and concrete*' [my italics]. Here the universal aims of myth are inextricably mixed with the local and the individual, which can be seen as another example of the hidden wealth to be gained from that personal and local experience of tradition and its hidden wealth.

Campbell addresses tradition specifically in his series of interviews, published as *The Power of Myth* (1991). In the chapter called 'The Hero's Adventure', he says that 'There is a kind of secondary hero to revitalise the tradition. This hero reinterprets the tradition and makes it valid as a living experience today instead of a lot of outdated clichés. This has to be done with all traditions.' (1991 edition). This is the lofty, or humble, intention of *Tradition in Creative Writing*.

My own journey to bring this back home began with my book on myth and creativity, which led on to a book about magic and writing. Both of these went parallel with my feel for tradition from my folk music background. Tradition tends to be ignored and is, as we have seen, hard to trace through any clear path of writers or thinkers. But I soon began to realise that myth and magic are in fact traditions in action and also that there was a creative force, rather than merely a preservative one, at the centre of the traditional.

The folk scene from the 1960s in England still had some of the older singers around, who seemed to have a grace and openness in their attitude to their material. They would sing popular songs of the music hall alongside traditional material and singing seemed to me to be part of their whole being, not a question of any measured authenticity. They lived it. Later, when I got to study and perform songs collected one hundred years previously in my home county, Essex, by Ralph Vaughan Williams, I heard of Charles Potiphar. This was the first man Vaughan Williams heard sing who was part of that living tradition. Potiphar himself referred to people making up songs about current events.

These old boys and girls lived in a living world of song and to themselves were no mere relics. My own creative practice evolved through these influences.

The point of this book is to reap the hidden benefits of this method so that tradition can be seen as 'active', in Raymond Williams' words. The aim is to show you what tradition, what becoming a roots writer, can do for you. The word 'roots' has given a positive feel to tradition, via Alex Haley's *Roots* (1976) and Primo Levi's anthology *The Search for Roots* (2001), where tradition was honestly and positively sought. The positive Jamaican use of 'roots' is echoed in British born rapper of Jamaican heritage Roots Manuva and his album *Brand New Second Hand* (1999) has the rooted old/new axis, so characteristic of positive tradition.

If your hidden wealth, your subject, is right under your nose and feet, the first thing it can do is to help you keep writing. The circularity of life is itself a subject and every season needs an old new song, every celebration needs re-celebrating, every loved thing needs its reminder, every spring its newness. Writing is about continuity, not linear progress or competition.

The second hidden wealth is connection to the world. Traditions, in all their variety, are a locally available universality. As Campbell indicates, they have a dual function, both local and universal. As soon as you stop trying to write for the world, you find you are doing so in your very humility. The need for tradition is both specific and common to all peoples. Even if your own connection to the past via family, place or birth is an uneasy or troubled one, you still have something there to grasp, some trouble to resolve or grapple with, to work on. Everyone needs the renewal of the creative tradition.

A third and related hidden wealth, seen via Lewis Hyde, and another by-product is that of escaping the tyranny of the market. If you write something for your family, for example, its value is beyond the monetary, if it connects. In ritual moments, even the non-religious turn to the usefulness of words beyond the striving for success. The right words at the right time show that writing is both more relevant and more powerful than we have been led to believe.

The hidden wealth of being a new traditional writer, of being or becoming traditional is then in such things as locality, family, identity, that old song renewed, that old recipe your Gran gave you. It is nearer to your own life and less some dream of self-aggrandisement and publishing deals. As Patrick Kavanagh says in his poem 'Pegasus', as soon as he stops trying to sell his horse which is his 'soul', then it takes flight: 'Now I may ride him/ Every land my imagination knew' (*A Soul For Sale*, 1947).

This hidden wealth, the secret of writing traditionally is that the tradition has the quality of reflecting on its own validity, on its own ability to return us to ourselves and to what is really valuable. The song everyone knows at New Year, which Robert Burns creatively adapted from traditional sources, asks itself in the first line about its own value: 'Should auld acquaintance be forgot ...?' Traditions must not only be useful, but be reusable. When someone returns to nature, nature returns them to their own nature. This returning we will return to, often.

The song lyric below reflects on something of value that stays valuable. The song it reflects on is itself about the value of love, home and nature which remain, even in a time of war. Tradition discusses and creates its own renewal in its world, where 'the task of the hero is that of restoration', as Jessie Weston says in *From Ritual to Romance* (1920, Chapter 2). Here words are 'worn new' as Edward Thomas says so succinctly in the poem 'Words' (2004), which, for me, both roots and elevates the idea.

There is an Irish flavour in my lyric, which is intentional, as the Irish can teach us much about how to live tradition. Yeats and Kavanagh were very aware of this, as we have already seen. The song mentioned in the lyric, 'The Wind that Shakes the Barley' (1861) was not, as many think, a traditional song, but a song written by Robert Dwyer Joyce, in the tradition. Both speak of youth and yearning towards a sense of roots and, for me, my own sense of connecting my writing to my life, of becoming a writer.

Author's Creative Example:

IT WAS A PLUMP AND JOVIAL ...

It was a plump and jovial
Chap at my first folk club
I was young and long-haired
In the back room of the pub
Instead of raucous chorus songs
Sung both late and early
One night, a change of pace, he sang
The Wind That Shakes The Barley

I thought it was an English song
Agricultural, dreamy
But the feeling of timeless romance
Captured my heart clearly
It caught a stillness, caught a grace
A seed was sown then surely
Both old and new and of the heart
Was the song that caught me wholly

He may not have sung all of it
But I expect he knew its history
Written by a clever Irish scholar
About rebellious glory
And perhaps the rebel in old Gil
To be a serious folky
Identified with all that stuff
In the song that caught me wholly

And now I like my whole mistake
With traditional creativity
I did not judge, discriminate
Through my ignorance heard plainly
A yearning for a truth and love
Beyond my day's empty glory
The renewal of the mind and heart
In the song that caught me wholly

So I thank that plump and jovial
Chap who sang so plainly
And I thank that little back room club
And the song that caught me wholly

And the wind that shakes the barley

Writing Exercise

Choose an object or event which represents some value beyond the monetary (not valuable; priceless) and write about it then, and now.

Reading

Auden, W.H. 1963. The Poet and the City. In *The Dyer's Hand and Other Essays*, 72–89. London: Faber and Faber.
Bloom, Harold. 1973. *The Anxiety of Influence*. New York: Oxford University Press.
Brande, Dorothea. 1983. *Becoming a Writer*. London: MacMillan.
Campbell, Joseph. 1969. *Primitive Mythology*. New York: Penguin.
Campbell, Joseph. 1993. *The Hero with a Thousand Faces*. London: HarperCollins.
Campbell, Joseph. 1991. *The Power of Myth*. New York: Anchor.
Eliot, T.S. 1944. *Four Quartets*. London: Faber and Faber.
Eliot, T.S. 1952. Tradition and the Individual Talent. In *Selected Essays*, 13–22. London: Faber and Faber.
Giddens, Anthony. 2002. *Runaway World*. London: Profile.
Haley, Alex. 1976. *Roots*. New York: Doubleday.
Hughes, Ted. 2007. *Letters of Ted Hughes*. London: Faber and Faber.
Hyde, Lewis. 1983. *The Gift*. New York: Vintage.
Joyce, Robert Dwyer. 1861. *The Wind That Shakes the Barley*. Traditional: Roud Index 2991.
Kavanagh, Patrick. 1973. *Collected Poems*. New York: Norton.
Levi, Primo. 2001. *The Search for Roots*, Trans. Peter Forbes. London: Allen Lane.
Manuva, Roots. 1999. *Brand New Second Hand*. London: Big Dada Records.
Thomas, Edward. 2004. *Collected Poems*. London: Faber and Faber.
Weston, Jessie. 1957. *From Ritual to Romance*. New York: Doubleday.
Williams, Raymond. 1976. *Keywords*. London: Fontana.

Wordsworth, William. 1904. *Poetical Works*. Oxford: Oxford University Press.
W.B. Yeats. 1959. *The Celtic Twilight*, 5–141. In *Mythologies*. London: MacMillan.

PART I

Literary and Historical Traditions

CHAPTER 2

Modern Traditionalists

Is this an old story or a new story? A gender-ambiguous star comes to town and all the women follow her/him up the hillside to take part in wild dances and strange rites. Is this a new story or an old story? A wild, green man arrives in the city to challenge everyone, coming from a higher power to overthrow the corruption that threatens to destroy them. A wholly black page interrupts a novel: is this a new novel or an old one? The point is that they all could be either and that their common theme of challenging the world is one universal in literature, now as then. I will return to these specific three examples later in the chapter.

To say that writing is a traditional activity could be seen as a banal observation, or as a threat to the newness of the present. Writers have expressed their concern about being overwhelmed by the past and critics have sought to challenge the perceived authority of the literary canon. 'Canon', though it sounds like something aggressive and archaic, in fact means books allowed by church law as acceptable and authentic. So its threat is double here: the brother of the huge old gun (cannon) and the books allowed, or not banned by Church law. All of this feels mighty heavy.

The novelist Margaret Atwood wrote a book about writing, originally published as *Negotiating with the Dead* (2002), later to be republished with its rearranged subtitle as title, *On Writers and Writing* (2015). Rudyard Kipling, in 'The Handicaps of Letters' (1928), from *A Book of Words* says writers are often more alive when they are dead and sometimes 'the longer … dead, the more alive'. Harold Bloom published *The Anxiety of Influence* in 1973. Subsequent editions have emphasised the subtitle, *A Theory of Poetry* and in *Poetics of Influence* (1988) he revisits his themes. Death and anxiety from the past can seem to dominate us, let alone the talk of 'dead white males' and the weight

© The Author(s), under exclusive license to Springer Nature
Switzerland AG 2021
A. May, *Tradition in Creative Writing*,
https://doi.org/10.1007/978-3-030-74776-3_2

of lost empires, suppression and domination. Is there yet a way to reclaim tradition and even make it inspirational?

How is the writer to relate to writers of the past? With respect or rejection? With a shrugging off or an embrace? Is it somehow possible to do both? There is a double-ness to creativity that suggests that a traditionalist is somehow paradoxically liberated by the past—is this possible? I say it is and the only bad thing you can do to the literature of the past is to ignore it. Even a total rejection is a move in response to it. Writers have always used the literary past and it is often the most radical who are the most traditional.

When I teach first-year undergraduates about the benefits of using old material, we tend to start with a group writing exercise. Taking the first ten lines, or 'proem' of *The Odyssey*, we get a plot summary and a list of themes. We invent an outrageous name and character, then pull the lines into all kind of unnatural shapes and directions to obtain something that does not even resemble the original in the slightest. I write it on the board, acting as editor or encourager of outrages and we aim to produce something wild and good for a laugh. One year, it was called 'This Bastard'. Thus we demonstrate not only the usefulness of the old, but a kind of freedom from it, which is also strangely of it as well. The intention is to free up the creative mind and see the fun to be had and that a writer does not have to reveal their sources at all. We also talk about Derek Walcott's *Omeros* (1990) which, though based on *The Odyssey*, reflects colonial experience as well as his immersion in the poetic tradition. I point out that Walcott used to be a visiting professor at Essex University, UK.

This tradition reveals or conceals a secret strength from an ancient writer present in your work. Language is old stuff itself and we must reuse it for it to be useful. Writing is an activity which contains its own continuity and being aware of this is a strength to the writer.

If we look beyond the first ten lines of *The Odyssey*, we find early a picture of another traditional figure beside the protagonist. Phemius is a folksinger. His name means 'the famous'. We have Prince and Madonna, so why not 'Famous', or just 'The Famous' as a band or person? We meet this bard singing an old song. He is also a writer/performer put in an awkward position. He embodies a writer's dilemma when confronted with the choice of what material to use.

As Alexander Pope's translation has it: 'Then Phemius was consigned the chorded lyre/ Whose hand reluctant touched the warbling wire' (1.153–4). Should he sing encouragement to the men who want to marry the absent Odysseus' wife Penelope or should he admonish them? The times are difficult for singers, who feel they should have something positive in a strange time. As they say, no change there, then. What is he to do? He sings an old song about returning from war, he expresses the hidden sadness of the situation as a reminder of humanity to a greedy world of men. In choosing this song, he has distanced himself from the immediacy of things and has chosen reminding them all of something bigger than them. Do, then, the ambitious men, the 'suitors', complain?

No, it is Penelope that hears the bigger picture and is affected:

> There from the portal with her mild command
> Thus gently checks the minstrel's tuneful hand:
> 'Phemius! Let acts of Gods and heroes old,
> What ancient bards in hall and bower have told,
> Attempered to the lyre, your voice employ;
> Such the pleased ear will drink with silent joy.
> But oh forbear that dear disastrous name,
> To sorrow sacred, and secured of fame … (I:325–32)

Here she does not start by telling him to stop, but suggest something even older, as if guessing his move into the traditional role. Phemius proves his worth in a difficult situation by sticking to his traditional role of revealing the old truths of human nature and, in *The Odyssey*, this proves lasting. He is one of the few spared at the end of the epic, when 'the suitors' are killed (22: 330–77) and he gets to perform a wedding song in Book 23. Here we see a traditionalist maintaining his dignity and long view and the integrity of his art in a subtle and intelligent way. He is no purveyor of nostalgia or whimsical, unreal heroics but someone who makes his art useful, attuned to the present but calling on the older song to retain a bigger reality.

A useful modern parallel might be in the Coen Brothers' film *Inside Llewlyn Davis* (2013), where the titular character, confronted with a crass commercial agent, resorts to an ancient traditional folksong. This audition struck me as very true to life, as I have personally known and experienced this kind of encounter. His failing of the audition, with a deliberate performance of something that goes totally over the head of the agent doing the auditioning, is a way of retaining his self-respect in a situation which could have no good benefit otherwise for him as an artist. The beautiful performance of the traditional song by actor Oscar Issac makes it even more poignant. This unusual sympathetic depiction of failure as a kind of personal triumph is all too rare in commercial film. The message is the same as the tale of Phemius: the song can be bigger than the situation and can inspire survival. Tradition is a survival system.

Nonetheless, persuading first-year students into the creativity of older material sometimes had its problems, as it seemed to them like mere history. For that reason, when I was once director of first-year literature, I would suggest the teaching of literature to be done backwards. It always seemed more organic to start from now and work back, so that the really strange and challenging stuff, like Greek Tragedy, would be arrived at in the third year of study. No one took me seriously enough to adopt my idea, but I was thinking as a creative writing specialist.

Jokes, that most traditional of forms (of which more in Chapter 7) are usually written backwards. You think of a punch line and work out how to arrive there. Some jokes, which seem so fresh, go back hundreds, if not thousands of years and are therefore definitively traditional. More of these reversals of time below.

I remember being very struck when writer and artist John Berger wrote in a newspaper article in the 1990s words to the effect that there is no progress in art. This thought, that art is not science and deals with what remains the same in the human condition through the ages, struck me as seismic and profound. The fact that it originates, so far as I can find, in the most experimental of modernist artists, will become significant later in this chapter.

The three old or new conundrums at the start of this section will now be easily answered by the careful reader up to here. They are all old, however told in a new way. The first is the plot of Euripides' *The Bacchae*, the second is part of one of the oldest texts known, *The Epic of Gilgamesh*. The novel is Laurence Sterne's *Tristram Shandy* (1759–67).

If Homer, the traditional and mythical bard of *The Odyssey* and *The Iliad* was the father of all poets and himself a reuser of old song and stories, then who is our first writer in the English tongue? Although he was writing in the common tongue of the time, not that recognisable today, the story of Caedmon (pronounced 'Cadman') is strange and inspiring. To me, he again has strong traditional traits which can be inspiring and useful.

Caedmon's story, Caedmon's song is his own. His life is an old tale and his work was also on the old themes. His tale is an example of the traditional creative process.

This is how the story of the first English writer, the first English poet goes, as told by the first great English historian, the Venerable Bede, in Book IV, Chapter 24 of his *Ecclesiastical History of the English People* (AD731). An illiterate peasant, who avoided singing even when asked, had a dream and was inspired by an angel to sing, which he then did. He sang of creation and kept on singing, inspired by God and the miraculous. The monks he sang to were astounded by his new, local-voiced, English versions of the old tales.

Caedmon's story is exemplary, as he is more like us than we might imagine and because he tells us what it is like to be a writer, trying to bring a fresh view to an old truth. His traditional status contains the promise and the mystery, apparently coming from nowhere, but with a power to revive the world's view of itself. I also think that, secretly, he had the writer's magic, in tune with something bigger than himself.

When we start writing, starting for the first time seriously, or just starting a new piece of work, we are like Caedmon again, knowing nothing. This is necessary, if we are to sing of creation, to make what we write fresh. As T.S. Eliot says in Part V of 'East Coker', from *The Four Quartets* (1959), we are always learning, with old things becoming new, in the writer's paradoxical, traditional way.

Caedmon was like us would-be writers, knowing much about his world, but singing the song of starting again, of self-creation. Among the many versions of the tale, or myth, in histories of English Literature, only Michael Schmidt's account in *The Story of Poetry* (2001), gives even a hint that Caedmon, so heavily and religiously patronised by history, might have known what he was doing, although 'we cannot advance beyond conjecture', as Schmidt admits. Looking at his story from all angles, however, might help us create a picture of someone who *appeared* innocent and use our conjecture to see some hidden strength in him. We might start by looking at a story in reverse order, too see its hidden meaning. This meaning could be another version of him, as Caedmon the folksinger, self-renewer, Caedmon the Magician who recreates himself.

To tell a tale, or religious ritual, backwards is itself a magical idea, something which undoes or undermines or reveals another side of the intention of the story. This is sometimes called a Black Mass. Creation and inspiration can work in many directions. So, we begin at the end. The use of tradition is the creative use of time.

The second and last miracle recorded by Bede about Caedmon, was that he had foreknowledge of his own death. This is not much mentioned in the books about literary history. But this knowledge of the occult seems to me a clue that his gift was not so naïve as Bede reports. 'For, when the time of his death grew near', as Bede reports, he asked for a 'resting-place' in the monastery's 'house to which all who were sick or were likely to die were taken', even though he appeared well. He waited until 'the brothers had roused themselves to sing God's praises in the Night Office' and then died peacefully. This is the first evidence of his power.

The middle part of the backwards story is the subject matter of Caedmon's songs. 'He sang of the creation of the world, the origin of the human race ... the whole story of Genesis' and he sang of 'the Last Judgement'. He chose, in other words, all the most traditional elements of the Bible, ones that deal with creation and destruction, with change and growth: the subjects of creativity.

Next, returning backwards to the beginning, comes his sudden inspiration, which might be a metaphor for all creativity. When it works, the angel seems to come to us, like the flowing of some pure source and no matter how much work or craft has gone into coming to that moment, something genuinely creative seems to have that freshness, like that of a first flower. There are many stories about sudden inspiration, too. The great blues artist Robert Johnson is said to have sold his soul to the Devil at the crossroads, as recorded in his famous 1937 song 'Cross Road Blues' (*King of the Delta Blues Singers*, 1961), which begins 'Went down to the crossroads/ Fell down on my knees'. He did actually vanish for a while, before returning to the world with an amazing improvement in his guitar-playing and singing, which gave rise to the story.

If Caedmon was already an inspired and magical poet, he knew that the story of sudden illumination was a good one to weave. The poet who knew of his own death and sang of creativity would be the first to know how to present his magical tale. It obviously worked. He had a safe old age in the protection of the monastery. He also fills the role of the Mentor figure, the older man with a purer, 'primitive' knowledge. Apparently simple, he weaves his creative story.

So we arrive backwards to his humble origins, so emphasised by the Bede and probably, from what we have conjured or conjectured about him, so emphasised by himself. To play the humble man of the soil is another traditional way to tell truths, to show wild inspiration in an acceptable way. To act simple is a way to access simple wisdom, beyond our tendency towards over-complication. Just like the Beatles using their Scouse accents to take the rise out of pretentious critics in the sixties, Caedmon the Traditional hid as a 'neatherd', as Michael Schmidt tells us, who looks after livestock. Knowing the animals is as aspect, too, of being a magician and a poet, in the Pastoral tradition. The pastoral, beginning as far back as the Greeks, sang about sheep and nature and drew peace and wise analogies of goodness from the contemplation of these simple things.

Part of the humble, innocent origins in Caedmon's tale is the story of him refusing the harp, as his turn came to sing. Here is another reluctant folksinger, like Llewyn Davis and Phemius. But does this really mean that this mature man, who refused to sing, was as yet no poet? 'Indeed it sometimes happened at a feast that all the guests in turn would be invited to sing and entertain the company; then, when he saw the harp coming his way, he would get up from the table and go home,' Bede reports. Does this mean he *could not* sing?

We might recognise his reluctance, when we bring our work to a writing class. But, also, knowing what we knew from his knowing story, seeing his creative tale reversed back on itself, he might just as well have gone home for the opposite reason. It might not be that he knew no songs, but that *he knew songs which were too strong, too magical, too powerful for the pious company to take*. He knew the old songs.

Part of tradition is knowing the way things happen, via the old patterns, you might say. If this is so, then it is a way of having foreknowledge. It seems likely, as a foreknowing and magical man, that he knew the old animal, ritual, pagan songs of the earth. He knew his own song and knew when to sing it and how to recreate it for the company he wished to be among. The Bede story was that he was their naïve pet poet, but I think they were his naïve, pet patrons and that he wove his own tale. He had the authority, he controlled the story, like a good storyteller needs to learn to do.

Caedmon's story, Caedmon's song is his own, old song.

The spell Caedmon wove is still with us and all the elements of the way tradition echoes and enhances the creative are still here. His life was a creative pattern and he sang of creation and destruction and of redemption at the end. His life has the beginnings and ends written well, as did his writings: his life and work are a unity of creative strength. The great comparer of world myth, Joseph Campbell notices the story's connection to 'the Chinese legend of the Zen patriarch Hui-neng, whose dates 638–731, coincide with those of Caedmon'. The two legends render the same doctrine of a wisdom beyond learning

...' he notes in *Creative Mythology* (1968), Chapter 3, Part III. The prophet arising from a humble source is a common trope of all myth, religion and literature, most obviously connected to the Christian myth in Caedmon's tale. In my native U.K. county, Essex, the composer Vaughan Williams was turned on to real folksong by an old, illiterate man, called Charles Potiphar. That the truth might reside in nature and in those close to it, and be renewed in nature is our own story of ecology. Caedmon has the wisdom and has become its literary embodiment.

The way I have tried to explore the story from a different perspective is also witness to the way old material responds to attention, to change, to the creative use of its possibility. Love, death and all human experience have much in common through the ages, which is why we turn to stories for a different kind of truth from the factual. This is a tale for all time and the spirit of Caedmon might be our mentor, as a 'new' writer, ready to sing at last, finding our strength in our link to the past which gave us birth.

Tradition is down to earth, like Caedmon, and the renewal of nature is never far away, as it deals with birth and death and tries to understand the world in the process. John Clare, the nineteenth century's 'peasant poet', yet another new Caedmon, talks in a prose fragment, of walking and hearing the songs of the lark and the ploughboy: 'Green into mirth with the sprouting grain the songs of the sky lark and the old songs and ballads that ever accompany field happiness in following the plough—but neither heard known or noticed by all the world beside' ('Prose on songs of the plough', 182?). The sense of renewal, of the old, hidden connections of song and earth recreating the world are inescapable.

The writer, then, is a traditional artist who deals with these serious issues of change, renewal, creation and its opposite. Caedmon's story, when he comes to join the world of St. Hilda's abbey in Whitby, having been, in Clare's words, 'neither heard known or noticed by all the world beside' despite perhaps his fullness of magical song, in my version, brings his gifts, in a fresh, new form, to a new audience.

This is how creativity brings the personal into the universal, and tells us about tradition and about publication, making work public, about connecting writing that speaks to a wide audience.

Edward Thomas, from the early part of the twentieth century, speaks of a natural, humble strength of writing in 'Words' (2004). In this poem, words are renewed. Thomas is doing what Caedmon did, and what we can attempt. In his wonderful oxymoron, 'worn new', the spring is renewed. And, here also is the renewal of the tradition and of the writer.

Persuading students to take the Bible as an item of interest to the writer took some doing. The trouble with the Bible is that people either hate it irrationally or love it irrationally. My lectures on the Bible became legendary for my mythic and dramatic take on Genesis, where I would overload the new cordless mic on purpose, with my growling, sententious 'voice of God' act. In effect, I played up fantasy genre credentials of the Old Testament, in order to get the students to see it as a collection of writings that showed various ways of expressing various kinds of truth, especially symbolic and mythic truth. I would also emphasise the language.

The language of the King James Bible is roughly of the same era as Shakespeare. It was revolutionary in its time, new and bold in English, though allowable and not in Latin. One piece of irrefutable evidence that tradition exists is how the language of the Bible is still there in how we speak and write today, as is Shakespeare. Words are traditional tools and we need to know about them and their uses. The Bible is extraordinary poetry, whatever else it is or is not. It is also a fantastic source book, if wrestled from the hands of the irrational atheist or ardent religious literalist. They are entitled to their views, but they ignore a great source book and great variety and even subtlety, beyond the prejudice of youth, or anyone else.

Of course, all great religious texts are as interesting, especially in their cultural context and I recommend you study them. However, the Bible, for writers in English, is indispensable, I believe.

My personal engagement with the poetry of the Bible comes through writing poems directly influenced by its strange tales and images. Although, since I last was director of first-year literature, at my own university, they no longer get much on the Bible (teachers are similarly prejudiced, in fact), some of my creative writing colleagues are devoted to working with old texts in new ways. I would recommend Philip Terry's *Dictator* (2018; a startling take on *The Epic of Gilgamesh*) and Chris McCully's 2018 version of *Beowulf*. One group of my own poems came from discussions of this.

When Chris McCully suggested, off the top of his head and partly as a joke, that I might write a version of Ecclesiastes, while discussing the reception of his own translation of *Beowulf* and Phil Terry's *Dictator*, two things occurred to me. First was a sense of exhilaration, especially as I had, a day or so before, used the first line of Ecclesiastes at the end of a song I was writing and that I thought it a fantastically great poem/Bible book already. The second one was of the futility of cover versions, especially of things that were already and untouchably extraordinarily good. Yet the ridiculous presumption somehow appealed to me, despite the dangers of aligning myself to the great in a kind of literary virtue signalling. There was something about the Book which had an appeal of being bracing, of counteracting the trap with some kind of unyielding honesty, which we imagine is quite modern.

I then began thinking about something appropriate in relation to writing from biblical sources and remembered my prized copy of *Peake's Commentary* (1962), which I got second-hand at a bargain price many years ago and had often consulted. A 'verse commentary' seemed to me suitably humble, where I might not be ventriloquising a dumb imitation or grandiose, delusional chumming-up with the great. Rather than just adding to a long line readers singing praises and raising questions.

It is possible that these thoughts on nomenclature gave me license to be as loose or ambitious as I liked? One thing was for certain, I was already doing it, whatever it was, with my thoughts and doubts of vanity, especially when I found myself scribbling verses and lyric ideas on the back of a pack of 'inspired bean burgers', as part of the label read.

Writing some sections addressed to royalty might be seen as the ultimate vaingloriousness and satire and I hoped these kinds of and/or move would work. The mood of this move suited my absurd or bold purpose. But again I found that even thinking about this folly of a work was entering the language and the world of the devastatingly undermining King James' poem-book which is Ecclesiastes. The author of the Book is said to be from at least a royal background.

Another way of writing from some other work is to use the word 'render', as Edward Fitzgerald did with his *Rubaiyat* (1859), 'rendered' into English. A rendering can be a humble offering up as well as a translation. Translation is well down the list of meanings and 'render' is a useful word for a writer, albeit out of fashion. I have used the word in the poems too, when referring to writing.

What I was offering up, giving, submitting or delivering is as various, aslant and free as a commentator might be allowed to be, I hoped. It is sweary but respectful; roughly reverential and thus has something in common with my work as a songwriter. My love for the King James Version is increased by my commentary and I have used it directly when I could, making it part of my word-world, as it already is in fact.

At times I found myself translating meaning, at times lifting phrases and rhythms, at times going off at an angle that suited me. I had no one method, which seems to be one of the benefits of writing as direct interaction with an existing text. Ecclesiastes himself is also at times direct and accusative, at times poetic, at times hectoring and blunt, at times obscure. He is obviously often repetitive too and the word 'vanity' chimes more often than the word 'God' and I do not think he is wrong about that.

The varieties of repetitions in the Bible are called 'parallelism', which to me seems a thing always present in the world of song anyway. I read a whole chapter of a book about biblical literature which did not once mention the comparison with song in terms of repetition. The rhythms and cadences of thought, of words and meanings, seem to me to be always like this, just that they are more obvious in this type of poetic language. Is there a fashion for non-parallelism in writing, which is perhaps a recent orthodoxy and one, which does not necessarily do us any favours, even among many Creative Writing conventions? We cut off our nose to spite our face; we cut off our blood to spite the page. The repetition supplies both warmth and humour and the texture of human thought and discussion. We are parallel.

Another kind of parallelism might be the Hebrew scholarship tradition of debate, which I think is called 'ma'amat', which means 'across from' or 'facing'. This is where two scholars sit opposite and debate textual meaning. The lovely image of this makes me think of being in debate with the world, facing it and sometimes also in opposition.

I did not much seek to replace 'vanity' which is a great word, rather vary it and play with it and even, in one case to add one to a chapter where none was present in my source. To accept vanity is to accept much.

Writing religious and poetic work does tend to make you sound a bit like T.S. Eliot. To this, I would say that there are worse people to sound like. Other influences might be Richard Brautigan's *A Confederate General from Big Sur* (1964; U.K., 1970), which I read in the 1970s. Here, Ecclesiastes is both a warning and an obsession. Just as Brautigan character counted commas, I counted 'vanity' and 'God' and knew I was getting obsessive. Pete Seeger's song of 'Turn, Turn, Turn' (written in the late 1950s) came up, as it is from chapter three of the book. When a friend asked me what I would do about this I somehow immediately knew the answer, which was to write about Seeger himself. He increasingly feels like more like a biblical figure since his death.

Letting the K.J.V. seep in has been my method in a sense and allowing meaning, however, misread, to emerge, my faith. On the other hand, I did have the New International Version to hand for reference to meanings and the website biblehub.com allows the instant comparison of many commentaries (though none in verse). Mostly I stumbled on in my own vain way. The worst I can do is draw your attention back to the text. There are some beautiful chapters, especially the last two, where to add anything seems cursed at least to failure. This did not stop me.

My 'pocket canon' tiny single K.J.V. volume of Ecclesiastes (1998, with an introduction by Doris Lessing) was my constant companion. You can still get one of these cheaply although they are out of print.

After finishing the first draft on Good Friday, I realised that the composition had run from Christmas to Easter, which felt natural at least. Writing runs from birth to death, all the time.

Curses were often added to texts in Biblical times to prevent the addition or subtraction to texts (see Revelations). The N.I.V. suggests this more than the K.J.V. and I have included something of it in my Envoy.

I like the feeling when writing that there is something *inevitable* about it and you cannot escape this feeling while Ecclesiastes is your traditional source. There is an expression in secondhand books, appropriately enough, usually abbreviated to W.A.F., meaning 'with all faults'. Needless to say, all faults were mine.

One lovely thing working from another text gives you is the feeling of surprising yourself, of something outside coming through. Even at times, I felt a long line of emboldened commentators, from the old, meek vicar to the tough hedge-priest to the non-religious ranter in the left-wing street, all standing behind me, joining in the chorus. Guess what word they are singing?

While I was excitingly writing my Ecclesiastes poems, I had been browsing in Alexander Pope's prose writing. His jokey take on how to write an epic was both funny and true, as he demonstrated in his mock-epic *The Rape of the Lock* (1712). I found this justification of traditionalism in literature brilliantly expressed if you take the time to fathom it out:

All that is left to us is to recommend our productions by the imitations of the ancients; and it will be found true, that in every age, the highest character for sense and learning has been obtained by those who have been most indebted to them. For, to say truth, whatever is very good sense, must have been common sense in all times; and what we call learning, is but the knowledge of the sense of our predecessors. Therefore they who say our thoughts are not our own, because they resemble the ancients, may as well say our faces are not our own, because they are like our fathers: and, indeed, it is very unreasonable that people should expect us to be scholars, and yet be angry to find us so.

('The Author's Preface to the Works', 1717)

One of the reasons I liked this so much is that it reminded me of John Berger saying that there is no progress in art. So far as I can tell, this remark, common in art criticism, comes from the artist associated with surrealism, Man Ray, in 1948, but I suspect it is older. It always seems that the most modern of artists turn back to the past for a sense of fresh knowing that the human condition is something of a continuum takes us away from the vanities (see Ecclesiastes) of the present day and its idea of the march of progress and change and growth. There is a humility here and a powerful sense of community with the wild old ancient writers, so unknowable and yet literally familiar.

Every artistic age renews itself from the more raw and direct expression, now seeming lost, but which in the past was so vividly present. I remember poet Norman Schwenk telling his MA creative writing students that he wanted to be part of a community of writers. That community was not only ourselves and our teachers, but our reading too and our feeling of belonging was one of being part of a tradition. These days they want you to be part of an industry.

While Wordsworth and Coleridge, in the preface to *Lyrical Ballads* (1801) wanted to reconnect with the vernacular truths that remained in folk and traditional material, likewise the moderns, like Picasso, Stravinsky and Pound, similar sought their justification in the vitalities of traditional arts. Writers have always used tradition and every innovation in literary history seems paradoxically reflected in older, universal concerns and methods of literary creativity. Writers are renewed by the directness and freshness found in previous works. For example, D.H. Lawrence's '[Autobiographical fragment]', from *Phoenix* (1936), presents an insight into how writers from the twentieth century, who might be called 'modernists', showed many aspects of the traditional: these include Kipling, Joyce and Eliot.

Lawrence's misnamed piece is so much more than mere autobiography. It combines autobiography with fiction, geography/geology, and futuristic science fiction. He describes returning to a childhood place of seeming magic, in some caves where items would become crystallised. He falls asleep and wakes up in a utopian future. The piece is strange and poetic and seems like a ritual of return and renewal. He returns to a place of origin and is reborn. I used this piece in a class on psycho-geography as an example of multi-genre work which addressed a traditional move of returning and renewal. It also seems to sum up the experimental aspect of writers of his time, who pioneered techniques of fiction we still find liberating. It is no coincidence that James Joyce's great experimental novel *Ulysses* (1922) derived in part and title from Homer's *Odyssey*, being the Roman version of the same name. A five-stage exercise, based on the Lawrence's piece, is among those below.

Recently Kate Tempest's work has been unashamedly classic and traditional in approach. This is especially true of her *Brand New Ancients* (2013) book and album, where she addresses an issue others often avoid in their adaptations: the gods. Her bringing home of the gods of Greek and Roman literature to the ordinary world of now is a triumph and her advocacy of myth is daring and exhilarating. You can easily find the opening tracks of the project on the internet. She is just one example of a serious and contemporary writing artist who seems steeped in the energy of tradition, like Seamus Heaney before her.

Once you begin to see tradition as valuable, you also begin to see it all around you, like an extra dimension, like a metaphor come to life in the world. As I write this, for example, a film of James Hilton's novel *Lost Horizon* (1933) is on TV. This is a story of a lost place where time seems eternal, where the timeless exists for the time-worn travellers who stumble across it. The novel is an image of a lost tradition still present in the modern world. The tale is like *Paradise Lost*, a deep meditation on good and innocence and the age-old verities of human life, always with us and available in literary as well as other traditions.

The most important thing for writers is that tradition is an active thing, a process rather than a fact, a practice not a formula. The traditional process is becoming aware of tradition and using it as a way of continuance and sustainability.

The traditional process is likewise a conscious and symbolic return to a lost home, which amounts to a remaking of the self. In this chapter, Phemius is a reminder of tradition amid the challenge to it and a story of traditional survival. Caedmon, from the people, brings the tradition back to the vernacular energy of honest religion and poetry, like another reminder of humility. Ecclesiastes is likewise a reminder of basic truths in humble honesty and his book ends positively, like a hard-won homecoming. Lawrence's piece projects a rebirth into a future, free from the wearying world of progress, via a return to childhood. These traditional motifs resonate in the heart as well as the mind and go deep into the places where creativity happens.

Author's Creative Examples:

IV: ANALOGUES ON ST GEORGE'S DAY

All other selves -
Hui-neng (638–713), Abbot Fursey
St Waltheow, Godric of Finchdale, Dunston
Elisha, when the minstrel played

The Piper and the Pooka in Ireland
Valmiki in the *Ramayana*
The underworld purification of Thomas the Rhymer
My John Banyard and Charles Potiphar
Robert Johnson on his knees down at the crossroad
The gipsies, John Clare and me
(and all the modern uneducated with degrees
who don't realise they're idiots in their seriousness)
The peasant poet, ancient mariner, idiot savant, noble savage
singing cowboy
and all the lovely oxymorons of
the suddenness of inspiration
make Cædmon multi-persons
and archetypal his story
of being the fool inspired beyond himself
tricked by muses and tricking to amuse
we hold the way open for writing
we let the animals go free
into the pasture
beneath the roof-tree
the low song from the high place
the high song from the low place

His is our song and his own
more foolish and more in control
than we know
our own mind's conjurer
orderly trick of inspiration
our utilitarian romanticism
making us humble wonderful

Maybe we should make him our Saint
and give him this day
with Shakespeare, also thought by snobs
to be too low to make the play
the sweetest high music of English day
April the twenty-third as I write
as low with potential as Cædmon might
He is unknowable, reflecting the light
offering song, sweetness and humility
infinite chances of discovery
to raise the song to a vantage point
the song unending knows its ending
singing its praise in the office of Night
the possibility of beginning

(From 'Caedmon's Own Song' in Ballads of Bohemian Essex (2011, Wivenhoe Books, Essex, UK))

TO YOURSELF (verse commentary on Ecclesiastes 5:1–20)

Keep your feet on the ground when you open your mouth
The rash row and dream hold divers vanities
And the man of words is the mouth of windy hot airs, insisting –
Hear the response, everyman's reply to the solipsistic prate –
You're talking to yourself, mate!

Newscasters, lecturers, loblolly men, spouters, shouters, dare I say long-necked screecher-preachers -
Don't blubber away to the closed world, you know what they'll say
Virtue signalling away makes you feel great –
You're talking to yourself, mate!

Shout your bleedin' head off at a god you're not ready to hear -
Better use a few words, pay what you owe
When many words and dreams fall from your pate –
You're talking to yourself, mate!

If you show that you are as foolish as those who buy a gilded mirror
And can't sleep for looking and
Those who gather money that shall not be satisfied with money
And their children shall show them nothing

Then rather eat and drink humbly, take your gift, your portion
Do not give thanks too late –
Or you will hear the all-purpose reply of god to the ungrateful inglorious ingrate
–
You're talking to yourself, mate!

You're talking to yourself, mate!

(from *Preacher: The Vanity Games*)

Writing Exercises

Write a work that uses the words 'canon' and 'cannon' to explore the weight of the past (research their meanings and etymology). Suggested title, 'Firing the Canon'.

Rewrite the first 10 lines of Homer's *The Odyssey*, the 'Proem', as film pitch, after reading as many translations as you can find. See Derek Walcott's *Omeros* (1990).

Write about a person or band called 'The Famous' and base the story on Phemius from *The Odyssey* (Homer, trans. Alexander Pope, 1726).

Use the ideas from the three new/old subjects given at the start of the chapter (*The Bacchae*, trans. Philip Vellacott, 1972), *The Epic of Gilgamesh* (trans. N.K. Sandars, 1960), and *Tristram Shandy*) to create something new.

Write one of the old magic songs that you imagine Caedmon the Traditional might have been reluctant to sing. This could be a song about soil, a song about animals and their lack of human pretence, a song of growing crops and harvesting, with a theme of sacrifice, or a song of his pagan gods, who inspired him to sing. See Bede's *Ecclesiastical History of the English People*, (731, trans. Shirley-Price and Latham, 1955, 1990).

Choose an animal or person or supernatural being or season to personify the arrival of inspiration and describe how they appear like a symbol of new life.

Research a visual artist, like Gauguin, Picasso or Paula Rego and see what influence traditional material had in their work and write about it as fiction, creative non-fiction or verse.

What would a contemporary Ecclesiastes write about?

Use this framework, based on D.H. Lawrence's '[Autobiographical Fragment]' (*Phoenix*, 1936), combining any genre, including fact and fiction: (1) Returning to a place of origin. (2) Describe the journey and landscape and the mixed feelings and associations of the experience. (3) Write about a meeting or arrival there and something unexpected happening and some secret, or secret place revealed. (4) Describe a change that happens. (5) Write a scene from the future, where change has affected you or the world around you.

Reading, Watching, Listening

Atwood, Margaret. 2002. *Negotiating with the Dead*. Cambridge: Cambridge University Press.
Atwood, Margaret. 2015. *On Writers and Writing*. London: Virago.
King James Bible.
Bloom, Harold. 1973. *The Anxiety of Influence*. Oxford: Oxford University Press.
Bede. 1990. *Ecclesiastical History of the English People*. Trans. Shirley-price and Latham. London: Penguin.
Brautigan, Richard. 1964. *A Confederate General from Big Sur*. New York: Grove Press.
Campbell, Joseph. 1968. *Creative Mythology*. New York: Viking Penguin.

Clare, John. 1966. Prose on Songs of the Plugh, 174. In *Selected Poems and Prose*. Oxford: Oxford University Press.
Coen Brothers. 2013. *Inside Llewlyn Davis*. C.B.S. Films.
Eliot, T.S. 1959. *Four Quartets*. London: Faner and Faber.
Euripides. 1972. *The Bacchae*. Trans. Philip Vellacott. Harmondsworth: Penguin.
The Epic of Gilgamesh, 1960. Trans. N.K. Sandars. Harmondsworth: Penguin.
Hilton, James. 1933. *Lost Horizon*. London: Macmillan.
Homer. 1872. *The Odyssey*. Trans. Alexander Pope. London: Routledge.
Kipling, Rudyard. 1928. The Handicaps of Letters, 41–44. In *A Book of Words*. London: Macmillan.
Lawrence, D.H. 1936. [Autobiographical fragment], 817–836. In *Phoenix*. London: Heinemann.
McCully, Chris. 2018. *Beowulf*. Manchester: Carcarnet.
Pope, Alexander. 1871. The Author's Preface to the Works, 1–16. In *The Works of Alexander Pope*. London: John Murray.
Schmidt, Michael. 2001. *The Story of Poetry*. London: Weidenfield and Nicholson.
Seeger, Pete. 1965. *Turn, Turn, Turn*. The Byrds. Columbia Records.
Sterne, Laurence. 2009. *Tristram Shandy*. Oxford: Oxford University Press.
Tempest, Kate. 2013. *Brand New Ancients*. London: Picador.
Terry, Philip. 2018. *Dictator*. Manchester: Carcarnet.
Thomas, Edward. 2004. Words, 77–78. In *Collected Poems*. London: Faber and Faber.
Walcott, Derek. 1990. *Omeros*. London: Faber and Faber.

CHAPTER 3

Not Just History and Ancient Inspirations

As I write, the U.K. and much of the world is under restriction in protection against the virus crisis of 2019–? As is so often the case, the restriction has proved a stimulus to creativity, good and bad. One positive thing is what I am calling the increase in 'hereness'. Local walks proscribed for health have made people aware of what is around them, where they normally might have travelled further to seek pleasure. Even for someone who is steeped in locality (see Chapter 8, Tradition and Locality) like me, new depths have been found amid the surface anxiety. Driven back on ourselves, we find our imagination moving in a different direction, reminding us of a past where people did not travel so much, rarely commuted and the riches they might have had in their apparent poverty. An awareness of past informing present usefully might be a definition of tradition in action in relation to history. If tradition is history, it is history in action, history brought alive.

The estuary is five minutes from my front door. It is the old dock area, only closed within the last twenty years, full of new blocks of flats, old industrial sites, houseboats, sewage works, a boat-builder, a potter, a reclaim building-materials yard and the ancient and modern side by side. The area, once full of sailors and pubs, ships and entertainers of sailors, has always felt to me as if it has the same rough and raucous energy, lurking underneath the surface. The house I have a place in was once the accommodation part of a pub called The Dolphin, and I imagine sailors and their women carousing away the evenings, as I sit quietly alone, thanking them for their ghostly company.

Recently during my constitutional walk, I noticed a wading bird with a long beak and asked my companion, a fisherman and someone who knows rivers and their wildlife well, its name. He told me it was a black-tailed godwit, a name I feel I should capitalise. It came to me that, aside from noticing obvious birds, like the little egrets arriving a few years ago, I was ignorant of seabirds. In the Hythe, as the area is called, freshwater birds like the ever-present and ancient moorhen, share water with birds of the sea, such as my godwit. Since then, over a few days, I have began to sport the binoculars I had all but forgotten I owned and look up birds in books. The black-tailed godwits have a history and a natural history. They are alive to me and offer me a hidden connection to where I live and a hidden depth to my local exercise period. 'My friends from the prison they ask unto me/ How good, how good does it feel to me free', as the traditional song goes. Tradition has me free in its chains.

What history offers the traditionalist is a kind of double lens. While a historian investigates the facts and sometimes even seeks disconnection from the present, the roots writer seeks images, metaphors, phrases and stories which offer a parallel or contrast with their own life. We look for the 'nowness' in the 'hereness'. Tradition as a word is often used as a synonym for history. Even those writing historical novels would argue their freedoms from the facts alone. Tradition seeks what is resonant and what offers a glimpse of depth beyond the self.

If you treat history like this, as a writer, you will be rewarded with images and inspirations that capture something of tradition itself, at the same time. You will find the timeless in the timely. The black-tailed godwit, to take one example of natural history, was once hunted almost to extinction, so its elegant presence here now in good numbers is an image of current good in terms of our relationship with the wild world. We see a tale of bad becoming good, something once present being brought present again positively. We see some use in history in a small exhilaration of the present—this is history brought alive: this is tradition in action.

Each U.K. county, I found out recently, has someone called a 'Bird Recorder', who notices movements, arrivals, departures and species. This might be a recent appointment but the profound role and title seem to me again significant of a change of attitude where someone would be given such a poetic name, with its traditionalist flavour inbuilt.

Here is a poem on the black-tailed godwit:
Author's Creative Example 1.

BLACK-TAILED GODWIT

At the old dock area in the Hythe
By the mess of old industry and new flats
The footpaths along the Colne are busy
With people exercising on foot and bike
Slow and fast, with or without kids
At times I step into long grass
So that others can safely pass

I notice an elegant wading bird
With a long beak; every twenty yards
As I go slow towards the lagoons
And realise my knowing my own back yard
Is limited in this avian estuarine direction

Told what they are, I take a lucky snap
On my way back and look up the name
Black-tailed godwit and you can hear
The 'wit' in their call but whence the god?

God in long elegance and delicate brown neck
God in long leg and reaching beak, in beauty overlooked
God amid the constant change of the estuary
God in my neglect, in subtle presence
God in almost disappearing by man's appetites
God in ability to return and remind
And seasonal changing raiment
God in sudden dazzle of black and white flight
God to us shamblers in the light
Clumsily rediscovering our footpath
With various forms of intention, resentment, ignorance, or delight

The intention of this poem is to show that history, and natural history, can be very much about now. It is written in the midst of the virus restrictions of April 2020. The history of the now closed dock area and the old and new worlds being side by side frame a rediscovered 'nowness' and 'hereness', which the narrator, among others, stumbles into.

Something of the history of the bird is there: how it was hunted almost to oblivion for eating in the nineteenth century. Likewise, there are details of its appearance. This is nothing like a purely historical poem or a purely nature-based poem. It tries to place the self and contemporary events in a historical context.

The poem also seeks to show the timeless in the timely, which is both historical and traditional. The 'god' with a small 'g' might be non-Christian or even pantheistic, but the line beginnings, with the subsequent capital 'G' are deliberately ambiguous. With luck, the literary reader might be reminded of T.S. Eliot's line about the river being 'a strong, brown god', from 'The Dry Salvages' in *Four Quartets* (1943).

The move in the poem is intended to be from oldness to newness, via the timelessness of nature. If this works, the poem becomes a traditional ritual which acknowledges the past and present. Other poems which do this might include Tennyson's 'Ulysses' (1842) and Mathew Arnold's 'Dover Beach' (1867).

Here is another poem that attempts a more historical, yet simple approach.
Author's Creative Example 2.

THE STANDING STONES

No-one owns the standing stones ...

No-one knows how they were moved
No-one knows how they were loved
No-one knows if they stood for life
No-one knows if they marked our death
Some say it's to do with the sun
And our rationality must be done
We can't help using the mind of today
Our only move is explaining away

No-one owns the standing stones ...

No-one knows why the stones are there
Their ancient message is obscure
But when I was low one bleak day
They reassured – Look how we stay
How we retain the mystery –
And I remembered my life, and forgot about me

No-one owns the standing stones ...

In structure and number of the two main stanzas' lines (not in metre), this is a sonnet. This one attempts a critique of history, which sometimes seems to be a seeking for answers to the unanswerable. Now and the personal come into it again, as does the sense of time. We seek the timeless in time and perhaps all writing has this function, or tradition. Wordsworth spoke of 'spots of time' in his great autobiographical poem *The Prelude* (1850). Seeing your life, the above poem seeks to imply, in relation to something bigger is a liberating traditional move.

Realising that the world is full of images and stories is liberating too and reading depth into your surroundings is always popular, at a local level. As philosopher John Dewey said, 'Locality is the only universal' ('Americanism and Localism', 1920). In the U.K., counties have their local studies libraries which are secret treasure-houses of information. They also have record offices, similarly amazing sources for writers of all kinds. I used to take my psychogeography students to the Essex local studies library and I could guarantee they would get lost and absorbed in such a wealth of material. They even had specialist librarians in those days, who would talk us through the scope of the collection and were like talking encyclopaedias of fascinating information.

Here the humility of the scholar meets the audacity of the writer. One of the paradoxes of writing is this balance between being humbly open to be inspired, coupled with the seeming arrogance of being original. For a roots writer, these two opposites are help in useful opposition, or balance. A roots writer moves from one to the other as part of the process. To be a traditionalist is to understand creativity and to become creative as a sustainable way of life.

It is my own creative practice of many years to be interested in the local as a way of living, as well as a way of being a writer more deeply connected to the world. I seemed instinctively drawn towards old buildings which had a purpose or function no longer fulfilled. I remember that, as a young man, I was drawn to an old abandoned cinema decaying on the street. This place, once so full of human dreams, seemed hugely poignant to me, with a sense of the sadness of time passing. Also, I found older people interesting for their history. My historical sense was then one of creative connection, not of fact or, at least, not merely of fact.

This is so much the case that by now it is my habit to have always in mind some aspect of history, often local history. At present, aside from the estuary birds, I have been fascinated by something in the south of the country of Essex. My fellow creative writing teachers and I made a trip to the Southend Museum about a year ago to see the Anglo-Saxon burial material from a grave discovered below a roundabout in Prittlewell, a town nearby, connected to the Southend area by urban development in south Essex. What had caught my attention was that this Prince or King was buried with both a sword and harp, or lyre nearby and how they symbolised a balance of war and peace. The fiddle and the gun was an image used in the U.K. during World War II and indeed is a song—'Fiddle or a Gun'—by a favourite band, Oysterband, from Kent, on their album *Deserters* (1992). The connections of Essex and Kent here might be from Queen Bertha of Kent's descendants, who moved to Essex, including the King I eventually chose as my subject.

I came by accident on a TV channel showing a programme about what they called 'The Prittlewell Prince' and discovered that my wonder at this had further evidence as to its significance. The fact that the sword was not inside his coffin was unusual and gave further reason to believe he might be an early Christian, in touch with peace. Speculations about who he was also intrigued me. At one time, historians thought he might be King Seebert of Essex, but some scientific dating has placed him earlier. With no historical certainty at all, he now might be King Saexa, son of King Sledd. A search on the internet soon revealed something else which got me more interested.

The buried Anglo-Saxon royal seemed to have galvanised a local protest group, against the road-widening scheme which the discovery has inadvertently brought about. Locally the royal had been called 'The King of Bling', where 'bling' is a recent slang word for fancy jewellery, not unknown in south Essex. The protest group won local support and the local Council withdrew the scheme. The museum we visited, owned by the local Council, did not mention this modern intervention at all. I am retrospectively unsurprised at this. So my imagination saw King Saexa as a man of peace for the county both in his time and, significantly, in the time of his rediscovery. This man of peace had a second coming. Seaxes are knives or small cutting implements which actually form part of the Essex county flag, so my prejudice is in favour of his name.

Perhaps inspired subconsciously by the Oysterband, I imagined a folk-rock song about this. Not based on fact at all, the lyric started as a jokey rhyme in my head and then became serious. I recommend this method of balancing the creative with the factual, moving from the child-like to the adult. Here's my lyric:

Author's Creative Example 3:

SAEXA

King of Essex, King of Bling
Had a sword and everything
Gold-fitted sword there in his room
But it was not inside his tomb
The warrior balanced weapons sharp
With a harmonious maple harp
King of balance, King of peace
With gold crosses on his eyes
 And even if it weren't his name
 He changed the world twice just the same

With his symboled wealth, like these
His resurrection caused surprise
For the money men who tried
To build a massive road and wide.
More than a thousand years ago
Saexa little thought that so
As he weighed up peace and war
Music song and fighting for –

The harmony of right and wrong
How he'd inspire a protest song
And keep the benefit of doubt
To expanders of the roundabout.
King Saexa rules with peace
Saved Prittlewell, its folks, its trees
So don't ignore the cool King factor
All sing praise to King Saexa!
 And even if it weren't his name
 He changed the world twice just the same

One thing that arose in the scribbled draft of this was the mistake of using 'weren't' instead of 'wasn't'. I quickly realised this was appropriate channelling of my unposh Essex past. It is what we would say. Also the sentence strung between two stanzas, when I began to think about stanzas at all, in the editing stage, seemed to draw attention to itself usefully, linking the disparate things as

I was seeking to do in the burden of the text. The chorus, in italics, came as an afterthought, or comment on the whole, almost a footnote. Often this kind of things shows a slant on the tale, appropriate to a chorus, even in the sense of an external voice or voices, as in Greek drama. These kinds of tuned-in 'happy accidents' seem to happen to writers all the time.

One problem for writers is that history is in the hands of historians—we might have to wrench it from them. Novelist Hilary Mantel says that when she began writing novels based on history, she felt inferior to both historians and literary novelists. These days she counts historians as friends and realises her past feelings were generated by what amounts to snobbishness. She now has a radical view of her craft, earned by her huge success, in terms of sales and kudos. 'History is not the past: it is the method we have evolved for organising our ignorance of the past', she says, again in her BBC Reith Lectures from 2017. Here she begins by quoting St Augustine, 'the dead are invisible, not absent', which is literally true, genetically, and in a liberating way for writers and traditionalists.

It seems to me that making friends with historians is a good idea. Finding a local historian and tapping into their wealth of stories is fascinating. Historians are often interesting characters too and you might try the exercise below.

Shakespeare wrote historical works, yet few criticise him. His sources are well known and can be found in any scholarly edition. Writing with a dimension of history can give an eternal or timeless insight into the human condition, which, to a writer, often feels like it makes you young, renewed with your story. This is true of my tale of Saexa, whoever he was.

Find out what writers are from your area and do a little historical research into their life and work. Again, from my own experience, I years ago read Sabine Baring-Gould's *Wuthering Heights*-like novel *Mehalah: A story of the salt marshes* (1880), set on Mersea Island, a half-hour drive from where I live. This for me is due a feminist re-reading, as the titular character wears a red hat as a sign of rebellion and independence. Modern reprints of this novel cost a fair bit, but I have an old copy from 1920, which I repaired myself, like an ancient relic. The 'marsh ague' at that time was really malaria and the locals were immune. Some would go to Colchester to find a new spouse, if they lost one to the disease. They still have fearsome mosquitoes on Mersea. Baring-Gould was Vicar at East Mersea church for a time and worth researching as a great traditionalist himself. He collected folk song and his collections are still published.

His book *Old Country Ways* (1890) is fascinating and full of material. The chapter titles alone tell you much: 'The Old Garden', 'The Country Parson', 'Country Dances', The Village Band', etc. In 'The Old Roads', he tells us how awful the roads were, muddy and often impassable. Carts would sometimes tow a fallen tree behind them for extra stability, to buoy the cart up from the mud.

Another Essex author, Jack Lindsay inspired a short story I wrote some years back. Some local friends told me that they had found out he lived in

Castle Hedingham in the 1970s. They also knew that he had been friendly with poet Dylan Thomas, much admired by such bohemians as my friends. They turned up at his door—his house was called Bangslappers—and invited him out for a drink. He agreed and they had a good evening. Lindsay was another polymath, who wrote many books, including a pioneering work on north Essex archaeology, strangely called *The Discovery of Britain* (1958). I recently alerted some folk who live in this area to the book, which resulted in all the copies on the internet suddenly selling. There is recently a website devoted to him: jacklindsayproject.com.

In the U.K., there are some classic works of personal, social history and I am sure other parts of the world have similar books to discover. Flora Thompson's *Lark Rise to Candleford* (1973) holds a detailed world of rural life in Victorian Oxfordshire. Many songs and plays have used it as a source but certainly not used it up. W.C. Hoskins' *Local History in England* (1959) is just one example of an academic book still useful. In film, a recent example, *12 Years a Slave* (dir. Steve McQueen, 2013) is based on a historical slave text of the same title by Solomon Northup (1853). Even an original script, like Spike Lee's *Do the Right Thing* (1989) has historical, traditional relevance in quoting at the end from Martin Luther King and Malcolm X.

One more example from today, as I write. I visited a 'car boot sale' (like a garage sale in a field) and bought a 9″ × 6″ photograph of an unidentified big band, I guessed from the 1950s. Ten minutes on the internet and I found that it is The Teddy Foster Orchestra, formed in 1945. I was immediately plunged into the world of U.K. big bands of my childhood and this kind of thing could easily inspire some writing. There is one black musician in the band and I am keen to find his story. A whole world is uncovered again, only going to prove something G.K. Chesterton said in his essay 'The Duty of the Historian' (1939), that the most profound aspect of history is good stories.

Writers turn history into dream and dream into myth. Tradition is not just history but history that remains useful. Historical creative work is not just history, but history with the added value of the repeating image in the ritual recapturing of a human quality, which is the quality to appreciate the timely in the timeless. This is also called tradition.

Writing Exercises

If you live in a brand new place in a brand new street, research the land before it was built on. For example, London Stansted Airport was built on land once called 'The Wilderness' and I wrote a ghostly tale which incorporated this. Write something inspired by the land.

Write about an old, abandoned cinema: what dreams come alive there?

Write a more considered story or poem about the King of Essex, who might not even have been a King.

Read Hilary Mantel's Reith Lectures (*The Day Is for Living*, B.B.C. 2017) and try writing a dramatic monologue from inside a historical character.

Interview a historian about their subject, but then write about the historian.

Use something from history brought up to date without mentioning the historical source at all.

Oral history (see next chapter): interview someone older about their part of history, say in music, and use that to start writing.

The song of 'The Bird Recorder'.

'Ancient' is a trendy word, as is 'vintage' and 'retro'. Research and write a dialogue about these difficulties and authenticity.

Write about a writer who lives close to you.

Reading, Watching, Listening

I recommend that you become a history book browser, as well as using the awesome archives of the internet to find old histories; full of stories waiting to be told and songs waiting to be sung.

Use local resources, research local authors.

Buy a book on your native birds and natural history for reference and sources.

Look at any old movies that are filmed or set in your area.

Baring-Gould, Sabine. 1880. *Mehalah*. London: Smith Elder.

Baring-Gould, Sabine. 1890. *Old Country Life*. London: Methuen.

Chesterton, G.K. 1939. *Selected Essays*. London: Collins.

Dewey, John. 1920. Americanism and Localism, 684–688. In *The Dial 68*. New York.

Hoskins, W.C. 1959. *Local History in England*. London: Longman.

Lee, Spike. 1989. *Do the Right Thing*. Universal Pictures.

Lindsay, Jack. 1958. The Discovery of Britain. London: The Merlin Press.

McQueen, Steve. 2013. *12 Years a Slave*. Fox Searchlight Films.

Mantel, Hilary. 2017. *The Day Is for the Living*. B.B.C. Reith Lectures. London: B.B.C.

Northup, Solomon. 1853. *12 Years a Slave*. London: Sampson Low.

Oysterband. 1992. Fiddle or a Gun. On *Deserters*. Cooking Vinyl Records.

Thompson, Flora. 1973. *Lark Rise to Candleford*. Harmondsworth: Penguin.

CHAPTER 4

Storytelling, Myth, Folklore and Magic

Stories within stories within storytellers: we are the creatures made of stories. We think in stories and live in them too. At the same boot sale (a 'car boot' in the U.K. is a trunk) as in the last chapter, I saw a man with a shovel in one hand and a radio in the other. My mind immediately and shockingly, to me, created a tale of a partner who did not like the noise of him listening to the radio. He intended to bury them with the shovel, then sit with his feet up listening to the radio chirp! This dark scenario came from my world of stories, unbidden.

Essex University in the U.K. was built in the 1960s and they say the modernist library was built upside-down. There is also the story of the 1960s student who still haunts the corridors, lost, trying to find their classroom in the confusing room-numbering system. These were just two stories I used to tell my first-year undergraduates. I will return to them later.

Narrative is hard to define and it is an adjective as well as a noun. It derives from the Latin 'gnarus', which means knowing and 'ignorant' comes from the same source. Narrative is another word for story and means just that, or a recital of facts. Although E.M. Forster, in *Aspects of the Novel* (1927) was more interested in 'plot', he had to admit, sadly, that the story was still the primal thing and a plot is only one way of telling a story.

To return us to the source, it is worth imagining what the world would be like without writing and without the technology of communication. We would be more what we already are, which is part of an oral culture. The problem with writing is that it is separate from us, which is both its boon and its problem. This is true for writers. I have always found that a return to the oral nature of creative writing is a good move. Tell yourself the story, sing the

© The Author(s), under exclusive license to Springer Nature
Switzerland AG 2021
A. May, *Tradition in Creative Writing*,
https://doi.org/10.1007/978-3-030-74776-3_4

song without accompaniment and recite the lines without putting them on paper. *The Translator* (2002) by John Crowley has a teacher who makes each student recite a poem at the end of the first term and how challenging and liberating this is.

A.E. Housman, author of *A Shropshire Lad* (1896), used to go for a walk and compose his poems solely in his head. He would not write the poem down till he got home. Sometimes I think the problem with writing is that it is as if in inverted commas. The self-consciousness of inscription comes between the teller and the tale. There is a need for writers to reconnect with their tradition of normal social interaction. We talk to each other. We still tell our stories.

Working as a 'Lecturer' (University teacher) is strangely close to the oral tradition. We do lots of writing and reading but essentially we talk for a living. Talk is human culture and narrative our primal form of thought and communication. Our attempts to capture that, in improvisation, in oral composition like Housman, or into a recording device or application, cinema *vérité*, taking notes from life, conversational realism, hard-boiled writing, is all to capture the same effect: liveliness. In this sense, tradition itself is liveliness. This is the stream of consciousness, the lost connection, the spontaneity which some think is the opposite of tradition.

There is a sense in which written texts are fixed. Traditionally, every teller would have their own version. A written text is merely one. Another misconception is that mere story is banal, but the subtly and speed of stories told and the enduring qualities of traditional material are what makes them endurable and re visitable. The world of story is open to us. As Angela Carter said in the introduction to her *Virago Book of Fairy Tales* (1990) it is not so much that you make potato soup but what your particular recipe is for it. A contemporary novelist who uses Native American storytelling traditions is Leslie Marmon Silko, as shown in her memoir *A Turquoise Ledge* (2010).

Religion created creative writing, or accountancy did, but the theatre and the church are two places where speaking takes precedence and where catchiness, much-derided but essential to a popular song and all music really, is not despised. Traditional stories are catchy, sticky, enduring and open up worlds of thought.

Wonder and the supernatural work in our verbal, oral world in a natural way and stories think with a different, more primal logic. The modern writer does psychology, while all that is there in the world of the story, represented by the supernatural. It was no coincidence that psychologists like Freud and Jung, especially, found correspondences in their worlds of thought, their stories. Stories remain in children and we fallen adults have sold out to the writing and to the machine. Our culture has been stolen and sold back to us. Our birthright is as creators not consumers, but it is hard to resist. It is worth reminding ourselves that Jesus and Socrates, two of the most influential thinkers still in our world, never wrote a thing.

Walter Ong, in *Orality and Literacy* (1982) points out that, in a 1971 study, of three thousand languages in the world, only seventy-eight had writing. There are different kinds of wisdom in oral cultures, of a kind that might be useful to us and remind us of who we really are, before writing conquered the world. Learning was by apprenticeship, by known sayings and stories, by experience. I used to remind my class that ours was an oral culture at root and us talking to each other was the way we really learn. The long memory of the Serbo-Croat singers in Albert Bates Lord's *The Singer of Tales* (1965), who could recall Epics of great length, is all but lost to us who have fallen into writing. To make our writing sing again in the air, we need the liveliness of our roots.

'If in doubt, read it out', I would tell my essay writing class. Hearing your essay reveals its strengths and weakness. In my oral literature classes, I would tell students to put away their evil paper and pens, their keyboards and machines. Then we would tell stories.

Storytelling in a group is most effective, as the stories seem to add to each other and a sense of community seems to emerge. It is easily done with two people, however and, with a bit of imagination, by a person on their own. With my class, I would give them no real rules but just that it could be anything: a family tale, an urban myth, a ghost story they had heard, anything strange or fascinating and they could even make it up. I still have my lists of the kinds of things they told and they show great variety and diversity. Subjects ranged from voodoo to family to Facebook. We have this as a natural or traditional gift. It enlivens writing. An adult group I once taught was becoming a little dull, as the students' writing tended to become a style, a class fixity that was more of the same. After we had told some 'strange but true' stories, a good proportion of the group began writing more like they spoke. Life came in to their writing.

Recording devices are very useful, as is a plain old notebook. Going out to record what you hear and see in the world is another method of doing the same thing, which is bringing the real into the writing. Robert Wolf's book *Jump Start: How to Write from Everyday Life* (2001) is good on the whole topic. Oral history techniques are worth investigating, likewise.

The other great faculty of the writer is memory, both in terms of having a good one and in terms of being able to remember your story. A 'pitch', as in selling a movie, is a useful oral skill to develop. Be warned that talking a story out can happen, however. If you tell your book or piece too often, it can become stale, but memorability is a kind of catchiness. Jack Kerouac, the great Beat writer, was known as 'memory babe' by his friends, as he was known to hold the memories, the stories, of his scene, so well. Can you recite your best paragraph? Learn it and see why it works.

Studying how storytelling works, with swiftness, with key repeated phrases like choruses is always useful. Rhetorical devices like anaphora, the repetition of a phrase from the beginning of a piece, as in the 'I have a dream' speech, still works well. Look up and use other rhetorical devices. Rhetoric was once one of the oldest subjects at a western university and arguably with creative writing, it has returned.

See if there are storytelling clubs near you, as the movement is a growing one. I know more than one professional storyteller. Go and see them do their thing and maybe even participate. Ask what a writer can learn from them. Stories are already within us, as often stories are within other stories, as you can see from Homer onwards. Make a frame for stories within yourself.

The stories of the university, the lost student and the upside-down library are all about student anxiety told into tales. These take us, in the words of Horace's *Ars Poetica* (poetic arts), *in medias res* (into the midst of things) which is where epics start. Try starting your story in the middle. Are you the narrator? Or is your narrator another self, perhaps 'unreliable'? Stories start you playing with persona, as well as straight into psychology, in the world of dreams with the tale swallowing itself.

The world of urban myth is a direct root into the strangeness of shared tales. Most places have urban myths of their own. This kind of material is again in you and all around you. With my masters-level students, many years in the past, I used a collection of urban myths about my own home university, which I collected anonymously and very easily over a couple of weeks. These modern pieces of folklore are potent if used inventively and if you can see the underlying role they perform, often in embracing genuine anxieties of the day, as the student ones above do.

You can treat urban myth as the stories that we hear, or as myths of the urban. An example is the beginning of the *Epic of Gilgamesh*, where the King has become corrupt and is acting crazily, out of control. The story of Sodom and Gomorrah in the Bible has a similar reflection of the real anxieties of the age of the urban world. Even these new tales are old things come again. In other words, they are traditional.

Urban myths, like myth itself are an external manifestation of some inner reality. The uncanny and subversive elements of the madness of the world made real is undeniably useful to the intelligent writer. Writers treat source material as equal and are concerned with a different kind of authenticity, which is a creative one and what I would call a traditional one. What is useful to you and hence to the world? A book that covers this well is Jan Harold Brunvard's *The Vanishing Hitchhiker: Urban Myths and Their Meaning* (1983). Arguably the ultimate urban myth is the dystopian future story, where all our apocalyptic ideas are rolled to one great end.

C.G. Jung's *Flying Saucers* (translated 1978) says we want to believe in them, as we need gods and archetypes so much. Our unconscious desires speak through these stories and tell us not just what our characters think they want, but what they really want without perhaps even knowing it. Likewise, Sodom and Gomorrah are about human desire and ambition not recognising the angels in their midst. Human frailty is to the fore and these tales confront it. Marina Warner in her brilliant *Managing Monsters* (1994) suggests in a way that we have monstered ourselves and asks why.

The story of the life of Buddha is an urban myth. He leaves his privileged life and seeks quiet enlightenment. Here he fulfils a religious, mythic and psychological function of the separation from the world. In what I would call a traditional way, he goes above the city and the world and moves back into himself to discover the roots of peace and true self-connection. Only then can he change the world.

The taxonomy of different types of story is only of limited use to the practising writer. While academics might be interested in the differences, we are interested in the commonality of all stories. If urban myths are the folklore of a kind and myth of a kind, that is fine. When I teach classes on myth I am at pains to tell the students that when they learn to think mythically, then everything is myth. However, I have come to believe that tradition is the operative and useful term which overrides all these things.

Myths can become static and mere history. When I first encountered myth myself, it was in the hands of allusive litterateurs who showed off their Classical knowledge and alienated the common reader. I had to learn differently and then taught that it was possible to use myth without even showing it at all, if needed. This stuff became my own and the rootedness of it in the human psyche was why I liked it. My thinking became mythic and my mythic pursuits became useful, that is traditional, in the way I see it now.

Tradition for me is then *myth in action*. Another way of saying this is that it is myth made useful. Tradition is experiential, not taxonomic. Tradition is inductive, coming from the inside of the writer and their roots, which myth can all to easily be deductive and seem as an imposed thing or theory put onto the surface of the world.

Folklore is myth without religion or unconscious material becoming myth slowly, or material turned from tradition into taxonomy. Tradition rescues folklore from becoming Myth, with a capital 'M'. Tradition returns myth from its extremity, its divorce from experience and folklore from its neutrality. Writing is a traditional practice, as we have said and our work reflects that. It can bring us home and revivify us.

To show this in action, we can discuss the myth of Diana and Actaeon. The myth of Actaeon (the hunter killed by his own hounds) seems to embody the baffling problem of masculinity and violence, which both turns on itself and presents an inevitably cruel fate. In the most famous literary version of the myth, Ovid, in *Metamorphoses* III, describes Actaeon the hunter chancing upon the sacred grove of the Goddess Diana/Artemis. She is bathing naked attended by her nymphs and throws water into Actaeon's face, whereupon he is turned into a stag and then killed by his hounds. Ovid himself is obviously fascinated by this baffling quality, when he says, with a kind of male innocence, as if voicing what Actaeon would say, that if he had not been struck dumb by becoming a stag, then he might just be unlucky.

The question, after the straight denial, gives us doubt and makes us wonder if losing your way is somehow more significant and serious, remembering also that Ovid was in exile when he wrote *Metamorphoses*. He shows a sense of being on the side of those who might be unfairly treated and taken from their familiar role. Exile in those times is known to be considered a terrible fate. As so often with Ovid, we get the feeling that he is telling us to look as this weird old mythic material and daring us and perhaps himself to dismiss it. Getting lost, we know from fairytales, is a significant matter, meaning that something good, or bad, will be found and confronted. Ovid then, from his introductory lines, tempts us and himself to take it seriously.

Another version of the myth, mentioned in Euripides' *The Bacchae*, has Actaeon boasting that he was a better hunter than Artemis/Diana, the Goddess of hunting.So, if there is a naivety about the lost hunter, there is a sense of arrogance, or naive masculinity somewhere at the back of the myth, which teases the civilised and exiled Ovid and his readers still. We are also reminded that the forest, the dark wood of fairytale, is also the place where transformations happen and where nature and beasts confront our superficialities. Actaeon is a civilised man and nature is his sport and his raiding is always going to be a challenge to the Goddess of hunting, and of the moon and nature. Something is lost by boasting, as it is by being lost. Kerényi, in *The Gods of the Greeks* (1951) reports that an earlier version has Actaeon in a stag's skin, stalking Artemis: in a later version, he intends to rape her. Elsewhere he is merely her suitor. Actaeon thus seems to be every inappropriate man, foolishly arrogant in some way, stumbling into something beyond him.

What is remarkable is that this is how it must often feel to be a man, given the evidence of artists and writers returning to the story ever since. There is something in the paradoxical seesaw or insistence of the myth, the faultline perhaps, that keeps us coming back. This quality, to attend to the most troubled of situations, to the central taboos of humanity, is what gives myths a godlike, eternal quality and the ability to invite endless interpretation, as well as retellings. Myths that recur have traditional resonance.

The whole of Robert Graves' *The White Goddess* (1948: 1961) presents a different picture of Actaeon being part of a tradition or ritual of annual sacrifice to the great goddess of both nature and writing. This is a conscious, non-tragic Actaeon, aware of the sacrifice, seeking a renewal through the encounter. There is a sense of a renewal also through the wildness, which could make us think of Actaeon, turned stag and killed and scattered like seed, being a version of Dionysus, another great myth of how to deal with the wildness and troubled rational opposites, or extremes, in men. The cruelty is ignored by the scorned hero, if the Goddess is both that of nature and of creativity.

The positive, seasonal sacrifice is sometimes quoted in the traditional English song, 'Hal an Tow' as it is in Shakespeare's *As You Like It*, where the connection to Actaeon is clear, 'What shall he have that kill'd the deer?| His leather skin and horns to wear.' Later comes the line, 'Take thou no scorn to wear the horn,' which calls to mind the alternative approach of Actaeon again, as well as the ritual humiliation which seems bound to the myth. There is poaching, hunting and the testing and ritualising of nature here, as well as a resorting to it. Other versions of this traditional song have a chorus about welcoming in the summer, a kind of Mayday festival of renewal, as well as the humiliation of horns, with its links to cuckolding. Graves refers to Artemis having him killed at her *anodos*, or annual reappearance, when she renewed her virginity in the holy water and then found a new lover. Here we have Actaeon emphatically connected to an annual nature-based mythic rebirth, as is Graves' dedicatory poem at the start of his book.

In this view of the myth as a traditional, seasonal action, we see more sense and more embodiment of the problems it addresses. Actaeon is stumbling towards traditional knowledge, acknowledgement and seasonal renewal. In this, we have the potential traditional, even comic, or positive, rebirth, rather than the tragic vision, which the myth might seem at first glance to insist is its dark message. It is Actaeon's very vulnerability with which we can identify and upon which we can reflect.

If Actaeon's story reveals stories within us and within other stories, so the portmanteau is common in early literary texts. The storytelling theme in *The Decameron* (1903) by Boccaccio is set in the time of plagues, where a group of people take refuge in a house to sit it out and tell stories, one hundred in all. I can imagine writing a novel set in the current pandemic, perhaps a writing retreat become more permanent than intended, which I will include in the writing exercises below. *The Decameron* stories are often sexual and contain an inner world, as well as looking out. One of the tales (day 4, tale 1) is the same story as one from the Child ballad collection (Child 269). Love is the theme and love has the greatest claim to be traditional, as we all recognise it as something constant in human experience. Love underlies the Actaeon tale of course. Man Ray's thought that there is no progress in art, says further that art is more like love in its infinite variety and sameness. Another great ballad that reflects this, and contains grand storytelling, the magical and the mythical is 'The Earl of Mars' Daughter'. Its final message is of traditional love.

I first read the story of 'The Earl of Mar's Daughter' in Joseph Jacobs' *English Fairy Tales* (1890). The text of the tale of the eponymous daughter and her bird-lover is given in full below. I was at once struck by its strangeness and already had a hint of the kind of high magic the story contains. There was something exhilarating about it and a bookmark stayed in my copy of Jacobs for some years. The fact that it is not a story but a ballad and not English but Scottish did not put me off. I knew, from my folk music background, of the great anthology of ballads gathered together by the Reverend Francis James Child and quickly found the source for Jacobs' perfectly good retelling, in 'Child 270', as the reference would be given. In the Roud folksong index it is number 3879. When I recently investigated the tune of this little-sung, forty-one stanza song and began to sing it myself, in an anglicised version, following Jacobs here, its curious high magic power began to work on me and make my admiration for it deepen and itself take flight.

The history and the music, the 'avianthropy' and the related bird prince tales, together with the height of the flight all led me to performing the long ballad in public and leading a discussion of its motifs and power at the University of Essex's Myth Reading Group.

Scottish poets were the prime collectors of ballads, rather than scholars like Child. Robert Burns, who was a collector, adapter and participant in traditional song, was the model for this. He died just before the end of the eighteenth century but his reach and model live on. Walter Scott published his *Minstrelsy of the Scottish Borders* in four volumes between 1802 and 1807, which included his own attempts at ballad poems. 'The Earl of Mar's Daughter' seems to have been first published by another poet, Peter Buchan, in his *Ancient Ballads and Songs* of 1828.

Buchan's notes regret the passing of magic and he claims that nobles were taught magic on Grand Tours of Spain and Italy, citing the name 'Florentine' as the bird prince's name as evidence of its 'highest claim to antiquity', as well as the uncertainty of the location of Marr. Mar was part of Aberdeenshire in the middle ages, and I must admit that I left the name Florentine out of my version, but the fact that poets were involved in a kind of rediscovered tradition of balladry brings in the question of possible fakery. This is a question to which I will return.

The definitive Child ballad collection was published between 1882 and 1898 as *English and Scottish Popular Ballads*. Child was no poet and never visited these islands, but was an American vicar and academic and the anthologist of some 305 ballads in his great book. The story of the collecting of ballads was then one of gradual wresting away from their sources and from their music. The music of the Child ballads was not published, shockingly, until between 1959 and 1972, nearly three-quarters of a century later.

Joseph Jacobs published his retelling as a prose narrative in 1890 and says in his notes that the ballad is 'clearly a fairy tale' and again cites the name Florentine as proving its pre-Celtic origin. While I enjoy its questionable origins, I believe that restoring its tune and somehow bringing it back to itself as a song adds significantly to its power, not least in its musical aspects.

The first thing the music can tell us is that each verse of the sung ballad contained two stanzas of the printed version, turning it into twenty eight-line stanzas with a four-line envoi. These structural shifts make the movements of the ballad clearer, its verbal and musical heights, so to speak, greater.

Another feature of the ballad tune, in common with other ballads, is that the melody is higher at the *beginning* of each verse, before settling for the second quatrain into a lower register. This is unlike most short songs which tend to build through each verse towards a higher cadence, sometimes in the repeated chorus. The effect of this high start is a driving on of the narrative, a beginning again and a heightened sense of the repetition in a long song, creating a trance-like state in performer and listeners, with a renewal of height appropriate to the ballad. The repeated phrases, another common element of ballads, and between ballads too, adds to this. For example, the lists of birds keep the ballad in the air, so to speak.

Common epithets, stock phrases and even whole verses, often called 'floating verses' (flying verses?) appear in many traditional songs and ballads. 'The Earl of Mar's Daughter' has much in common with 'The Gay Goshawk'

(Child 96), as the title of the latter appears, for instance, in the former. The Gay Goshawk features a talking bird messenger and is not nearly so high a subject, favouring to my mind the absurd above the high-flown love story in 'The Earl of Mar's Daughter'.

In common with other performers of ballads, I use what is called an open tuning on the guitar as accompaniment, coupled with often modal chords. This means, at one level, chords that are neither straight major nor minor in sound and often have the third note of a chord absent. The effect of this is to repeat many notes as chords change, which also adds to the drone-like effect of the tune. This, I believe adds to the trance-effect which suspends the performer and listeners in a 'once upon a time' time and mental space, with the repetitions and high restarting mentioned above.

The length of the song and the time it takes to sing add again to this continuum. The various song lengths present in ballad collections and collections of other traditional songs show how the song has been dominated by technology in recent times. Bob Dylan, another poet with a deep interest in the tradition, has notably broken this taboo in popular music with the hypnotic and building flight of 'Like A Rolling Stone' (1965), which was a single of over six minutes, roughly twice the normal length. He also had 'Sad Eyed Lady of the Lowlands' (1966), which covered the whole side of an LP record, lasting about twelve minutes. 'The Earl of Mar's Daughter' takes me about eighteen minutes to sing. Dance music DJs obviously know the trance-like nature of long mixes of various tracks and the 'prog-rock' cliché of the long ego-trip of a song must, I hope, give way to the suspension of the ego where, ideally, the singer and listeners get lost in the flight of the sung story.

'The Earl of Mar's Daughter' is not often sung. I think this is partly because of its daunting length. Modern singers like the more realistic, dramatic, or even violent tales of song and the more harshly romantic tales. Its extraordinary nature makes it a bit forbidding as does its positive ending, I suspect. It might be too high, too absurd, and therefore too difficult to approach. It is, properly, a comedy, having a happy ending and teeters on the brink of absurdity in magical love and flying metamorphosis. Anyone interested in modern singers of ballads could do worse than to listen to June Tabor's album *An Echo of Hooves* (2003) or Pete Morton's *Trespass* (1998).

The fast-paced immediacy of ballads and their fantastic elements have been labelled 'tabloid' by some, but for me, the immediacy and the familiar cadences of words and music have an extraordinary power which, in the case of this ballad, echo well its avianthropic intensity. These are all aspects of the height of its flight.

Its story is the opposite of Icarus and there are interesting relatives of its tale-type and motifs worth exploring, not insignificantly in the symbolism of flight. This is one of our most common images of imagination, even of achieved imagination, if we consider that the sky is full of our mechanical birds. Love and birds are also inextricably linked in folksong, 'turtle doves' are often symbols of love and the bird and the nest are folkloric symbols of the male and female anatomy. The folksong 'The Cuckoo's Nest' is a traditional example. The fluttering of wings is that of hearts and sexual movement in symbolic form. One might fall into love but even that implies the flight of love to begin with, albeit perhaps unrealised. The bird is often the soul, or the mind, the flight of the intellect and of imagination. The element of air is nearer to the gods and the Holy Spirit is 'blowing in the wind'. The flight offers ascent as well as descent, performing the metamorphosis in the heights and bringing it back down to earth, to live in the world transformed. The bird on the head is often a symbol, in the visual arts especially of the Holy Ghost descended. No other version of avianthropy has such a powerful flight, as we shall see.

The novel *Sex and Sunsets* (1987) by Tim Sandlin has a rescue from a dull marriage by her foolish lover hang-gliding and crashing into a barbeque. The whole atmosphere of this strong comic novel has a real rescue finally, but again, nothing can match 'The Earl of Mar's Daughter' for the height of the flownness of the tale, save perhaps that of Cupid and Psyche, in its supernatural elements, as discussed below.

The Arne-Thompson tale-type 432 is that of the Prince as Bird. 'The Blue Bird' is the classic one of this type and was, traceably, a literary fairytale by Madame d'Aulnoy, first published in 1697. It did not appear in English until 1892, however, but might have entered or derived from the oral tradition anyway. In this, the Princess is called 'Florine', which might be the source of the 'Florentine' in the Earl of Mar's Daughter, by whatever route. Princess Florine is locked in a tower and her bluebird Prince visits her at night, bringing eggs and singing together. In this tale, as in many versions of the motif, the theme is of imprisonment and of the bird himself being under a curse. The variant in our ballad is that no one is cursed. Coo-my-dove is threatened but that is all. The flight of love is again unsurpassed and the high, matriarchal magic is always going to win. The matriarchal magic might also be a better claim to its antiquity.

Other examples exist in fairytale across the world: the Russian 'The Feather of Finest the Flacon'; the Danish 'The Green Knight'; the Mexican 'The Greenish Bird' and the French play 'The Blue Bird of Happiness' (1909) are all variants.

Again, it is possible to see the French, literary and romantic sources as suspect, but arguably part also of a long tradition of tale and imagery. Another motif from fairytale and myth is that of the 'the magic flight'. This is usually comic and shape-shifting but the outcome is an exuberant flight of escape and transformation, as in the tale of Taliesin. Here the pursued and pursuer keep changing form, like Proteus or Thetis, in a kind of contest.

For me, this again elevates 'The Earl of Mar's Daughter' towards being a story of high love-magic. In the way myths often seem to be about myth, in that a myth is in meditation on itself within its narrative, so here in this ballad. The long song takes its form and enacts its purpose of courtship, maturation and freedom from confinements and is therefore a flight of high marriage in the power of the traditional realm. Though the bird prince's mother says 'this things too high for me', she knows where to go to get the height from, 'an old woman /Who had more power than she'. Supernatural help is there until the 'dancers' and 'minstrels' are enabled, as the celebration builds.

The only other positive bird-as-prince tale I could find was Grimm's 123, 'The Old Woman in the Forest', which is about a young girl who hides in the forest, while all her companions are murdered. She is then tended by a dove and by the trees. Tree and bird symbols are common to both. She visits the old woman of the title, having been told by the bird to take the plainest ring from the old woman's house. She takes a birdcage from the house, wherein the bird has a plain ring in its beak. She leans on a tree which embraces her before turning into a prince, which had been cursed by the old woman into a bird and tree. This is a wonderful story, but still contains a curse and is not a self-willed transformation, as in 'The Earl of Mar's Daughter'. But freedom through love is a shared motif, however.

Cupid and Psyche, as told within the magical Apuleius' *The Golden Ass*, a work originally called 'Metamorphoses', similarly has a human girl, perhaps trapped by the world, who is, after many trials, made supernatural and united with her high-flown magical lover, who is the god Cupid. Her father wants her to marry someone unsuitable, in Psyche's case a monster. Her real husband is the son of a similar matriarchal power: Venus. The occult loves of the couples are rescued by the supernatural. Both couples enact the stages of initiation: separation, initiation, return. This is the great love-work of the alchemists and, as St. Thomas's Gospel says, 'When you make two into one/ Then you will enter the Kingdom' where opposites are unified. The long flight of the sung ballad enters into this process.

There is nothing fake about this for me: it is a high achievement of the ballad maker's art. The possibility of a literary original, the posh names and the poet-collectors all seem to raise the possibility, as does doubt of scholars about the whole romantic field of folksong, but it is not so easy to fake traditional material convincingly. The whole idea of faking traditional material is also arguably a suspect one, as it assumes that traditional material is inert. The whole question of tradition meaning simply something passed on implies creativity. If the old singers were part of tradition, my own experience of such people is that they were creative people, not historians. I intend to discuss this more fully later in the book.

The question of fakery is well addressed by a story told me by songwriter and traditionalist Roger Watson. Roger visited a folk club, some time in the 1970s, and heard a chap singing a song Roger himself had written. In the interval, he greeted the singer and told him that he was talking to the creator of it. 'Get lost – it's a traditional song!' the chap said, or words to that effect. Roger told me he'd never been paid such a big compliment.

The time-refined tone of traditional material is not easily faked. Someone wrote it originally for sure; songs are written by people. But the language and tune of the song seem to me of a piece with other very old stuff. The ballad is exceptional, in my view, but only in the way that all good work is exceptional. The transcendent and fertile, metamorphic take on love takes its long flight in the air and finds its unity at the end, which was never in doubt. It has its own kind of authenticity, where it comments on itself that 'this thing's too high for me', while it patently is not. A good song creates its own authenticity As the bird prince says to the Earl's daughter's disbelieving rationalism, 'Let all your folly be'. Rationality, including questions of what is fake, is folly in the mythic realm.

The traditional ritual of the flight of the tale is evident and has a domestic resonance to balance its magic. The use of the tale is still obvious. Here is my text:

Author's Traditional Example:

The Earl of Mar's Daughter

1. It was into a pleasant time,
All on a summer's day,
The noble Earl of Mar's daughter
Went forth to sport and play.
    And as she did amuse herself,
    Beneath a green oak tree,
    There she saw a sprightly dove
    Sat on a tower so high.

2. 'O Coo-my-dove, my love so true,
If you'll come down to me,
You shall have a cage of good red gold
Instead of a simple tree:
    'I'll put gold hinges round your cage,
    And silver round your wall;
    I'll make you shine as fair a bird
    As any of them all.'

3. But she had not these few words well spoke,
Nor yet these words well said,
Till Coo-me-dove flew from the tower
And lighted on her head.
    Then she has brought this pretty bird
    Home to her bowers and hall,
    And made him shine as fair a bird
    As any of them all.

4. When day was gone, and night was come,
About the evening tide,
This lady spied a sprightly youth
Stand straight up by her side.
    'From whence came you, young man?' she said;

'As if from out of nowhere;
My door was bolted right secure,
What way have you come here?'

5. 'O hold your tongue, you lady fair,
Let all your folly be;
Mind you not your turtle-dove
Last day you brought with thee?'
    'O tell me more, young man,' she said,
    'This does surprise me too;
    What country have you come from?
    What pedigree are you?'

6. 'My mother lives on foreign isles,
She has no child but me;
She is a queen of wealth and state,
And birth and high degree.
    'Likewise well skilled in magic spells,
    As you may plainly see,
    And she transformed me to this shape,
    To charm such maids as thee.

7. 'I am a dove the live-long day,
A sprightly youth at night;
This does make me appear more fair
In a fair maiden's sight.
    'And it was but this very day
    That I came over the sea;
    Your lovely face did me enchant;
    I'll live and die with thee.'

8. 'O Coo-me-dove, my love so true,
No more from me you'll go;'
'That's never my intent, my love,
As you said, it shall be so.'
    'O Coo-me-dove, my love so true,
    It's time to go to bed;'
    'With all my heart, my dearest dear,
    It'll be as you have said.'

9. Then he has stayed in the bower with her
For six long years and one,
Till six young sons to him she bore,
And the seventh she's brought home.
    But when every child was born
    He carried them away,
    And brought them to his mother's care,
    As fast as he could fly.

10. And when he had stayed in bower with her
For twenty years and three;
There came a lord of high renown
To court this fair lady.
      But still his offer she refused,
      And all his presents too;
      Says, I'm content to live alone
      With my bird, Coo-me-doo.

11. Her father swore a solemn oath
Among the nobles all,
'The morn, before I eat or drink,
This bird I will go kill.'
      The bird was sitting in his cage,
      And heard what they did say;
      And when he found they were resolved,
      Says, Woe is me this day!

12. 'Before that I do longer stay,
And thus to be forlorn,
I'll go unto my mother's bower,
Where I was bred and born.'
      Then Coo-me-dove took flight and flew
      Beyond the raging sea,
      And lighted near his mother's castle,
      On a tower of gold so high.

13. As his mother was walking out,
To see what she could see,
And there she saw her little son,
Sat on the tower so high.
      'Get dancers here to dance,' she said,
      'And minstrels for to play;
      For here's my young and only son,
      Come here with me to stay.'

14. 'Get no dancers to dance, mother,
Nor minstrels for to play,
For the mother of my seven sons,
The morn's her wedding-day.'
      'O tell me, tell me, my dear son,
      Tell me, and tell me true,
      Tell me this day without a flaw,
      What I will do for you.'

15. 'Instead of dancers to dance, mother,
Or minstrels for to play,
Turn four-and-twenty big strong men

Like storks in feathers gray;
    'My seven sons in seven swans,
    Above their heads to flee;
    And I myself a gay goshawk,
    A bird of high degree.'

16. Then sighing said the queen herself,
'That thing's too high for me;'
But she applied to an old woman,
Who had more skill than she.
    Instead of dancers to dance a dance,
    Or minstrels for to play,
    Four-and-twenty wall-wrought men
    Turned birds of feathers gray;

17. His seven sons in seven swans,
Above their heads to flee;
And he himself a gay goshawk,
A bird of high degree.
    This flock of birds took flight and flew
    Beyond the raging sea,
    And landed near the Earl's castle,
    Took shelter in every tree.

18. They were a flock of pretty birds,
Right comely to be seen;
The people viewed them with surprise,
As they danced on the green.
    These birds descended from the tree
    And lighted on the hall,
    And at the last with force did flee
    Among the nobles all.

19. The storks there seized some of the men,
They could neither fight nor flee;
The swans they bound the bride's best man
Below a green oak tree.
    They lighted next on maidens fair,
    Then on the bride's own head,
    And with the twinkling of an eye
    The bride and them were fled.

20. There's ancient men at weddings been
For sixty years or more,
But such a curious wedding-day
They never saw before.
    For nothing could the company do,
    Nor nothing could they say

> But they saw a flock of pretty birds
> That took their bride away.
>
> 21. When the Earl of Mar he came to know
> Where his daughter did stay,
> He signed a bond of unity,
> And visits now they pay.

My previous creative two writing books have covered myth and magic but it has been a gradual process of learning to combine my interest in tradition with them which has taken me as far as this book, to arrive home and, in a sense, where I have always been. This is the traditional process. Magic is itself a tradition, so *The Magic of Writing* (2018) was a step towards making the message found in myth of all kinds, including folklore and fairytale, actually useful in life and hence in writing. The ballad above provides a link with the next section of the book, where song becomes the focus, as it seems a constant, like love. Tradition is the overarching useful element and it is vital that we reclaim it, especially as it is already ours. The 'hereness' of tradition makes it the common, ultimate subject for me.

Writing Exercises

Ask your family and neighbours if they know any urban myths or strange tales about your kin or area. See if you can use them in your writing.

Tell 'strange but true' stories to yourself or in a group. Record them and listen. How can you get that liveliness into your writing? Try it.

Invent your own urban myth which connects with the anxieties of your day.

Combine two or reverse one urban myth to cast more light on its traditional reminders of human folly.

A tale of a city with a special vice (as Sodom and Gomorrah, Genesis 18–19).

Turn Actaeon's myth in a ballad. Call it 'All Men Are Actaeons'.

Find a ballad from the Child collection that links with a contemporary news story. Combine the two, using ballad language and motifs (easily researched).

Start a novel, based on *The Decameron*, set in the 2019–? Pandemic, called *The Writing Retreat*, where a bunch of locked-in writers tell tales. Write the first one.

Invent a story of animal transformation to aid love; or a flight towards unity in love.

Invent a 'fake' story, as singer Peter Bellamy used to call his own folksongs, written in the tradition. Make it as 'authentic' as you can, including some fake record of its collection.

What is a constant in your life? Write a tale about it that speaks of it.

Reading, Listening, Watching

Apuleius. 1932. *The Golden Ass*. Trans. Jack Lindsay. London: Paul Elek.
Boccaccio. 1903. *The Decameron*. Trans. J.M. Rigg. London: Everyman.
Bronson, Bertrand Harris. 1959–1972. *The Traditional Tunes of the Child Ballads*. Princeton: Princeton University Press.
Brunvard, Jan Harold. 1983. *The Vanishing Hitchhiker: Urban Myths and Their Meaning*. London: Picador.
Buchan, Peter. 1828. *Ancient Ballads and Songs*. Edinburgh: Laing and Stevenson.
Carter, Angela. 1990. *The Virago Book of Fairy Tales*. London: Virago.
Child Ballad Collection. 1882–1898. www.sacred-texts.com/neu/eng/child. Accessed 17 June 2020.
Crowley, John. 2002. *The Translator*. London: Harper Collins.
The Epic of Gilgamesh. 1960. Trans. N.K. Sandars. Harmndsworth: Penguin.
Euripides. 1972. *The Bacchae*. Trans. Philip Vellacott. Harmondsworth: Penguin.
Forster, E.M. 1927. *Aspects of the Novel*. London: Edward Arnold.
Graves, Robert. 1961. *The White Goddess*. London: Faber and Faber.
Grimm's Tales. 1987. Trans. Jack Zipes. New York: Bantum.
Horace. 1965. *Ars Poetica*. In *Classical Literary Criticism*, 98–110. Trans. T.S. Dorsch. Oxford: Oxford University Press.
Housman, A.E. 1986. *A Shropshire Lad*. Edinburgh: Ballantyne Press.
Jacobs, Joseph. 1890. *English Fairy Tales*. London: David Nutt.
Jung, C.G. *Flying Saucers*. 1978. Trans. R.F.C. Hull. Princeton: Princeton University Press.
Kerényi, C. 1951. *The Gods of the Greeks*. London: Thames and Hudson.
King James Bible. Genesis 18–19.
Lord, Albert Bates. 1965. *The Singer of Tales*. Cambridge, MA: Harvard University Press.
May, Adrian. 2011. *Myth and Creative Writing*. Harlow: Longmans.
May, Adrian. 2018. *The Magic of Writing*. London: Palgrave.
Morton, Pete. 1998. *Trespass*. Harbourtown Records.
Ong, Walter. 1982. *Orality and Literacy*. London: Routledge.
Ovid. *Metamorphoses*. 1986. Trans. A.D. Melville. Oxford: Oxford University Press.
Sandlin, Tim. 1987. *Sex and Sunsets*. London: Collins.
Shakespeare, William. *As You Like It*.
Silko, Leslie Marmon. 2010. *The Turquoise Ledge: A Memoir*. New York: Viking.
Tabor, June. 2003. *An Echo of Hooves*. Topic Records.
Warner, Marina. 1994. *Managing Monsters*. London: Vintage.
Wolf, Robert. 2001. *Jump Start: How to Write from Everyday Life*. New York: Oxford University Press.

PART II

Folk and Song Traditions

CHAPTER 5

Folksong and Creativity

Robert Burns, song collector, poet and still hugely popular hero remains the model for writers influenced by tradition. His modern parallel is Bob Dylan who cites Burns as a major influence. The importance of these and some other key figures for us writers is that they make it clear, despite every narrow-minded view of tradition or even of folksong, creativity was always part of it. This is what tradition has always been, a kind of cultural survival system. We began to see this is the last chapter, where we encountered the mythic, storytelling world of the ballad collectors and singers. As an alternative to the commercial world of the buying and selling of copyright and other crassness, the folk model still offers a viable alternative.

My own study of Burns began when I noticed how 'Auld Lang Syne', amid its ignored ubiquity, was all about tradition. So I became very much an Englishman in unlikely search of the great Scots icon, Robert Burns.

England, famous for self-hatred, has an uneasy relationship with its Celtic neighbours, Wales, Ireland and Scotland. In fact, it has been said that England, language aside, is just as Celtic as elsewhere in these islands. The original Celts were European, so we might have even used this reason to stay in the European Union, as many Scots voted to do. I have always liked the way the Scots were able to be themselves defiantly, in a way that seems out of reach for the English. Burns is surely part of this defiance, for a start. Burns has a night, while Shakespeare only has a day and, although shared with St George, we do not celebrate it much. It is not a night or a Bank Holiday.

For an Englishman in the contemporary world, approaching Burns is difficult. John Cooper Clarke complains of having to share a birthday with 'that fookin' Jock' and yet is not Burns the father of all traditionalists? Is he not the first real 'peasant poet', a songwriter, a collector of old songs and a hero

© The Author(s), under exclusive license to Springer Nature Switzerland AG 2021
A. May, *Tradition in Creative Writing*,
https://doi.org/10.1007/978-3-030-74776-3_5

to the likes of Bob Dylan, Keats and maybe all folkies and would-be popular poets? What is hidden behind the plastic Jockery and the heritage industry, the reputations, poetic and personal?

Part of the reason he is hard to approach is his ubiquity, which has rendered him somehow invisible. Scots singer Eddi Reader says 'We are all Robert's babies', in the sleeve notes to her album, *The Songs of Robert Burns* (2008) and it was hearing the delicacy and tender quality of him sung that started me seeking him. First was, some years back, hearing the late Scots songwriter Michael Marra sing 'Green Grow the Rashes, O', and live versions of this are easily found online. Next, it was Burns the collector, enthusiast for and user of traditional songs that caught my attention, as he seemed to have been a pioneer of this activity, who many are indebted to, know it or not. It has been said that the Ossian poems of James Macpherson created the dream of which Burns became the reality. His invisibility then made him all the more intriguing for me. Arguments still surround him from other writers, especially poets. He might still be too popular to be taken seriously, or taken as a whole. But a distant tourist image can still clear quickly to discovery.

The one thing other writers agree on about Burns is his width and his ability to combine opposites. He had the aspect of traditionalism about him that combines the high and low, the rich and poor, the past and present. He makes human life bigger. W.E. Henley (in 'Life, Genius, Achievement', 1897) talks of 'the amazing compound of style and sentiment with gaiety and sympathy, of wit and tenderness with radiant humour', while Don Paterson ('Introduction' to *Robert Burns Poems selected by Don* Paterson, 2001) speaks of 'the most remarkable linguistic resource any Scottish poet has ever had'.

What other poets disagree about is the turning of Burns to song, which he did with passionate energy, saying in a letter that he was 'absolutely crazed about it'. Paterson seems fine with this, saying his 'revitalisation of Scottish song was so pervasive that its extent can never be fully known'. For me this applies to his influence on subsequent tradition enthusiasts, while his devotion to it makes him the model for the authenticity and complex depth a traditionalist aspires to.

Paterson, though, does still insist on the 'status' and on the un-obvious nature of poetry making it different from song. Surely this is not absolutely true, as the boundaries between song and poetry are not so clear as he might like. Songs can hide their agenda too and poems can be obvious and some really interesting work goes on in the borders between them. I would say song is the prime medium and poems are a literary off-shoot, sometimes better and sometimes not—'status' is somewhere else. It strikes me that poets who emphasise the difference and status of poetry are often those who have had little luck themselves with songs.

Paterson's 'Introduction' is excellent anyway and he does add to Burns as a widely traditional figure 'still burning more fiercely than all the others' and quotes Duke Ellington on needing 'the street and the conservatoire'.

Paterson also recommends, as I do, Dick Gaughan's 'Westlin' Winds', again easily found.

Sometimes a glint of his achievement comes in the most obvious and easily overlooked things about Burns. 'Auld Lang Syne' is almost invisible in its universal use, but it strikes me that this is a song about tradition. To have the world singing about the value of 'auld acquaintance' makes it the unconscious traditionalists' hymn. 'Old Long Since', as the literal translation goes, was a favourite, resonant phrase in Scots for Burns, often said in conversation. Many poets and singers had written or sung the phrase but it was not until Burns heard an old singer's version which he adopted and adapted into focus that it came alive. Is this adapting a case of more or less merit or talent? From a traditional viewpoint it is more, I think, and the popularity of Burns' version might be over-familiar and hence invisible but it is not to be ignored. There is a good live version, with an alternative tune, sung by Eddi Reader, easily found, which gives the song fresh life.

Traditional songs often speak of themselves remembering, so a successful popular traditional song about tradition is an extraordinary achievement. The English folksong from the Copper Family of Sussex, 'Spenser the Rover' speaks of the titular character with 'The thoughts of his babies lamenting their father', which urge him to return. Another song of theirs, often called 'The Wedding Song', begins, 'Come write me down ye powers above/ The man that first created love', again calling on the past to justify and return to the present. Like 'Auld Lang Syne', these songs enact the traditionalist philosophy in remembering—giving us back our lives in a survey of time and a place of reflection. Perhaps all art does this at best.

It is the largeness combined with small, telling detail that Burns does so well. The stanza about each 'auld' acquaintance buying their own drinks but taking 'a cup o kindness yet' is a metamorphosis from material independence into something larger held in the vessel of common cheer. The reminder that 'old' means familiar as well as just old seems timely. Burns' own thoughts about the song and its title remind me of Ralph Vaughan Williams' feeling when he first heard a real, old folksinger. All his fears of folksong dying out were put to rest, he reputedly said. Burns really did have everyone with him when he made the song, which might be a definition of traditional virtue.

One work universally liked, even by other poets and critics, is 'Tam o' Shanter'. This song-like poem also argues for Burns as a model for traditionalists. It is a fine example of making the most of your own world and harks back to his childhood female influences. His mother, who sang, and especially his mother's storytelling cousin Betty Davidson were sources of local folklore and Burns' psycho-geographical use of his own world was deep and exemplary. In this poem, he also shows none of the piety or humourless quality of some recent examples of that kind of work. It is a model still worth following: lots of local detail, inventiveness and a feeling of the particular in the archetype of an encounter with the dark side.

While some biographers have used the poem for Freudian reductionism, making him counter-intuitively afraid of women, they tend not to deny its power. When the dead hold the lights for the living to celebrate raw liveliness in what the drunk man sees, and all the horrors of life are on the 'holy' table, Tam's 'stomach' is not on the 'turn', however. Life somehow, however raw and frightening, seems to reassert itself in the humour and in seeing too much. Tam's cry of 'Weel done, Cutty-sark!' ('Well done, Short-shift!') is the turning point and all goes dark. It is Tam's shout of approval before all disappears, which is an approval of seeing everything at once and overcoming it with a kind of affirmative 'enormous yes', as Larkin wrote of his jazz hero Sidney Bechet. The other thing it reminds me of is Douglas Adams' 'Total Perspective Vortex' in *The Hitchhiker's Guide to the Galaxy*, where Zaphod is able to look at everything and not be thrown, where most would be driven mad.

'Tam o' Shanter' taken seriously, as comedy should be, is a version of the Dionysian Greek tragedy of *The Bacchae*. Here the uptight King Pentheus is tempted to see the Dionysian women's wild rites. He ends up dead but Tam, like a Dionysus himself, or a trickster, evades capture by his open attitude. If you wanted more classical reference points, he might be an escaped Actaeon. However comic, Burns' breadth takes in the bigger themes.

If Burns then begins to look like our father, what are we to do, especially in darkest England? For a start there is a problem with finding readable editions of his work, as biographer Robert Crawford points out on the first page of *The Bard* (2009). Burns has his wide talent and perspective in his non-posh roots, in common with Shakespeare and Blake. My feeling is that Arden-like editions, with glossary beside and extensive notes below, style texts would work. I love my old four-volume centenary edition of *The Poetry of Robert Burns* (1897) edited by English poet W.E. Henley (of 'England, My England' fame) and T.F. Henderson, rescued from a charity shop sale. This has ten pages of notes on 'Tam O' Shanter' and includes some tunes to the songs. On the net, robert burns.org is good, but it is not a book. So a student-centred edition, or series, like Arden or Signet, with all the information before you at once, would make a big difference. The various selections, with bits of the life and the cheap reprints with bad or no indexes, do not help us take him seriously, or show us the humour and energy that reached the world.

To give credit to Burns' passionate conversion to song, the books might include a compiled album of songs, like the brilliant versions suggested here. I would volunteer to be involved. The three performers I mention are crucially all songwriters themselves and steeped in tradition and knowledge. There is an element in Burns of the clarity and simplicity of late style, sometimes indicated by the Japanese word 'shibumi'. This seems to be a concept that would be aspired to early in a traditional education and by anyone who recognises the refined lyrical strength in the older songs and singers. 'Shibumi' recognises 'Old Lang Syne'. Poets often begin and end in song and Burns was already there.

Every age claims Burns, it seems. The Romantics can be represented by Wordsworth's two poems at his grave and in Keats, as well as John Clare, while Modernists such as Yeats and Eliot might claim him too. Poetry, despite its wrenchings and protestations of progress, is a traditional art.

Burns is that good, then, and he grows on you if you find a way in. Then you find that he is already part of you, part of your tradition, or all traditions, like Shakespeare. In England, there are plenty of Burns Nights. A search revealed one less than a mile from where I write, in dark Essex. The BBC website had a list of the elements you need in order to hold one. While these seem to be an excuse for an expensive meal at worst, at best they actually celebrate a poet, which is no mere thing. At root, Burns Night is a genuine popular festival celebrating poetry.

April 23rd in England needs to be a Bank Holiday and we need something I might call Shaky George Night. There should be tales of and from the various St Georges and his countries; there should be bits of Shakespeare and his songs and some bits put to music (the sonnets work well). There should be strangers to bless from outside and 'see ourselves as others see us' with their own dances, stories and songs. We could have fun planning it and keeping it from the clutches of the partial, making ourselves as broad and universally local as Robert Burns himself.

We know what Burns thought of us English from his poem 'The Author's Earnest Cry and Prayer', addressed to parliament (primarily but perhaps not exclusively to 'Scotch representatives') in St James', Westminster:

> In spite o' a' the thievish kaes,   [jackdaws]
>   That haunt St Jamie's!
> Your humble Bardie sings and prays,
>   While Rab his name is.

Burns 'sings and prays' for us all in these islands and we can hear him from England—even from darkest England.

Woody Guthrie is the most famous influence on Bob Dylan, but Dylan is interesting to anyone around today, as he is the link with the great influences of the past, and arguably, gave popular culture licence to take itself seriously and traditionally. Guthrie was an enigmatic figure of self-invention and traditionalism, who showed other key figures, like Pete Seeger, how inventive tradition allowed you to be. In Seeger's Foreword to *Bound for Glory* (first published 1943; 1969 edition) he tells of not being able to tell if Guthrie's stuff was old or brand new, as his imagination was very much in his own highly traditional place. He seemed like the real thing and Seeger's thought on hearing of Guthrie's death in 1967 was that the songs were immortal. Guthrie's final song was called, 'I ain't dead yet', he reports. Seeger notes his influence on Dylan and also compares him to figures like Robert Burns and Taras Shevchenko from the Ukraine. The immersion in the tradition is what impresses about

Guthrie. He was impressively prolific in writing poems and songs and his autobiography is illustrated with his own drawings. Recent years have seen unused lyrics being recorded by artists like the band Wilco and the U.K.'s Billy Bragg.

The Carter Family were also a great influence in the world and are linked with the recording industry and its use of folksong. *Will You Miss Me When I'm Gone: The Carter Family and their legacy in American music*, by Mark Zwonitzer and Charles Hirshberg (2002) is an exhaustive exploration of their craft and lives. Two strong women, Sara and Maybelle, the main singer and musician, respectively, and their elusive main collector, assembler and writer, A.P. Carter present in this book a picture of the magpie collecting/ reinventing/ creating axis which is a tradition in action. The fact that they were doing it for commercial ends makes no difference. The fact is they created a body of work that others have drawn on massively, and still do, as shown in the documentary film, *The Carter Family Documentary* (Ken Burns, 2019). The book's chapter called 'Home Manufacture' illustrates how they worked and the piece on the assemblage of 'Sweet Bird' is instructive. The informed invention of A.P. seems familiar to anyone in the creative tradition.

In one of the chapters towards the end of *Will You Miss Me ...*, we get a picture of A.P. responding to young singers but not to serious, detail-driven, folklorists of the academic kind. They realised that he was all of a piece and someone who himself realised the value of what was around him, which others had mocked when he told them of his plans to record songs. Then they all went out and bought them. The power of tradition in action then overcame the commercial or humble orthodoxies that surrounded him and his family.

Edwin Muir's poem 'Complaint of the Dying Peasantry' regrets the passing of songs from bar to library, from oral to written, but, I would say, in writing it, his own work's liveliness derives from the Scotland that grew him. The old stuff was in him too. Something is lost for sure but something is preserved and learnt in Muir's own work and in Burns and Guthrie and the Carter Family who took the liveliness of tradition out into the world and trusted in their vision and their material. Muir's best poems, like the wonderfully apocalyptic 'The Horses', where all is lost but a new beginning comes from the blessing of the ancient beasts who blessed us with their presence for so long. In this poem, the horses are tradition and give us a way to go on.

With Muir's work seen through the song element, we can come to the idea that poems need to sing too, in order to take flight in the imagination. Poems, if they move far from the lyrical, from the memorable or haunting qualities, become only writing. Even novelists need this singing quality, according to E.M. Forster in his influential *Aspects of the Novel* (1927). In Chapter 7, 'Prophecy', he uses the word 'song', associated with voice. Perhaps the cliché of 'finding a voice' that creative writing types talk of might be better put as finding a way off the page, somehow into the oral world of story and song.

Talking about Bob Dylan has never been easy, as everyone seems to have an opinion about him, even those who have not listened to his work. He has had more books written about him than any other comparable artist in popular song and this shows no sign of stopping. One thing I would say is that in the kinds of literature and writing departments of universities I have worked in, it is hard to find anyone who is not a fan of his work. Despite this, when I, only partly joking, suggested we did a class on 'Bob Dylan studies' a few years ago, no one joined me in enthusiasm for the idea. Something so immediate and slippery, something so song-like, was beyond us, it seemed.

The best guide to Dylan, though, is his own work. In *Chronicles* (2004), he leaves no doubt of his being steeped in tradition and that this is a constant in his career, in his methods and in his thought. This autobiographical work, which amounts to a tale of the 'growth of a poet's mind', to use Wordsworth's line, which was the subtitle to *The Prelude* (1850), is instructive. In part 5, 'River of Ice', he is honest about his debt to Guthrie and he tells of an encounter with someone he identifies as being a member of 'the folk police'. This is a well-known phrase among folk musicians, which I have used myself for many years. Anyone who sees themselves as an unappointed guardian of something is called the something police: hence jazz police, poetry police and so on. Dylan's conclusions about this person are telling when he says that he was not sure if the person was trying to help him or condemn him out of hand. Dylan catches their ambivalence and shrewdly puts it down to snobbery. Without underplaying his own naivety, he emerges enhanced from the experience, being more in tune with the songs and singers he learns about than with the self-appointed guardians of the scene. Dylan's attitude to the material was one of someone determined to be steeped in the source of real power, in the tradition and in the songs themselves.

The one commentator I have seen who is good on this aspect of Dylan's work is Michael Gray, author of the monumental *Song and Dance Man III* (2000). There may be an updated version of this by now. Significantly, chapter one of this book is called 'Dylan and the folk tradition'. This leaves us with little doubt. Gray sees that tradition is the source of Dylan's creative work. I would go further and say that Dylan is a traditional singer and that tradition is in his practice as well as his roots.

This is not to say that Dylan was not influenced by those around him. Black topical and protest singer Len Chandler figures prominently in *Chronicles* (2004). Chandler was quoted by Martin Luther King in his 60s speeches. Another big influence was his girlfriend from a radical Italian background, Suze Rotolo, as told in her memoir *A Freewhelin' Time* (2008). The radical black and European traditions were well to the fore.

If you want to see how traditional an artist is, seek a work by them where they seem to have looked for a reconnection to their origins, their inspirations or their home territory. Obviously, this can only be done with an artist of a certain career longevity. In 1967, when others were moving towards complexity and multi-coloured elaboration, Dylan released the album *John Wesley Harding*, which, as Gray says, was a move towards simplifying his work. It was a return-to-roots album. It is interesting to note that his friend

Robbie Robertson of the Band says, in his own autobiographical book, *Testimony* (2016) that Dylan had not meant the album to be so simple in musical texture. Robertson reports that Dylan asked him and other members of The Band to add parts to the original tracks with just bass and drums. They then told Dylan they did not think it needed anything further. Dylan surrounded himself with people who could see where his feeling for a renewed simplicity could take him.

John Wesley Harding for me amounts to a manifesto for tradition. Going through it track by track for traditional elements is instructive. The title track is an outlaw ballad, in the tradition of Robin Hood, or Guthrie's 'Pretty Buy Floyd'. This is followed by the most traditional line known to start an Anglo-American folksong, 'As I Went Out One Morning', with its talk of damsels. The third track, 'I Dreamed I Saw At Augustine', is Biblical, but based on an old union song. The fourth, 'All Along the Watchtower' is biblical again. Towers often figure in writers' work as symbols of tradition and we only have to think of Yeats for the imagery of an ancient vantage point. The tower enables you to see the future by being elevated from the past itself in the building. This manifesto for tradition could not be plainer. There may be a confused age in front of him but he is seeking clarity through tradition.

He follows this with a long narrative ballad, with his strange storytelling art to the fore. 'The Ballad of Frankie Lee and Judas Priest' is again in search of clarity in a confused world and in search of home, which is where tradition starts and ends. There follows a deeper exploration of traditional ways of escaping the greed and confusion of the world, with a series of portraits of victims of the world. In the final track of side one, 'The Drifter's Escape', we have a Western, a cowboy film of the validity of being an outsider. Such problems are continued in characters on side two. 'Dear Landlord', and 'I Am A Lonesome Hobo' have their traditional elements of home and homelessness, while 'I Pity the Poor Immigrant' seems to be about the whole of America in a kind of vagrant view, to the tune of 'Come All Ye Tramps and Hawkers', a traditional Irish song. His final comment in track ten is through the character of 'The Wicked Messenger', with another biblical and traditionally simple message of open-heartedness. The final two tracks, 11 being 'Down Along the Cove' take love to heart, then to home in track 12 'I'll Be Your Baby Tonight'. The former has a blues structure, a traditional form rarely absent from any Dylan album or show, while the latter points towards that most traditional of American art forms, the country song with its links back to the Carters and further.

Thus every single track on the album is a musical and lyrical tribute to the healing and renewing power of the tradition. I have a friend who, when I last checked, had attended every Dylan tour in the U.K. who told me that Dylan always did at least one traditional song during shows that he has seen. Consciously or not, Dylan has spread a message of the vital importance to his art of the traditional. This he continues to do, in his recent, almost historical work, like 'Murder Most Foul' from 2019. Dylan is unlike Burns in that he is not a field collector of songs. However, his 'Theme Time Radio Hour' shows (2006-9), amounting to one hundred hours of selected songs, tells us something of his fundamental interest in the tradition of song. Tradition for Dylan is his whole art.

Dylan's endless fascination and depth need little further explanation in my view. The *John Wesley Harding* album alone shows and explores a journey home, which is the crux of tradition. It is an image of the exploration of the self and its place in the world.

Moving to my own background, within a few miles of where I was born in Essex, U.K. is the place where, around the turn of the nineteenth century, a classical composer was undertaking a similar journey into his roots. Other composers were doing this across Europe. Ralph Vaughan Williams came to Brentwood, a short bus ride from my home, to lecture on folksong, as told in Sue Cubbin's *That Precious Legacy* (2006) and was approached by a local vicar's daughter, who said she had experience of what Vaughan Williams only knew in theory, real folksingers. Eventually, he visited the vicarage at Ingrave, a village nearby. Among the singers he met was one who would not sing in the vicarage but invited Vaughan Williams to his cottage, which still stands. This was the mysterious Charles Potiphar, an allegedly illiterate labourer, who sang, when visited, several wonderful songs which changed the composer's life.

The image of the toff Vaughan Williams inspired me to join Sue Cubbin and her husband John in the group Potiphar's Apprentices, which made two albums of songs collected by Vaughan Williams in Essex. Our name came from this apprenticing of the educated to the folksong artist and in reference to one of the songs he sang on that first encounter, 'The Sheffield Apprentice'. The song makes us all apprentices in life and tells this story into song.

Author Creative Example:

Mr Potiphar's Apprentices

Young Vaughan Williams was a learned man
But he could tell something was missing, as a wise fool can
One day in Ingrave he heard an old man sing
And he knew it could link him back to everything

Charles Potiphar couldn't read or write
But he had the songs and he sang them right
Like a light going on in the soul was this
Being one of Mr Potiphar's apprentices

I was searching for my own soul in the 70s
And I knew the Music Hall held some promises
I met Leslie Sarony and I heard him sing
And I knew it could link me back to everything

Chorus - Just like one of Mr Potiphar's apprentices

I went to a party, someone said to me
I only know of singing through technology
If you switch it all off and let me hear you sing
You may find it can link you back to everything

Chorus - We're all Mr Potiphar's apprentices

If you think you know it all, it may not be that way
We all have to fight the prejudices of our day
Everybody tells you that the old stuff is gone
But though it hides its purpose, it still lingers on

Chorus

WRITING EXERCISES:

England and Scotland have a neighbour/ other, or even love/ hate relationship. Who is your 'other' neighbour? Explore your feelings for them and them for you. Personify the places, if that helps.

Write a piece based on this folk tale, from the same letter where Burns told the story of 'Tam O'Shanter'. From Burns, Letter to Francis Grose, 1792:

> On a summer's evening, about the time nature puts on her sables to mourn the expiry of the cheerful day, a shepherd boy, belonging to a farmer in the immediate neighbourhood of Alloway kirk, had just folded his charge, and was returning home. As he passed the kirk, in the adjoining field he fell in with a crew of men and women, who were busy pulling stems of the plant ragwort. He observed that as each person pulled a ragwort, he or she got astride of it, and called out, 'Up, horsie!' on which the ragwort flew off, like Pegasus, through the air with its rider. The foolish boy likewise pulled his ragwort, and cried with the rest, 'Up, horsie!' and, strange to tell, away he flew with the company. The first stage at which the cavalcade stopt was a merchant's wine-cellar in Bourdeaux, where, without saying 'By your leave,' they quaffed away at the best the cellar could afford, until the morning, foe to the imps and works of darkness, threatened to throw light on the matter, and frightened them from their carousals. The poor shepherd lad, being equally a stranger to the scene and the liquor, heedlessly got himself drunk; and when the rest took horse, he fell asleep, and was found so next day by some of the people belonging to the merchant. Somebody that understood Scotch, asking him what he was, he said such a-one's herd in Alloway, and by some means or other getting home again, he lived long to tell the world the wondrous tale.

Find a Burns' poem or song and translate into a modern lyric.

Write the 'sleeve notes' to your 'back to my roots' album.

Write about an encounter with an old singer does not understand the concept of copyright or buying and selling a song.

Read the two Edwin Muir poems and write a bridging poem, which links the 'peasantry' of 'Complaint of the Dying Peasantry' to the post-apocalyptic world of 'The Horses'. (Edwin Muir, 'Complaint of the Dying Peasantry'; 'The Horses' in *Collected Poems*, 1963).

Where are your own roots of song? Find a song from your childhood or growing years and write a response or tribute to it.

Listen to the Carter Family and update one of their songs, available on the internet (see *Complete Songs of the Carter Family* at bluegrasswest.com). Listen to Len Chandler's 'Beans In Your Ears' (1964) and see if you can write a topical song like him.

Is there someone who broke the law for good in your culture? Write a tale about them in the manner of 'John Wesley Harding' (*John Wesley Harding*, album 1967).

Reading, Watching, Listening:

Burns, Ken. 2019. *Country Music*. Episode 1. P.B.S. Television.
Burns, Robert. Poems. robertburns.org. Accessed 22 June 2020.
Chandler, Len. 1967. *To Be A Man*. Columbia Records.
Chandler, Len. Beans In Your Ears, 1964. New York: Broadside.
Carter Family. *Complete Songs of the Carter Family*. bluegrasswest.com. Accessed 12 January 2021.
Crawford, Robert. 2009. *The Bard*. London: Pinlico.
Cubbin, Sue. 2006. *That Precious Legacy*. Chelmsford: Essex County Council Sound Archive.
Dylan, Bob. 2004. *Chronicles*. New York: Simon and Schuster.
Dylan, Bob. 1967. *John Wesley Harding*. Columbia Records.
Dylan, Bob. 2006–9. Theme Time Radio Hour. Sirius XM Radio.
Gray, Michael. 2000. *Song and Dance Man III*. London: Continuum.
Guthrie, Woody. 1969. *Bound for Glory*. London: Picador.
Forster, E.M. 1927. *Aspects of the Novel*. London: Edward Arnold.
Gaughan, Dick. 1981. *Westlin' Winds*. On *Handful of Earth*. Topic Records.
Henley, W.E. 1897. Life, Genius, Achievement. In *The Poetry of Robert Burns*. Volume IV, 233–348. London: Caxton.
McAlpine, William. 1968. *William McAlpine Sings Robert Burns*. E.M.I. Records.
Marra, Michael. 2010. Green Grow the Rashes. On *Recorded Live On Tour*. Delphinian Records.
Muir, Edwin. 1963. Complaint of the Dying Peasantry, The Horses, 262, 246–267. In *Collected Poems*. London: Faber and Faber.
Paterson, Don. 2001. *Robert Burns Poems Selected by Don Paterson*. London: Faber and Faber.
Reader, Eddi. 2003. Auld Lang Syne. In *Songs of Robert Burns*. Rough Trade Records.
Rotolo, Suze. 2008. *A Freewhelin' Time*. New York: Broadway.
Wordsworth, William. 1904. *The Prelude*, 494–588. In *Poetical Works*. Oxford: Oxford University Press.
Zwonitzer, Mark, and Hirshberg, Charles. 2002. *Will You Miss Me When I'm Gone: The Carter Family and Their Legacy in American Music*. New York: Simon and Schuster.

CHAPTER 6

A Songwriter in the Tradition: A Creative Folk Life

I have already spoken of the first local folk club I attended and played at, in Chapter 1, the introduction to this book. Folk clubs were my first university, you could say, as I learnt a huge amount from the first places I took my writing into the world. If publication means simply 'making public', I have come to value these humble places and this humble beginning very highly. My experience of the clubs and other performers are still with me and, as I try to show, have informed much of my work and life since then.

In the U.K. folk and especially folk clubs have an ambiguous reputation at best. In a current music journal, I read of someone having to play 'dreary' folk clubs. Folk, in the market and envy driven music industry and the culture it dominates is here still denigrated and seen as partly a joke and for the feeble-minded. Fighting against this has been a motivating power, as well as occasionally a source of despair to me. What it did do was enable me to seek a workable alternative, which has been a source of creative energy throughout all my subsequent life.

My friend had written one song and a half. I had written one song. We were the same age and had about the same ability on guitar and some experience of playing in bands, which would have been called 'beat groups' in those sixties' days. I helped Clif finish his half a song and we tried them out at Harlow Folk Club, in the backroom of the Queens Head in Churchgate Street, Old Harlow, Essex, U.K. We went well with the audience, who I suspect were tolerant of young people showing interest and a certain local creativity. The folk club was a tolerant place, where you might hear someone playing classical guitar, reciting a poem or singing an unaccompanied traditional folksong, all in the half-hour of 'floor' singers, up to when the paid guest came on. This width is still a rare thing, catered for a bit these days by 'open mic' events. But this was in a back room, with no bar, so listening was paramount.

The first folksingers I heard were English ones who did American style folk/blues. I admired them but knew somehow I could not do the same. We probably all saw the influential **1964** Granada T.V. (U.K.) special called *Blues and Folk Train* (producer, Johnny Hamp), where artists like Sister Rosetta Tharpe and Muddy Waters played live. For older singers, I think it made them want to play this material. For me, it strikes me now that the singers on the screen were very much themselves. This did not make me want to imitate their style but emulate their sense of self-identity. It is interesting to note that Joe Boyd was involved in that tour, who was later to encourage Fairport Convention, who he managed, to be more English, resulting in their album *Liege and Leif* (1969).

Clif and I were always joking and making up parodies of songs in our talk, whereas our three songs were poetic and slowish. As winter came on, the lack of efficient heating in that small back room became noticeable and it happily occurred to Clif and me to write a balancing comic song, to add to our otherwise thoughtful repertoire, so we concocted a comic item called 'Cold Song'. This was a jolly piece of nonsense but none the less valuable for that. The spoof middle eight started, 'Give me an electric fire, baby …' Not the greatest thing ever written but fun and, most significantly, it brought the immediate world into our writing. This was a very folk, a very traditional thing to do, which I think we somehow knew instinctively.

Another thing we were doing here was cheering ourselves and our community up. This seems to me no mean thing. We had become, however falteringly, part of our audience and part of the celebration of diversity and goodwill which songs engender. However 'dreary' to the starstruck outsider, this little back room was the womb that gave birth to my lifelong and fruitful interest in creativity. 'Cold Song' got huge laughs and loud applause, like a heroic deed on a tiny scale.

To be cheering up and cheered up from our youthful melancholy was there in our first few songs. Clif and I were using tradition to overcome the melancholy that is part of creativity. This feeling of isolation is common to writers and is a stage in the separation towards some new insight which is what the tradition of the creative process offers. We found our way to what has been shared via the simplicity of what is shared. We were keeping warm. The writer needs to seek warmth by way of acknowledging the cold. This is not stretching the analogy too far, but the strength which tradition offers. Voicing the suffering is what artists do and the work is more honestly arrived at if the difficulty is worked through from darkness to light. However small, this was a sure step.

Here, we have only got to the part of the evening where the 'floor' singers and residents (like Gil in Chapter 1, the introduction to this book) had finished the first section before the main guest came on. These also showed great variety. One singer I do remember was Cyril Tawney (**1930–2005**). He was a songwriter who played the guitar, as well as singing unaccompanied, but very much someone who had written songs in effectively traditional mode. His early life had been in the merchant navy and his songs reflected his life there and were written to be sung to his shipmates. He was already famous for his catchy song, 'Sally Free and Easy', recorded by many folk artists. Most of his songs came from earlier in his life but they varied from sea-shanties like 'Chicken-on-a-raft', as sung by The Young Tradition, about egg on toast to narrative songs of love like 'Sammy's Bar'. He was a convincing real-life folksinger who seemed all of a piece, demonstrating the usefulness and honesty of his method.

He had something we had yet to arrive at, singable choruses. Everyone sang in folk clubs or at least chorus singing was expected. When I first was booked to do a solo gig, this was one of the things I was notable for myself. I am still a devotee of the chorus. The fashion for choirs seems to fulfil this need to sing now, as does fans who knew every word of, say, Arctic Monkeys' first album. Folk clubs were there first, along with the traditional chants of soccer fans. Cyril Tawney, with his sea-shanty style, had this quality that made his songs fit seamlessly with the folk tradition.

We were already listening to traditional music, as well as songwriters who took their licence from Dylan's work to be intensely poetic as well as tradition-influenced. We saw Roy Harper in London clubs and concerts, writing longer and more political songs, like 'I Hate The White Man', but we also had an L.P. by the English unaccompanied trio The Young Tradition. 'Sampler' albums were cheaper and *The Young Tradition Sampler* (1969) was an experiment worth hearing. At first, we did not really get it. How could this alien material be our own? We knew it was somehow important, even though it reminded us of school, where poshed-up versions of old folksongs were spoilt with of-their-day piano accompaniment, as we remembered. Somehow we got the feeling that we had been hasty in our naïve feeling that only pop music counted. The key was how singable the songs were, as well as how infectious the performances.

The cover has a picture of the hippy-looking group sitting at a pub table with two men of an older generation and one other young man. These are Bob and Ron Copper and their son John, from the singing Copper Family of Sussex. The Coppers had a family songbook that went back a couple of generations and was the inspiration for the harmony style of The Young Tradition. It seemed a radical thing, this picture, a bold statement of intent, of roots and seriousness. The 'generation gap', often spoken of then, was swept away and somehow our prejudices about our own world were challenged. The songs found their way in.

Clif and I, along with our more intelligent girlfriends, who seemed to get it more easily than us, at times harmonised the songs in the car, on our way to see other artists' gigs. The singable quality became part of how we thought, along with the choruses designed for real joining in. Later, in a group myself that did lots of harmony, singing in the car featured again. I recommend it.

When I came to teach songwriting, the repeating line or chorus would be one of the first things I would seek to communicate. Finding what I called 'a verbal riff' is a good step towards making your own songs. Slightly changed clichés can work, as can phrases with double meanings, good names, words that roll off the tongue well, even nonsense. In a class a few years back I used the name of a Professor whose room was just down the corridor from the classroom, someone I had never met, to invent jokey rhymes and keep returning to. This was a fun game and got us working in a singable and repeatable manner.

There was, however, an undeniable gap between the old material and our own sensibility. One of the keys, it seems to me now, as then, was to be widely open to influences. Peter Bellamy, the main melody singer with The Young Tradition, depicted on their L.P. cover in flamboyant hat and flowing clothing, always did such a variety of material. When he went solo, he would do, all in his pronounced English style, cowboy songs, anglicised blues, music hall, poems set to music, all as well as traditional English folksongs. Finding out how to bridge the gap in sensibility between the old material and the new has been a useful problem to push against and work with. In a way, I am still trying to answer the seeming oxymoron of Bellamy's group's name, The Young Tradition. It seems now that the task is this—how to make yourself singable.

A few years later, I had a breakthrough on all this, which resulted in going solo myself. It came, strangely, via America. As well as listening to my own tradition, I had become impressed with how American writers and artists managed to be very much themselves. The joke here was that American places were romantic sounding, as reflected in popular song, while writing a song about 'Chelmsford' would sound feeble. I wanted to confront this 'English cringe'. Embracing the irony seemed to be the key and when someone lent me a copy of Randy Newman's *Sail Away* (1972), the title song gave me a way into writing about England, resulting in my song 'Little England'. This was coupled with my learning another song from a Peter Bellamy solo album, where I played the melody of the tune on the guitar while I sang it. Between these two things, I created a style of my own. It was a useful way of bridging the gap between myself and the old world, via tradition and the new world of the ironic songs of Randy Newman.

I had also begun to listen to old music hall and variety artists from earlier artists who used this material, like the Bonzo Dog Band, who plundered 78s of variety material to do in their mix of old jazz, comedy and pop music. These seem to me the key influences I still carry. They each involved bridging between old and new, in other words behaving in a traditional manner, although I might not have seen that specifically at the time. When, a decade later, I came to make my own L.P. record, *Anarchy In The Ukelele* (sic, 1984), the sleeve notes talk about what I was trying to do. My little manifesto still seems pertinent:

After every line, nearly, when I first tried to write songs, I used the word 'babe', uncomfortably trying to copy my heroes of the time, writing with an American accent. The search then started, which is every serious writer's search, for an honest voice of my own, that would express my place and time in the way I thought and spoke. Wading through a sea of pop and other musics, I started to pick out some little bits of English sound that had yet to be lost in the great U.S. take-over, or had been created recently by songwriters who felt, in some way, the same. For example, Syd Barrett was an early influence.

Humour crept in early as part of this, inspired by the Bonzos and others in the sixties (people forget the amount of humour in the so-called 'hippy' era) and I quickly developed a hard shell to some of my mates' mild scorn, because they preferred the undeniable if suspect power of untra-American rock and roll. I liked it too, but was set on my own quest.

When I first began to sing solo in folk clubs, it was great to discover other writers daring to do similar foolish but necessary work in this cultural underground. We were bound to be only partly successful, if that. Some would say we were all failures, from Richard Thompson and Steve Ashley down. I disagree, and we have some good stuff and a lot of fun and still a workable alternative view. And there is life in it yet. A lot of modern pop is proof of that, feeling around the same honest and fertile areas. So it is not in vain and in confusing times it is more important than ever to try for the natural voice.

So writing and performing these songs has been a journey of discovery for me, into the past and into the present. In the past I found forms and styles of songs that fitted better than rock my native speech rhythms and thought. Into the present because I tried to use these forms to write about now.

Music hall and traditional songs were an influence, but the area I got most from was the popular music of the early part of the century that I suppose you might call 'variety'. Also the unbroken tradition of comic, satirical, social comment songs that stretches from trad. to Leslie Sarony to Paddy Roberts to the more articulate pop writers of today. Punk, for example, was an attempt to make rock more real and expressive, and in a way similar to what I was trying to do with my old/ new songs. Hence the title of the record, which seems to sum up the little passé rebel responsible. Puns (pun rock?) and ukes and tame rebellion are my magic spells against the worst, though most of the songs have serious points too.

I offer these explanations to anyone interested, because no-one now seems to bother much about saying what they are up to and why – probably they don't know! I hope the songs are good enough to be enjoyed with or without this personal memo, but it might help. Thanks for listening.

Not having looked at this for many years, I am amazed how much it still describes my method and how what I now think of as traditional in method it is. I do remember someone reading it and asking what university I had attended. The truth was I had not been to university, and, as I said at the time, 'I've got the ignorance to prove it!' The folk clubs were my university and my manifesto, I now feel, was more than a 'memo'. I was a 'little passé rebel' but I was also a radical traditionalist.

I mention punk, which had been around in Britain for a while and, to me, had a lot in common with folk. The main obvious difference between the old rock groups and the new was the length of their material. The short, punchy song made a comeback. I was reacting, as a new soloist on the folk scene in the 70s, to the sitting-down, self-indulgent, lovelorn songwriter who was a cliché. These English singers sang in the U.S. accents of their heroes. In the early 70s, I had already seen the Essex band Dr. Feelgood. They wore suits, moved to their music and did short, punchy version of old and new blues/rock songs that we in the U.K. called R. & B.

On the folk scene, I had heard singers like Vin Garbutt, who was from Teeside in the North-East of England. He stood up, sang in a loud voice and in his native accent and wrote songs about the industry in his area, as well as singing traditional songs. His performing style had a great influence on me when I started doing gigs myself. I found a loud voice by not using what is known as a 'head voice', but singing lower, from the diaphragm. Many mic-singers use head voices. This was like blasting a new voice altogether, as I remember the singer-songwriter Maggie Holland saying, when we discussed this self-discovery. No doubt a good voice teacher could have advised me but finding out for myself was a blasting through to something new that sounded new. The keys of my songs changed.

I shortened and simplified my songs. I learnt to edit my own work and cutting for directness and singability. I stood up and sang loud. I put a limit on love songs. I had read Rilke's *Letters to a young poet* (1929) where he advises avoiding love for many reasons, plus I had my own desire to avoid the singer-songwriter lovelorn cliché. One love song per gig was my rule. I even dressed differently. I wore the clothes of someone from the English countryside, which I was.

My friend Roger Lee and I had been to a free concert in a local new town, where we had stood on a hill and looked down at the audience. It was a sea of denim. 'I don't think this denim thing is going to catch on,' Roger said, to my great amusement. I wore cord trousers and a tweed jacket. I carried it off with a gipsy-like neck scarf and an old knitted yellow waistcoat that my deceased mother had made for my Dad. Malcolm Burch, who I was in a pub band with, called it my 'young farmer' look. Maybe it was the flat cap. I even wrote a song about wearing a flat cap.

These new simplicities took me further than I had ever been artistically. I began to be proud of my completeness and the gap between me and the world provided endless material and a useful opposition, a standing place to see things clearly.

Another breakthrough came later, during the eighties. Writing about place, specifically the roads of Essex, became a focus. I spent much time in the car, driving to and from gigs and odd jobs, between the rural and urban worlds. The simplifications outlined above gave me a way in. It was to do with writing about what is in front of you, seeing the wood for the trees, the immediate. It began with noticing a distressed woman beside the road and wondering if she were a ghost. This opened a floodgate of songs, about a bus service, about the new M25 motorway around London, about home and the strangeness of the 'roadscape', as I called it. My cassette album *Roadworks* (1989) was the result.

The punks sang in strong English accents too and I began to be influenced by younger people, as I kept my eye on the pop world and some similar trends to my own solo and humbler furrow. The synth-bands sang in English too, like Depeche Mode, who were from where my brother lived in south Essex. Later I was to hear my friend Pete Morton, whose positive attitude inspired me. Alex Turner of Arctic Monkeys wrote songs on their first two albums that were as Yorkshire as my own contemporary Jim Eldon. Recently I love poet-musician Kate Tempest, very much their own person and again uplifting in epic story-poems.

It was later still when I felt confident enough to perform traditional material myself. Singer Sue Cubbin had written a songbook with a collection of old Essex folksongs, collected by Ralph Vaughan Williams. When we began performing them, the unaccompanied song and the old singers who sang them became central in my mind. I began trying to write songs that were simple and direct enough to be sung without instruments. This was yet another simplification and attempt at direct communication. My mission was renewed and my own voice grew stronger and less self-conscious. The directness of the naked voice, its freedom, its concentration on the words has the ability to command attention. A good recent young singer who sometimes sings unaccompanied is Richard Dawson. Listen to a recording of Phoebe Smith, the great English gipsy singer, if you want to feel the power.

This is the most autobiographical chapter here but I do feel that the growth of my own writer's mind has helped me move from being someone searching for a way to write that would be close to my own real life, towards something more useful. It has led me to finding a workable method that has carried me for a long life in writing, performing and teaching. If writers are people who find their own vantage points, I found one and I am still noticing insights and visions from where I stand. I now realise that what I have been doing is very much working in the tradition.

When the group I sing old folksongs with, Potiphar's Apprentices, recently performed at the Museum of East Anglian Life in our adjoining county, Suffolk, Sue Cubbin introduced Vaughan Williams' meeting of the old singers in the early 1900s. 'We are those old singers!' I interjected to diverse laughter. What I captured in my absurd suggestion was the feeling of what power there was in having a traditional attitude. I feel it coming through me now, as I write this.

Below are a selection of three songs from my writing life, as outlined above. 'Don't Tie Me Down' is about someone I worked with when in my youth, a traditional craftsman and the sense of freedom he was always seeking, though settled. It was the first song of mine that got covered by others on the folk scene. There are old and new elements here.

'The Back Roads' is from the *Roadworks* project, which describes the strange mix of urban and rural where I still live. 'Making Good' is about a traditional attitude to life, one of simplifying and improving rather than innovating or 'progressing'. This is from the more recent unaccompanied songs from the 2000s. The themes of these lyrics are reflected in some of the writing exercises below.

Author's Creative Examples:

DON'T TIE ME DOWN

I am a carpenter, I work in the town
In the old people's houses, I work with my hands
You ask if I'm happy, I tell you I am
Though I often think of the past

Don't tie me down, don't even try
To beg me to stay with a tear in your eye
I may sail away or else I may drown
But I'll take my chances, so don't tie me down

I once love a woman as rare as can be
But she found another when I went to sea
I travelled the world, in my youth I was free
And I'd like to travel again

In the war I was shipwrecked, my nerves are not strong
So I'm still as restless as when I was young
I still like a drink and I still like a song
Though my time is slipping away

With my agéd parents, I live here alone
I don't have a wife but my life is my own
I dream of the freedom that I've sometimes known
And no-one can tie me down

THE BACK ROADS

I was born out in the country
Though I've lived in the city and town
I still can find my way around
The lonely places

    The big wide road is moving
In processional ordered routine
But all that it really means
Is still more sameness
It's fast and famous

I prefer the back roads
Full of danger and beauty it's true
It may not be the quickest way through
But it's the pretty way, the old way
The hard way, the dark way, the sly way
And if you like the wide, bland highway ...
There's no point in me going with you
'Less you prefer the back roads too

Not far from all the new world
The old one still quietly lives on
Adapting like foxes have done
To human wasteland
      The shy ones and the brave ones
The gipsy still strolls in the lane
As if we had slipped back again
It's still real knowing
The way you're going

We're robbed of fascination
On every no-stopping straight road
Where everybody has thrown
Their dirt and money
      I can't afford a cottage
But how can the wild be tame
Somehow we will always remain
Among the strangers

MAKING GOOD

It was time to decorate the room
my father said to me
Son the best work you can do's
mainly preparatory
Fix that wooden shelf and fill
the holes just like you should
You must spend most of the time
in merely making good

Making good's the thing to do
where craftsmanship still counts
maintaining and improving in
slow but sure amounts
This was the attitude to use
in life, in paint and wood
You must spend most of your time
in merely making good

Robin told me Don't be daft
you know she still loves you
and I was sensible enough
to know that this was true
and although I lost her in
the end I know you should
work at your relationship
the same, by making good

Making good's the thing so your relationship still counts
maintaining and improving in
slow but sure amounts
This is the attitude to use
in love, in life and wood ...

I try to write, I try to sing
for strangers and for friends
for to make a song that's good's
a task that never ends
It can be much more pious
soft or painful than it should
you have to spend most of your time
in merely making good

Making good's the thing to do
where the song still counts
maintaining and improving in
slow but sure amounts
This is the attitude to use
in song, in life and wood ...

So I'm cooking soup for Cathy
and I'm phoning my old mate
Trying to make a bit of love
before it is too late
Mend my old guitar case
so it functions as it should
even trying out this song
is merely making good

Making good's the thing to do
when everything still counts
maintaining and improving in
slow but sure amounts
The only attitude to use
it's love, it's life, it's food
and I'll still spend most of my time
in merely making good

Writing Exercises

Write about the room you are in; its feel, temperature, view and what you love/ hate about it. Or about an article of clothing that says something about you.

Write a manifesto—what do you want to do with your writing and how you try to do it?

Write a song to be sung in the car. Give it a singable chorus, about joining in.

Write something, then edit to make it more simple, more direct and shorter than your usual work.

Create a new, strong voice and use it to be the writer or narrator of a piece of writing.

If you do not write about love, what else do you write about? List some and choose one.

Write about a person you know and their work and life.

Write about the roads and infrastructure where you live.

Write about something worth preserving against the newness demanded by the world.

Write about a strange conjunction of the old and new.

Write a writers' survival guide to keep you writing.

Reading, Listening, Watching:

Reading, Listening, Watching

Arctic Monkeys. 2006. *Whatever People Say I Am That's What I'm Not*. Domino Records.
Arctic Monkeys. 2007. *Favourite Worst Nightmare*. Domino Records.
The Copper Family. 1971. *A Song for Every Season*. Topic Records.
Dawson, Richard. 2017. *Peasant*. Weird World Records.
Fairport Convention. 1969. *Liege and Leif*. Island Records.
Hamp, Johnny. 1964. *Blues and Folk Train*. Granada T.V.
Holland, Maggie. 2007. *Bones*. Proper Records.
May, Adrian. 1984. *Anarchy In The Ukelele*. Mayday Records.
May, Adrian. 1989. *Roadworks*. Mayday Records.
Morton, Pete. 2020. *A Golden Thread*. Further Records.
Newman, Randy. 1972. *Sail Away*. Reprise Records.
Rilke, Rainer Maria. 1929. *Letters to a young poet*. Trans. W.W. Norton. New York: Norton.
Smith, Phoebe. 1989. *The Yellow Handkerchief*. Topic Records.
Tawney, Cyril album *The Song Goes On*, 2014.
Tempest, Kate. 2013. *Brand New Ancients*. London: Picador.
Tharpe, Sister Rosetta. 2015. *Complete Sister Rosetta Tharpe*. Varese Sarabande Records.
The Young Tradition. 1969. *The Young Tradition Sampler*. Topic Records.

CHAPTER 7

Protest Songs and the Comic Connection

All songs are protest songs. They protest their love, they protest their feelings, their celebration. Songs are not about weak feelings, though in fact, you could also protest that. Some songs are just more pointed than others. There are problems with them and there are techniques for overcoming these, but starting with the comic is not a bad way to start.

In the last chapter, my own L.P. sleeve notes describe the comic song as 'an unbroken tradition'. The sheer silliness or sheer pointedness of the comic and protest are closely aligned and it is easy to overlook the comic as unserious. Anyone who has studied Shakespeare or literature generally knows however that comedy is a serious business. Comedy turns the world upside-down, so we can see it better and comedy, in the Shakespeare sense, has a positive ending. These two purposes are not unserious at all. I love the fact that an old comic song can still get a laugh. The tradition is alive.

My comic song hero was well known for a silly traditional song, 'The Old Sow'. This begins with 'There was an old farmer who had an old sow …' and follows on with a series of grunting and snorting noises, never known to fail to tickle an audience. The singer was Leslie Sarony (1897–1985), who wrote many classic silly songs, such as 'I Lift Up My Finger', 'Why Build A Wall Round A Graveyard' and 'Jollity Farm', which was an 'answer song' to the U.S. comedy number he also recorded, called 'Misery Farm'. I heard of him from the Bonzo Dog Band's version of 'Jollity Farm' and finding an old 78 rpm record or two around in my Dad's old cupboards. I began collecting his 78s at second-hand shops and markets. I wrote a song about him, which I often followed with one of his songs. I wrote a piece about him for a long-gone journal, *Folk Review* and I sent this to his home address and received a nice reply, in 1978.

Later someone tipped me off that he was recording a TV special about old variety artists and I managed to get a ticket to go and see him live. Already in his eighties, he was sprightly and brilliant. He played the ukulele and, backed by a trio of double bass, drums and piano, he began with 'I Lift Up My Finger', which went on ... 'and say tweet-tweet, hush-hush, now-now, come-come'. He told stories and recited a rude monologue about a dog, 'Piddlin' Pete'. I had met some of the film crew in a fish and chip shop nearby, before the gig, and they had encouraged me to try to meet him after the show.

Jimmy Perry, one of the creators of the hit BBC TV show *Dad's Army* was the M.C. and was still on the stage at the end of the triumphant evening. I was, at thirty, the youngest member of the audience by far. I approached Mr Perry and asked if I could meet Mr Sarony. I explained that I had written an article about him for a folk music journal and his suspicious look softened and he ushered me into Leslie Sarony's dressing room. Leslie had already changed out of his stage trousers and I think he explained that the trick was never to sit down in them, so they looked neat on stage. It was a thrill to meet my hero and we discussed the fact that no records of his were available at the time. 'After I'm dead I expect the bastards will be falling over themselves to put my stuff out!' he said and we laughed. He was charming and funny and I felt amazed and exhilarated to have shared a few moments with him.

I remember telling a fellow musician, into the blues, about meeting him and I said it was for me like meeting Muddy Waters might be for you. Over the years I helped other people interested in him and even planned a show based on his still neglected songs. A few years after I met him though, the comedian Roy Hudd, back in the eighties a well-known enthusiast for old songs, did oversee an L.P. of Sarony, which I still have: *Roy Hudd Presents Leslie* Sarony (1980). As well as some of Sarony's old songs, it contained a song he wrote in 1961, called 'Yer Gotta Get Aht' (You've Got To Get Out), which Leslie himself says in the sleeve notes is 'a protest song really. It was my reaction to seeing what they've done to my beloved London'. It is also a cockney song, hence the dialect title. So again, very much in the tradition. The brutalist modernisation of London was a subject later taken up by critics of architecture and seems prescient, even now. I also note that Sarony, ever the old pro, recorded the album in one day, the 4th of October 1979; all the songs were first takes. A triumphant end to an often unremarked career of someone I am still proud to call my hero.

The sleeve notes tell us the story of Leslie writing a parody of a popular song of the day and teaching himself to play uke, as the pianists in the clubs were not up to busking an accompaniment. This is still a good way to start songwriting, especially comic or protest songwriting.

Leslie Sarony had been a star of 78 rpm records and probably his most famous hit was 'Ain't It Grand To Be Bloomin' Well Dead'. This song was banned by the BBC, always a boost to sales, as children used to follow funerals singing it. I want it played at my funeral. So controversy and taboo subjects are never far from the comic song and jollity and sheer seriousness are close. There is something here of the distortion to restore proportion dynamic, a phrase I associate with another comic songwriter from the early twentieth century, Joyce Grenfell (1910–1979).

An early film of Sarony exists, easily found by searching for 'Hot Water and Vegetabuel', where the young comedian starts unpromisingly, with ritual-like misogyny before a jolly positive song, 'Hot Water'. 'Don't Be Cruel to a Vegetabuel', which I have the sheet music for hanging on my wall, follows, which is itself an ironic protest song. Even his song about death is somehow positive, as he seems always on the side of life. Was 'Ain't it Grand …' a protest song? Yes, in a way.

Parody and irony are two ways of writing comic and protest works but at their root are hyperbole and litotes, or simply distortion. Hyperbole (look up how to pronounce it) is bigging up and litotes (look up again) is its opposite. If someone says you are a 'not bad' writer, meaning you are good, that is litotes. If someone says your worst thing is a work of 'sheer genius', they might be using hyperbole. Choose a subject and ask if making it bigger or smaller will make it funny and/or bring out some hidden truth in it, or, restore some proportion. Comedy and protest deal with making the ordinary extraordinary and vice-versa, which is both comic and a root of all art. As Arthur Koestler said in his classic on the creative process, *The Act of Creation* (1964), the comic analogy is the root end of the poetic metaphor. All creativity is about these dynamic opposites which make the world fresh. It is a traditional ritual of laughter and tears.

Another type of distortion in comedy can be to create pure silliness and nonsense, which I believe is particularly a feature of English and Irish comedy. This is usually 'all over the place' and for all kinds of effects, but the distortion motif still applies, as silliness is deflative. The picture of the fool with a bladder inflated is a classic symbol of inflation and deflation. The world blows itself up with pride and then goes pop, like a trickster. This again is a traditional function. An example of a litotes absurdist comedy song man is Sam Mayo, from the English Music Halls. His droll songs were flat and banal at times and he was famous for never smiling, all of which made him funnier.

Another aspect of the comic which is essential, especially to the comic song, is the relishing of the verbal. This relishing, of even, or especially of bad words masquerading as good can be seen in the workmen's version of 'Pyramus and Thisbe' in Shakespeare's *A Midsummer Night's Dream*. The absurdity and relish go together. Great poetry can also be funny, as we recognise the truth in its painful honesty. However much comedy distorts, it has a relish of language and its ability to get near to some truth, howsoever distorted. Comedy gets you back to the roots of creativity as well as to the roots of the relishing of good writing. The hip, witty quality of black U.S. songwriter Oscar Brown Junior and of Ted Joans, the black beat poet I saw live, impressed me early on.

If we take a song like Tom Lehrer's 'National Brotherhood Week', written for a topical show in 1967 and easily found online, we see the link between comedy and satire, which is the connection to protest. Thus protest, the latest thing, is thoroughly traditional in nature. Lehrer builds up the idea only to deflate it and the song is still funny and pertinent today. This is comedy, satire and protest against hypocrisy and it might be arguable what type of satire it is. Satire aims at the follies of the world and Horatian satire is said to be more gently mocking, while Juvenalian is darker and more bitter in tone. Lehrer always has dark elements but, at the same time, is not extreme in attitude. Satire is a whole subject and tradition and its name seems to come from cooking, which could be the cue for a little satire itself.

The comic element in satire could help protest not sound too pious. Protest can sound like virtue signalling or propaganda and that is perhaps why so many avoid it. For me, though, protest is an ancient form and can change minds and focus intelligence. There are folksongs I know about poverty that remind you of something you need to be reminded of, like 'All Things Are Dear But Poor Men's Labour' and 'Working Life Out To Keep Life In'. Work songs themselves often express something which needs to be expressed, as seen in 'chain gang' songs and chants. In the 1930s the songs about the Depression and tramps were genuine expressions of the feelings of the general population. Yip Harburg, lyricist of 'Buddy Can You Spare A Dime' used to say in interview words to the effect that before his song there *was* no depression, with comic hyperbole.

The danger in protest and comic song alike, as well as other types of writing, is that of shallowness. It is all too easy to skate on the surface of subjects with a sneer of virtue signalling superiority. This, incidentally, is also the danger of the internet and computer culture generally, while people are often hasty to judge and prejudice is rife. To write well, you need to go deep. To protest, to be funny, you need your frivolity but also to go much deeper. The internet is also good for research, if you know the right sources. Use university resources and good reference sources. Do some in-depth research and base your most easy-seeming writing on hard work as well as inspiration. If you look at a manuscript page of P.G. Wodehouse's fiction, so light as to almost be evanescent, it is the most highly worked on text you will see. It takes masses of hard work to make something look effortless and this pays off.

The folk revival grew out of protest in the 1950s and 1960s, with singers like the great Pete Seeger, influenced by his mentor Woody Guthrie. Seeger's song 'Waist Deep In The Big Muddy' is a good example. I recommend listening to Richard Shindell's 2004 version. On the surface, it is a ballad that tells the story of a foolish army sergeant drowning his men by crossing a river at the wrong point. We are left to make the analogy ourselves between this and the political situation in muddy Vietnam. The final verse even says he will not tell you what to think. This allegorical action makes the song all the more effective as it makes the audience think. This is a great example of one way of writing a protest song.

This story song highlights the ballad approach which is narrative. Often, telling the story plainly is effective, if the story gives its own message. The English folksinger Chris Wood's song 'Hollow Point' (2010) shows this effectively. Here he tells the tale of John Charles De Menezes, shot by police in London (2005), after being mistaken for a terrorist. He uses a traditional ballad form and tells the story plainly but in fourteen verses. It is chillingly effective.

By contrast, the greatest protest song of the twentieth century might be 'Strange Fruit', as sung by Billie Holiday. This was written as a poem by Abel Meeropol in 1937 and his wife Laura Duncan helped him put it to music. The song is so closely associated with Billie Holiday that it seems her own. She persuaded a record company boss to record it after singing it to him without accompaniment. This brought him to tears. The song operates on that central analogy of fruit hanging from a tree to the lynchings that were common in those days. A powerful image is its method and this can work well for a writer. It has an original title and memorable quality. Again, this takes the song out from mere sermonising or propaganda, which protest songs must avoid to be effective.

Comedy and protest are closely aligned in that they challenge conventional views with their pointed and relished use of language. They seem to be the yin and yang of creativity too in their power. They are easy to get wrong and it is easy for people to mistake irony for sincerity, for example, in satire. I wrote a song called 'Isn't Love Disgusting?', which parodied censorious puritans, but sometimes people thought I agreed with them when the opposite was true. Some listeners think songs should be of good cheer only and avoid the political. You might also be 'preaching to the converted'. But using the methods and warnings here can give you the power to write something which captures a mood of seeking the truth amid a world blinded by convention and power. My argument would be that we need these songs as part of the useful resistance to the stifling of true voices. It is a traditional role to write comedy and protest injustice and it reminds us of our human propensity to folly and even to evil and the need to counteract it. The latest thing is the most traditional and the traditionalist challenges the world.

The first of the four songs below shows an example of having a song hero. I used to go straight from this song into a comic song by Sarony when I sang it myself as an opening number, or statement of intent, in folk clubs. The second song is a tribute to another English comic songwriter, Noel Gay, who wrote many songs about sunshine, including 'The Sun Has Got His Hat On'. The title is taken from yet another comic, Old Mother Reilly, as played by Arthur Lucan. In an old obscure film, the name of which I have long forgotten, he says the title phrase.

The third song is influenced directly by 'Strange Fruit' and talks of the practice of taking prisoners aboard to enable 'legal' torture. This is an example of using an image to focus the attention. The fourth song is about an immigrant to the U.K. who was found murdered on the Queen's royal estate in Norfolk in 2012. The message here is 'It's such a long way down from high to low', as the song says, but essentially it merely presents the facts, which have a strange contrast built-in.

Author's Creative Examples

The King of Comic Song (1979).

Some folks have heroes, so famous or so strong
But my own hero is strong in wit and song
He's entertained us for seventy years
The world's full of laughter when he appears

He's Leslie Sarony, the King of Comic Song
He's entertained us so well and for so long
He's eighty plus but he's still going strong
He's the King of Comic Song

Right from the days of the good old music hall
To the TV now, he's done them all
Singing and writing his tunes and his words
You will be brighter if you have heard ...

He sang 'Ain't it Grand to be Bloomin' Well Dead'
He took us from 'Misery' to 'Jollity' instead.
You may hear him sing on a 78.
But a good laugh cannot be out of date, with ...

He'll still do a monologue on the stage
He'll sing and he'll dance like a man half his age
The world must have changed since he's been on the boards
Except for the laughter and the applause, for ...

SMOTHER MY SMALLS IN SUNSHINE

Smother my smalls in sunshine, simmer my socks in smiles
Semaphore semolina sandwiches all the while
Don't tell me the bad news when I'm feeling vile
Smother my smalls in sunshine, simmer my socks in smiles

Summer was saturated, spring was soggy too
Winter has been backdated and I feel that way too
Atom bombs activated, everyone's got a gun
Everyone's aggravated; we've lost our sense of fun, so ...

Everything is against me, walls are closing in
Everyone is pretentious, life's a looney bin
Everyone looks so gloomy, everyone looks so wet

But I'd rather be a looney that agonise and fret

But I'm not advocating wearing a phoney grin
I just find it grating being miserable as sin
And if we've lost our gumption, we've still got our smalls
So put away that truncheon, and sing with lusty balls

Smother my smalls in silly soppy sunshine
Simmer my socks in silly sunny smiles
Semaphore sticky sickly semolina
Sandwiches scrumptious scoffing all the while
Don't tell me the bleeding bally bad news when I'm feeling violent and vile
Smother my smalls in silly soppy sunshine
Simmer my socks in silly sunny smiles

STRANGE TOURIST

Strange tourist passing through the airport
All the brochures never mention
You'll be handcuffed to an armed secret agent
or 'extraordinary rendition'

> Strange tourist, flying away
> To somewhere you can be free
> Free from laws that stop you being tortured
> Free from the land of the free

Strange tourist, paranoia's scapegoat
It could be you on that flight
Hypocrisy is democracy's big promise
And no-one cares what's wrong or right

> Strange tourist, flying away
> No travel agent ever spoke
> Of these flights away from human rights
> Or that freedom's just a joke

Strange tourist, passing through the airport
Security services don't mention
How we all could become estranged as you
And dream of revolution

And no-one's free until he's freed
Strange tourist indeed
And no-one's free until he's freed
Oh a strange and bitter tourist indeed

QUEEN ALISA (Alisa Dmitrijeva, 17, found January 2012)

Royal connections only when she died
quite the opposite of wealth and pride
and it's a long way here from Latvia
to the grounds of Sandringham where they found her

Near where the shooting parties sometimes stalk
found by someone taking their dog for a walk
you made the news because it seemed to show
it's such a long way down from high to low
Queen Alisa

> *Lost in the summer, no-one saw her face*
> *And four long months went by till she was found*
> *Then winter came to that exclusive place*
> *Poor murdered girl on the cold royal ground*
> *Queen Alisa*

Your folks were immigrants here, where slaves seem free
Mum works in the food-processing factory
You dreamed of a better time out on the town
away from where low wages keep you down

But this is no wonderland that you had found
this England won't turn fortunes upside-down
once from the rich and powerful in their shame
you stole the limelight; you deserve the name
Queen Alisa

Writing Exercises

Who is your writing hero? Write about them as an introduction to an example of their work, trying to capture something of their flavour in your writing.

Write an 'answer song', like a 'Stand By Your Woman' to a 'Stand By Your Man' (Tammy Wynette and Billy Sherill 1968).

Write a comic portrait about your own home place and what is good or bad and what has changed about it. This could be a celebration or protest, or a combination of both. You could use the old songwriters' trick of writing of a place as a person (they also use person as place).

Find a phrase from a surreal comedian you like and make it into a song, or other piece, with 'patter', with relish for the complex pattern of words and a high proportion of nonsense.

The Portuguese traditional form 'Fado' often had two sets of words, one safe and one political. Write an example of this kind of 'contrafacta'; a set of political words for a love song you know. 'Contrafacta' is the art of writing alternative words to songs (singular is 'contrafactum').

Write a parody of a well-known song, making nonsense of its sense.

Find an image for an injustice, inspired by 'Strange Fruit' (Abel Meeropol 1837) and create a piece of writing.

Research a story from the news in-depth and write it as a narrative, inspired by ballads like 'Hollow Point' (Chris Wood 2010).

Write about a vain leader, distorted into even more grandness, to the point of hyperbolic absurdity.

Write a love song that uses litotes, with a title such as, 'I Like You Very Slightly'.

Reading, Listening, Watching

Brown Junior, Oscar. 1996. *Sin and Soul ... and Then Some*. Sony Records.
Holiday, Billie. 2015. *Strange Fruit*. On *Gold*. Not Now Records.
Joans, Ted. 1970. *Afrodisia*. New York: Hill and Wang.
Koestler, Arthur. 1964. *The Act of Creation*. London: Hutchinson.
Lehrer, Tom. 1967. National Brotherhood Week. On *That Was The Year That Was*. Reprise Records.
Sarony, Leslie. 1980. *Roy Hudd Presents Leslie Sarony*. E.M.I. Records.
Shindell, Richard. 2004. *Waist Deep in the Big Muddy*. On *Vuelta*. Koch Records.
Wood, Chris. 2010. 'Hollow Point'. On *Handmade Life*. Ruf Records.

PART III

Tradition, Self and Nature

CHAPTER 8

Tradition and Locality

To start to talk about the local, I want to begin with two quotations which are local to me. When asked, at an academic conference, away from my home university, for an introductory blurb from a chair of a session, I used to tell them to say this: 'Adrian May is an over-educated skinhead from Essex'. The other, specific, incident happened when I moved from my native Bovinger, near Ongar, thirty miles north in Essex, U.K., to Halstead. I overheard an elderly woman who lived opposite saying, 'He don't belong round here; he's from Ongar way'.

Both of these lines are about ambivalence. The county of Essex has a reputation as the place of the 'Essex joke' and every area has its scapegoat place of the roughest and most working-class one around. My line is a joke about baldness also, but, in the main, it is a way of embracing the public image in a mild form of defiance, a way of subverting prejudice, while clinging to the positive side of the toughness, the common energy, which belongs to Essex. I bring myself home and locate myself with that most traditional form, the joke. Jokes assume knowledge, that which is passed to us, which is a definition of tradition. Jokes also contain thinking on two levels and enact a journey out and back.

Not belonging thirty miles from where I was born is a bit more tricky. If the word 'belong' means the same as 'being from', as in its Old English etymology, then she was precisely right. The ludicrous nature, to my younger self, of the remark, which made me remember it, is now superseded by this sense, and a sense of ambiguity. It still strikes me as funny, but as poignant too. She must have had a stronger sense of traditional connection than I will ever have. She was perfectly nice to me, too, incidentally, and I came to feel

© The Author(s), under exclusive license to Springer Nature
Switzerland AG 2021
A. May, *Tradition in Creative Writing*,
https://doi.org/10.1007/978-3-030-74776-3_8

very much that I belonged to Halstead, perhaps partly because of what her remark triggered, slowly, in my consciousness.

We all tend to be ambivalent about the local. On one hand we discuss 'food-miles' and say 'think global, act local', while a popular 'cool' film of not so long ago was *Borat*, where the whole premise mocks the parochial. Performance and all kinds of art are often thought of as a universal language, even as an active political tool to emphasise what it means to be human, although art itself often finds renewal in rootedness. Writers like Yeats in Ireland and the Americanness of Philip Roth, for two well-known examples, are among many who illustrate this paradox.

Our traditional connection, or belonging, to the local is something that needs this performance of its ambiguities to become real. The idea of tradition, of examining what connects us to each other, can be a radical, rather than reactionary, way of responding to a world where 'local' is a joke. The communal and tribal continues to hold strength and perhaps a real sense of truth resides only in traditional gratuity, in what is passed to us.

If the traditional is what is passed over to us, it can be seen, in this sense, as what we take for granted, the habits and ways of behaving and thinking that come from the world we live in and the people we know. The problem here is that what we are talking about gets harder to define, more abstract, rather than moving towards the simple, or the truth about what we are, as defined by what we are given. So, in a sense, we already are local. Here we are, inhabiting the space we are in, on this concrete, this board, this walkway, this grass and this earth. Likewise in this body, this life, this imagination, this relation to others, this connection or lack of it. We tend, or have tended to of late and in England, to do everything we can to somehow deny this 'hereness'.

We are talking mythic simplicities here, about Nature versus abstraction, about 'getting back' to something we already have. Sometimes the name of that something is Home.

So, before making any elaborate claims about the local, to start from home, capitalised or not, is probably the best place, as you have to start from somewhere. Homelessness is something we fear and a home, a lair, a nest, a bower, an Eden of some kind is something we do not care to do without, by instinct, by homing instinct even, and by practical and everyday needs and universal practices.

The culture, as opposed to the tradition, we find ourselves in, values, above all, the escape from home. Partly this is also an instinctive thing. We only value what we take for granted by what we put in contrast to it. But I am suggesting that the commercial world, the public world's urge, is towards using our desire for escaping from the banal as a way of controlling us for commercial and political reasons. So I will try not to push the political point, just to suggest that we are overwhelmed by notions of escape. Youth culture, fashion, multi-national popular arts, the TV, the internet—all these things are holidays abroad. All the things you connect to are things that disconnect you from the nourishing banalities of home.

The problem with the world getting smaller, the global village model of Eden, is that if anywhere is home, no-where is home. Not only is there then no home, there is no elsewhere either. So, if home means anything in this context, it must mean the reality of the particular over the general.

Part of this feeling is exacerbated by the individualistic emphasis which goes with the exotic, escape-driven, view of the world. People 'go for it' and want to 'fulfil their potential' and 'live the dream'. As Wordsworth said, 'The world is too much with us' and our worldly drives have taken us to a place where, for example, the ultimate triumph of men over women seems to get them to agree that the home was worthless, to sell out feminism by joining the masculine world outside. So individualism is not crushed by the imagined holiday in the world of adventure, but by the limiting idea of individualism. The imagination has failed to ground itself, to tell itself the story of what is really of value.

If the world is smaller, it is also further away. Globalisation, relativism, where everywhere is of equal value, individualistic escape are species of hunting culture at best. It has energy, but no vision of synergy or cyclic fertility. The tradition of locality is maybe the next stage. We cannot, in fact, live without locality, as I said. We are where we are, despite our strenuous technological and mechanical attempts at omnipresence. As with other elements of the traditional, we find we are already there.

If there is value in locality, how deep is it and how deep should it be? Are we to be like a religious anchorite and chain ourselves to one place? Are we in danger of indulging in nostalgia and, worse, a prejudice against other places and peoples?

Literature, from Genesis and Homer, is so often about home and about feelings of belonging, which is something given, passed to us and therefore traditional. The paradoxical nature of our attitude to our place somehow only reveals the kind of taboo, or special, nature of the relationship. In a world where movement and change is vital to the commercial imperative, our ignorance, lack or rejection of our place of origin makes us all the more ambivalent, like adopted children who seek to reject their parents completely or seek them earnestly. The violence of those who seek to enforce a local identity, where they fear the lack of any identity or who seek to manipulate the need for identity for corrupt means, makes us all the more ambivalent. But this ambivalence at last only acknowledges the importance of local identity by being unable to deal with it, like a trauma which blocks acceptance. And a feeling of acceptance, of belonging and being ourselves part of the tradition of a particular place in the world, is what we block. The simple nourishment of the earth, with every resonance of 'dung and death', but also of growing and standing (when 'everybody's got to be somewhere') is only ignored as a matter of pride or of an inability to see what is underneath our nose. It seems a secret peculiar to our time.

Like many natural, or basic, base aspects of life, which reveal sentiment, we like to call a local sensibility provincial (to where exactly?), sentimental, nostalgic, Romantic. The tendency to blame Romanticism for all our just or unjust sentiments is more dangerous than any honest, homely nostalgia or sentimentality. While no-one reads *Paradise Regained*, accusations of nostalgia mask the mindless, inflexible orthodoxy of the present. Like Odysseus at the start of his epic, we have yet to get home from this war. We do not even know that there is a war. We do not know, consequently, that there is a home to go back to. Yet in these primal texts, as in the work of the Romantics, there is a clue as to how you find home again.

Home, locality, is only found in the journey away and then in the process of coming home, or becoming home. Home is the alpha and the omega, the process, the place from where you set out, so that you can remember it, away from the fixed worlds of violence in war, or sexual obsession, with Calypso, or drugs, with eating Lotus flowers. These things that so much exercise us, which seem so beguiling are all fixed outside of the homely world of maintenance, in their quality of the everlasting present. Just as we blame Romanticism, this old thing of the fixity of seeming movement in drugs and sex and war, we tend to label something like 'modern',which makes them seem inevitable.

In the local, tradition is not then a boring repetition of an old routine, but the very place where the future can be rediscovered. This is not discovering something old and praising it as a relic (called 'revivalism'), but tradition in an active, processive sense, the place where change is made sense of, adopted, because it is where contingency is allowed. The prodigal son has the rejoicing because he has restored himself.

In these mythic, traditional tasks, we are strangers to ourselves, as Ted Hughes indicates in his essay 'Myth and Education' (1976). In terms of our sense of place, in our ignorance of local history, nature, folklore, we are often demonstrably so, yet this rich resource waits for us, like an undiscovered or parallel world, while we search the web for some virtual connection.

Wordsworth's *The Prelude* is so much about this, in that it describes his return from the revolutionary age to a new sense of home. Away from 'vain conceits ... of self-applauding intellect', he returns to home, literally and imaginatively, to where—

> Were re-established now those watchful thoughts
> Which, seeing little worthy or sublime
> In what the Historian's pen so much delights
> To blazon – power and energy detached
> From moral purpose – early tutored me
> To look with feelings of fraternal love
> Upon the unassuming things that hold
> A silent station in this beauteous world (1850, Book XIII, 40–48)

The attention to place, to home, to 'the unassuming', is 're-established' by 'watchful thoughts', the humble lessons already there, 'early tutored', ready for the cycle or ritual, of reconnection.

As Wordsworth indicates in the one word title of Book XIII, this is also a story of the mediation, of the education of the 'imagination'. Imagination needs to be rooted in place to perform its transforming function, otherwise it has nothing to transform. That prime text of shadows and doubts about imagination, Shakespeare's *A Midsummer Night's Dream* also asks the same questions.

The famous speech at the beginning of Act 5, where Theseus shows how he thinks the whole story 'More strange than true' is often thought to be a positive view of the imagination, by compilers of quotations especially. 'The lunatic, the lover, and the poet/ Are of imagination all compact' sounds pretty, but really he is saying that poetry and love are nuts. The voice of reason in the play will have none of it, until his wife, in five short lines, manages to make more sense than in his twenty-one lines, and to provide a proper place for the imagination at the same time. Thereby the play of love and madness is brought back to the great hall in the palace of the Duke and given a home, intellectually as well as actually, in a wedding, the traditional, ritual way of coming back home which ends the formal genre of comedy. Here is what Hippolyta says:

> But all the story of the night told over
> And all their minds transfigured so together
> More witnesseth than fancy's images
> And grows to something of great constancy
> But howsoever strange and admirable.

The last line echoes and rewrites Theseus' 'More strange than true', in its re-enactment of the cycle of the comedy, the 'bringing it all back home' to quote another poet. She suggests that the strange can be admirable, if given its proper place. Theseus' speech ends with a brash, male rhyme: 'Or in the night, imagining some fear,/ How easy is a bush supposed a bear!' Just as she rewrites his beginning with her end, she rewrites his end with her beginning, picking up the challenge implicit in his rhyme and transforming it into a soft, feminine and communal couplet. This turns the story 'over', until the community is at home with its imagination, 'together'. What is 'transfigured' returns them to their homely world, and the homely 'mechanicals' come on to do their own transforming of a love story, their own 'story of the night told over'.

The problem then, as the problem is now, is one with rationality, in its tendency to want to isolate its meaning, risking becoming simplistic and narrow, just in the way that it accuses religion, for example, of the same thing. This is Theseus versus Hippolyta again. The shrillness of the rational hides the harmony of the contingent.

The local is not then the safe alternative to the life of endless choice, endless adventure. It is the hard way, especially now that it seems a place of 'fear', where the 'bush' becomes 'a bear', the narrow, provincial place of dullness which cannot be embraced. The 'mechanicals' are the dull made fresh, the opposite route to taking the fear out of the bear, representing the rootedness and universality of the imagination's journey back home.

We can find a sharp indication of the disillusion with the world of choice in the poem 'Dover Beach'. This 'world which seems/ To lie before us like a land of dreams,/ So various, so beautiful, so new', as Mathew Arnold put it in 1851, is one where he needs to find a confession of loss making its home in the place of departures and arrivals. Home is what you re-make, even if you reject it utterly. The rich man builds his castle, his traditional stronghold of authority and safety, in spite of his poor beginning, or, exactly *because* of his birth-locality. But if we are disillusioned with the base reality, this un-losable root, how do we learn to embrace it, or find it useful?

One thing seems certain, the cycle of adventure and return, the narrative of tradition, of making what is passed to us an act that can be ritually recreated, must be at the root of it. Tradition, in this sense, seems to need to be performed, in order to be active, not a museum piece. That dull place where you were born has to be told into a story, the darkness of it, its invisibility, must become 'the story of the night told over'. My brother lived in a modern flat on the edge of the old 'New Town' of Basildon. By accident he discovered that the particular area used to be called 'Plotlands', and was full of self-built houses of migrants from London, looking for a new life. The wild, self-made hopefulness of the old place captured his imagination and he sought out older people who remembered the pioneering days, collecting their memories and the songs they sung. He is no academic, no folklorist, but he has found a way of imaginatively connecting to his place.

Types of home are all around us, taken for granted, overlooked. To be local is to slow, even stop and look down, in detail, as when reading over a rich poem. The great thing of sinking in like this is that it somehow is not exclusive. To be where you are, to see how really 'various' this is, as opposed to 'the world', with Arnold and Wordsworth, is to include the rich variety of a handful of soil. The maintenance of the rooted, the re-enactment of the adventure out and back, is at the root of societies where the traditional is valued. The music must be played. Do we need to go to a distant tribe for this? About an hour's drive from Colchester, in Essex, where I write, there are traditional musicians who still perform their works in a particular way.

In *The Fellowship of Song* (1980), Ginnette Dunn offers an academic, yet still useful, view of this local tradition. On an evening she describes, the local singers perform traditional songs with mutual respect, taking turns to strike up, while some visiting servicemen from a nearby airbase would like to play their banjo and guitar continuously in a monopolistic way. While it might be all too easy to read too much into this, and it is worth pointing out that there were some sensitive foreign servicemen also present, the clash of cultures is striking. The local singers have status via their local reputation with a song, while the insensitive-types have a more commercial, competitive attitude, not tempered by the communality and ease of accepted status of the natives.

What interests me particularly about these singers and musicians is that they rarely make distinctions between old and new material. While the old songs last, there is no exclusivity about this and creative work is not excluded. Jeff

Wesley, an older singer I have met from Northamptonshire, who mainly sings unaccompanied traditional songs learned from his family, told me that he both writes and adapts songs. I did not tell him that his practice as an artist was like that of writers of the past, such as Shakespeare, but I thought it.

There is something of the idea of mending and restoration here, which is essential to a local attitude. Mending and restoration have much in common with the mythic or ritual journey away and back to home. Something, say a song, becomes broken, perhaps by the loss of a few verses in oral transmission or loss of memory. Part of the song has journeyed away. The restoration work brings the song back into a sharper, reanimated, focus and the remaking of home is complete. The interest in genealogy and in TV shows on archaeology and the history of houses particularly show how deep this instinct is. Restoring the old, beloved object is a re-enactment of the making of home. Maintenance, even D.I.Y. in this way, is a human need. The pleasure it gives me to consult my Dad's long-broken old copy of *Lempriere's Classical Dictionary*, which I rebound myself ten years ago, is better than buying a brand new edition, as it carries us both with it, connecting me to my birth and, as important, with the fact that my father helps me carry on learning. This, too, is a re-enactment, a reminder, a remembering of the father–son tradition, a passing on of value, which brings value to the present.

These connections can sound dull from the outside, as if a xenophobe had entered the room, huffing and puffing about the old days. Surely, you might say, getting away from the past is as important, or even the whole point, rather than coming back. Obviously I do not think so, but the prophet of perceived dullness, poet Philip Larkin has grappled often with this, or his, problem, especially in *The Whitsun Weddings* (1964).

His most specific comment, in a collection which seems continually to be on the theme of home, is in 'The Importance of Elsewhere', about his time in Ireland. Again, the importance of home *in relation* to 'not home' is there. Again, too, it enacts the journey of elsewheres to bring home a sense of home. As so often in Larkin's work, the positive is carefully hidden in the insight that learns from its opposite. The poem being the bringing back home of this thought about 'elsewhere' and in this way being a triumph of 'here', a work which enacts its difficulty. It says that it is harder to be here than elsewhere and yet this poem has done the job.

This poem, the twenty-second in the book, takes us naturally back to the first poem, in many ways on the same theme, with its easily overlooked, up to now, but obviously carefully chosen title, 'Here'. This poem itself announces the book's achievement and theme, in contradiction to other poems, especially 'The Importance of Elsewhere'. 'Here' is very much a landscape poem, a poem of psycho-geography, full of rich descriptiveness, in celebration, however downbeat, of Hull, avoiding the word and its obvious echo of 'dull'.

'Here' ends with its chorus of three uses of the word in eight lines. Again, it would be easy to sense a closing down, an over-reticence, but if 'Here' is both town and country and metaphor, then freedom is found in the poem, brought back here to home, freedom to see something sunny, and even beyond the poem itself, which is the fruit of rootedness.

Even at its apparent bleakest, the whole collection is a triumph of the poetic over the daffodils of deprivation, the paraphrase Larkin's dictum that deprivation was to him what daffodils were to Wordsworth. For me this means that he finds flowers, or poems, of a positive nature, in spite of, or because of the journey *from* deprivation. Even the bleak 'Home is so Sad' says that home should be joyful, however distant.

The final poem, 'An Arundel Tomb', on the 'hereness' of death and love, ends the whole collection with an assertion of love. For a start, the poem ends with the word 'love', but this love is arrived at, like a homecoming, qualified by its human, and humanely sympathetic twin guards, called 'almost'. If getting past these guards is hard, it seems worth it to bring it all back, as, in this reading of it, to a book of verses about the small epic of home, where 'love' has the last word.

This ritual journey, this adventure which balances the outward with the return is spelt out best for me in mythographer Joseph Campbell's *Primitive Mythology* (1969), in a paragraph from 'The Functioning of Myth', in the 'Conclusion' (p. 462). Here he says myth takes you to the universal but that this must be via the local and particular. So Campbell, in his quest to find the universal language of myth, insists on the locality of the function, while highlighting the need for this 'antinomy', or paradoxical law. The potential for misunderstanding in this paradoxical, or circular, narrative journey is also emphasised.

Something in the American experience, the seeking of a new home, seems to make some U.S. writing aware of this. Bob Dylan, a great traditionalist, with the antinomy of being often topical and political, embodies the problem in his song 'I Pity The Poor Immigrant', as discussed in Chapter 5. In some ways *John Wesley Harding* is his Larkinesque album, with its dark, serious tone masking a playfulness and emphasis, finally on love. 'I Pity The Poor Immigrant' is one of the darker songs.

The sorrowful tone does not spare the listener from the negative message, except that we remember that America is the land of immigrants, Dylan included. The self-criticism is characteristic of Dylan's work and the song seems to be about what happens if you cannot root yourself. Remembering your roots positively, as in the old tune, with its tone of 'pity' can help you make an art that remakes you into being at home, even while 'hate', 'fear' and 'death' are close by. The work is cathartic then and not racist or anti-immigrant, while its condemnation of the dangers of a lack of acceptance of the local, both in the past self, now lost in the mere nostalgia, and the current thoroughness of evil, is Biblical. It could be a sermon from a founding father preacher, working towards a new life with a reluctant, resentful, disappointed flock.

Dylan is accepting the land that gave him birth, America, and the uneasy relationship with his immigrant roots here. To accept that somewhere gave you birth, that you do belong somewhere, is a deeply resonant psychological move, that liberates you from Arnold's 'world that seems/ To stand before us like a land of dreams' back to where, being away from the deathly 'poor immigrant' attitude, being awake and being at home is possible. Being 'just local' is not what it is about, in a market-driven world of shiny packaging where 'local' means 'no good'. Marrying the boy or girl next door is not merely a convenience or lack of imagination or education, but could just as easily be an acceptance of and the restoration of home. In other words, it could be the grounding ritual of the imagination in its proper place. In a way, the person one marries *must* be next door.

The old East Anglian fairytale, 'The Pedlar of Swaffam', tells of a man dreaming of treasure, who, on visiting London, is told to go home and dig in his own garden. The whole of a popular novel called *The Alchemist* is taken from this motif of the journey away heralding a return, a reminder, that the treasure is present all the time. The idea of treasure brings us to the concept of the traditional and local as being a gift, as opposed to an aspect of monetary culture. Lewes Hyde's book *The Gift* (1983) outlines this concept. Our locality is a given, our tradition is what is passed to us. Our locality then is one thing that gives us this gift, of the timeless and the temporal together, to paraphrase T.S. Eliot. We do this anyway, unthinking for the most part, but this process of 'defamiliarisation' is to reanimate the familiar, to make it strange in parallel with its familiarity. Hence we 'make ourselves at home'. The local is found by re-finding it.

The human tendency is to imagine alternative worlds but not to be able to imagine here. To find yourself alien is the first step to finding home, as Dylan imagines in 'I Pity the Poor Immigrant' and throughout *John Wesley Harding*. In a world of too much choice, it can be a way of deciding on using or accepting what is around you as the most radical move. A traditional idea of locality is a way of concentrating, a kind of pantheism, a depth of planting that rewards with nourishment. To work imaginatively with nature, with the earth under your feet, is to work with human nature. This is not a way of anthropomorphising nature but rather a way of acknowledging that we are part of it. You are where you are.

The more I think about this, the more it seems to me that writers have continually discussed this relation to place, as they themselves find a place with writing. Thomas Hardy puts it explicitly in *The Woodlanders* (1978), one of his novels 'of character and environment' and one which 'eco-critic' Jonathan Bate discusses to great effect in *Song of the Earth* (2000). Hardy's spelling out of the importance of locality to character comes in Chapter XVII.

> Winter in a solitary house in the country, without society, is tolerable, nay, even enjoyable and delightful, given certain conditions; but these are not the conditions that attach to the life of a professional man who drops down into such a place by mere accident ... They are old associations – an almost exhaustive biographical or historical acquaintance with every object, animate and inanimate,

within the observer's horizon. He must know all about the invisible ones of the days gone by, whose feet have traversed the fields which look so grey from his window; recall whose creaking plough has turned these sods from time to time; whose hands planted the trees that form a crest to the opposite hill; whose horses and hounds have torn through that underwood; what birds affect that particular brake; what bygone domestic dramas of love, jealousy, revenge, or disappointment have been enacted in the cottages, the mansions, the street or on the green. The spot may have beauty, grandeur, salubrity, convenience; but if it lack memories it will ultimately pall upon him who settles there without opportunity of intercourse with his kind.

This might seem so alien view to a current reader that it seems at first sight possibly trite or sentimental. Yet, it now strikes me, in the light of these thoughts, as profoundly and radically true. Nor is Hardy unaware of the effect on the character of being cut off from one's continuum. He describes the desperation felt by those cut off in such a way, leading to embracing 'any impostor' who looks like a friend. We seek connection so eagerly, having cut ourselves off from it, that we invest our uneasy relationships with more value than they can bear.

Poet Gary Snyder, about whom Jack Kerouac wrote *The Dharma Bums* (1965), an early environmentalist who has written much about Native American culture, believes that part of the answer to our problems with the environment is our lack of stillness. In recent writings he suggests that staying at home is the most radical thing you can do.

To love your own place does not mean having no respect for other places, but rather increases your respect for others' own places too. As the old saying goes, 'go abroad and you'll find news of home'. This is the journey out and back. As philosopher John Dewey said, 'Locality is the only universal' ('Americanism and localism', 1920). Aboriginal Australian writer Bob Randall echoes the deep tradition of place in his culture, in his use of the phrase 'the Land owns us' (*Songman: The Story of an Aboriginal Elder*, 2003).

This is not a kind of back door to nationalism, but a kind of backyard patriotism, a loving of your own place for the sake of love. For me, this might, with D.H. Lawrence be 'the tough old England that made me' (in his poem 'As For Me I'm a Patriot', 1929), or even being 'an overeducated skinhead from Essex', but belonging is important and I am still finding out where and what I belong to and it is a fruitful journey of discovery. As T.S. Eliot puts it in Part V of 'Little Gidding', from *Four Quartets* (1944), we must keep on with our 'exploration', the result of which is that we know home properly at last.

Author's Creative Example:

ENGLAND IS DIFFERENT

The tribal real American

Came to Essex Uni
And said This is who I am
Who are you – can you tell me?

Imagine the embarrassment
When no-one there could tell
All thrown into question
He made the point well

But England is different
In its humble pride
Like English poetry
Or countryside

Can't say what it is,
But must say what it isn't
Others salute
But England is different

We shouldn't rise up
Or be just like them
But more like that tribal
American

To be like some others
That would be a shame
Let them be like that –
England's not the same

Tell me what's English
And I'll disagree
It'll change like the tides
Of a surrounding sea

Some say it's a joke
Or say God save the Queen
I say England is different –
Know what I mean?

We like to be different
That is our essence
Let England be different
Embracing all difference

Writing Exercises:

Find someone who has lived in your area a long time and hear their memories. Note down key phrases that might make a title and any prejudices worth exploring, then write something which contrasts your life with theirs.

Are there jokes or urban sayings about where you live? Explore their ambivalence.

How much is the life around you an escape from where you are?

Write about an imaginary life away, then a return home.

If you live in a new place, find out what used to be there and describe that trip to the past.

Describe mending an old thing to be useful again.

Read the Larkin poems (*The Whitsun Weddings*, 1964) mentioned above and write a response to them, with your own ideas of home.

Do you know someone who hates where they are from? Write about this in the first person, exploring the reasons for their strong feeling.

Reading, Listening, Watching

Arnold, Mathew. 1993. Dover Beach, 76. In *Selected Poems and Prose*. London: Everyman.
Bate, Jonathan. 2000. *The Song of the Earth*. London: Picador.
Campbell, Joseph. 1969. *Primitive Mythology*. New York: Penguin.
Dewey, John. 1920. Americanism and Localism, 684–688. In *The Dial 68*. New York.
Dunn, Ginette. 1980. *The Fellowship of Song*. London: Croom Helm.
Dylan, Bob. 2004. *Chronicles*. New York: Simon and Schuster.
Dylan, Bob. 1968. *John Wesley Harding*. Columbia Records.
Eliot, T.S. 1944. *Four Quartets*. London: Faber and Faber.
Hardy, Thomas. 1978. *The Woodlanders*. London: MacMillan.
Hyde, Lewis. 1983. *The Gift*. New York: Vintage.
Kerouac, Jack. 1965. *The Dharma Bums*. London: Mayflower-Dell.
Larkin, Philip. 1964. *The Whitsun Weddings*. London: Faber and Faber.
Lawrence, D.H. 1929. As For Me, I'm A Patriot, 125. In *Pansies*. London: Martin Secker.
Randall, Bob. 2003. *Songman: The Story of an Aboriginal Elder*. Sydney: A.B.C. Books.
Shakespeare, William. *A Midsummer Night's Dream*.
Wordsworth, William. 1904. *Poetical Works*. Oxford: Oxford University Press.

CHAPTER 9

Self and Family Trees

Dolly Parton, herself a very traditional artist has said, in several interviews something to the effect of 'Find out who you are and be that on purpose'. This is reflected in her song 'Coat of Many Colours' (1971). But how do you do that? It is not that easy, as in a way it is like allowing things to come to you or acknowledging what is under your nose by a slow alteration of mindset. Part of this is because the world seems set on nurturing ambition to be what you are not, to aspire to be shining in the media rather than in the real.

Alan Watts writes, in the Preface of his book *The Taboo Against Knowing Who You Are*, of the way we are encouraged to think of ourselves as 'a separate ego'. He points out that this is not a reality supported either by Western science or by religions or philosophies from the East. He calls it a 'hallucination' and the result of this is a denigration of nature and an over reliance on badly used technology.

He goes on to say that, as this is the case, we need a different view to replace this odd alienation from ourselves and our world. This could have been written by a current environmental campaigner, but what is astounding to me is that the Preface is dated 1966, when the book was first published. The problem is one that has been with us a long time, perhaps since the disruptions of the industrial world's emergence and collapse of faith in the nineteenth century.

Many of our concerns about our blind spots in our relationship to ourselves seem now even more pressing in an age dominated by the internet and a sense of community being atomised and anxiety dominating isolated consumers.

Watts goes on, in Chapter 1, to argue that the mysteries of selfhood are important and that a materialist view of life only gives the sense of 'a growing apprehension that existence is a rat-race in a trap'. It is better to see life as connected, 'marvellous' and 'odd', rather than as 'futile'. We still have a strange relationship with the world we are part of, where we seek to impose our material, linear, rather than circular, ideas on it via ambition and ego. If we are part of a bigger completion of nature and the world, then our habit of building up and punishing the ego is a mistake. Rather than the 'reductionism' of Freud, we need to escape the ego, as a bird does its egg when it takes flight and becomes part of something bigger.

The strangeness, even absurdity of life is more convincing than materialism and Watt ends his first chapter with a very Zen saying of his own: 'The less I preach, the more likely I am to be heard'.

His work fits the traditional model of the self as connected to useful familial and cultural sources and calls for ways of connecting which acknowledge this. D.H. Lawrence's poem 'Trust' (from *Pansies*, 1929) talks about trusting the sunny quality in each other, which might be bright or dark at different times, but is natural and not one-sided. One of the traditional functions of writing is in exploring how we reconnect the alienated self back to the world.

More recently, Adam Curtis' documentary series *The Century of the Self* (2002) shows how we have been sold an idea of individualism in order to sell consumer goods to us. The paradox is that we are buying into a kind of mass idea of the self as struggling to express itself. Arguably since then this sense of isolation has increased and we are unable to see ourselves, as Watt says, in any other way. We are led to believe we are different, when we are made all the same by the world.

There are obvious, practical thing we can do to get back our connective selves. The easiest way to access the hidden self is via family. Guy Garvey of the band Elbow made a recent radio programme about interviewing his father and making recordings of these conversations and how important it was to make the effort: *Recording Dad* (BBC Radio 4, 2018). Families tell stories and use language in particular ways and these are fruitful areas for writers. Traditional folk singers speak of the spirit of older singers with them as they sing an old song, who give them strength in continuity. I often feel my musician mother and my poet father with me, as well as my two comic-songster grandfathers.

Troubled family relationships can be a source for writing. How can we be so related and so divergent? Bridging that gap with writing can be healing but writing should not just be a pouring out of bad feeling. Some healing, however arrived at, is needed to actually connect us. My own 'Sons and Fathers' below, echoes Turgenev's *Fathers and Sons* (1965) and Lawrence's *Sons and Lovers* (1913). The poem below this lyric, called 'The Bohemian Swerve' is perhaps more accepting, in the image of an invisible oak tree.

Transactional Analysis is a therapeutic model where the individual is asked to seek a relationship within themselves with their inner child. If the inner child has suffered traumas or other difficulties, often a dialogue with the adult self can be healing. Sometimes a letter to the inner child can bridge these hidden aspects of the self and serve to integrate a person, both within themselves and their family. This deepening of the self is always fruitful for a writer.

My feeling is that the idea of public life, as well as private, has broken down, as people increasingly interact via media. So we have somehow lost both the private and the public spheres to media and isolation. Once, on buses, if one person had already rung the bell to stop, others would not do so in unnecessary repetition. Nowadays, each individual feels they must ring the bell. I sit there thinking, are we so alone?

For me, a traditional reconnection to self and family is a step towards rediscovering the positive side of 'identity politics', so often used to accuse or divide people. Even if you hate your family, you have a place to start from, especially as a writer. Who is in your family? Who is your eldest and how much do you know them? Knowing who your parents are is important and even, or especially if you do not know, vital. These belongings or connections, or their opposite, make us who we are.

I remember a spooky, good feeling, when my father pointed out to me that both my grandfathers sang comic songs, as I do. Have you got connections like that? Thomas Hardy was a writer always interested in these matters, as with Tess finding she was from an older, more prosperous family. His poem 'Heredity' (1976) explores what might seem a mixed blessing, with its emphasis on 'the family face':

> I am the family face;
> Flesh perishes, I live on,
> Projecting trait and trace
> Through time to times anon,
> And leaping from place to place
> Over oblivion.
>
> The years-heired feature that can
> In curve and voice and eye
> Despise the human span
> Of durance—that is I;
> The eternal thing in man
> That heeds no call to die.

Is there something gloomy and inevitable here, or is there dark humour too? For me it is the detail of the 'curve and voice and eye'. There is a blessing and a curse, surely, which makes me think of Dylan Thomas's great poem 'Do not go gentle into that good night', where he asks his dying father to 'curse, bless me now with your fierce tears, I pray'.

Thomas wrote elsewhere about family and his poems often have an in-depth look at a simple subject. 'Fern Hill', about innocence and childhood and Eden, is intense and subtle and detailed and never a clichéd view of innocence. A lesser known poem, 'This Side of the Truth', written for his son Llewelyn, is an even darker view of life from a father, contemplating his son's journey into life, though it ends with the memorable phrase 'unjudging love'.

Names are given by families and we have a feeling about our own names and what we prefer to be called. Changing names can be a potent denial of family, or having a family nickname embraced or denied can also be revealing. Your own name has a meaning and a source. There is such a thing as 'nominal determinism' and I remember Martin Amis commenting, not entirely seriously, that someone called 'Tim' could never win anything, speaking of Wimbledon and Tim Henman.

Some years back I discovered there was a place in Scotland called the Isle of May. It had a saint, a martyr called Saint Adrian. A few years ago I went there and the first thing I discovered was that, due to an oft repeated mistake in an old manuscript, it was really Saint Ethernan who had lived there. Nonetheless, there are lots of streets in towns on that coast called 'St Adrian's Road', so I had fun finding out and taking photos. Researching your name's Saint is easy online and Saints often have interesting stories. The Isle of May is a lovely bird sanctuary and I could write a good, partly comic piece about my whole trip up there. This included, on the ferry back, the releasing of orphan puffins at sea to save them from predators, which seems to me a potent parallel with stories of parents and children. Our care for nature is our care for ourselves.

Try sacred-texts.com and search for Butler's *Lives of the Saints*. Your birthday will have a shared Saint and you might find a good story there, even if your own name does not reveal something useful. Local Saints can be good too and local churches are all named after Saints. I have written about St Leonard, who frees prisoners from chains, as my nearest church is in his name. *Chambers Book of Days* from the late nineteenth century (thebookofdays.com) is another great resource for birthday research. If you know what day of the year you were born, see what god oversaw your birth, for another source of delving into yourself and your world. Each day, each month has a meaning.

Rites of passage are connected to self and family, which often seem to enact a ritual of separation, before a return to reunite the world. This is the plot of *The Odyssey*, for example and of the English folksong 'Spenser the Rover'. The full 'individuation' of a character seems to involve a wrenching apart from one's roots before a clear view and reunion is possible. These growing pains are part of everyone, as are ways of being stuck. This is the growth of self and family. Can you make your work reflect on this most ancient and new tradition of initiation? Dolly Parton's idea of being who you are on purpose enacts the separation and return motif in thought and reminds us too of our tendency not to be able to see ourselves. As Robert Burns says, 'O would some power the giftie gie us/ To see ourselves as others see us' ('To A Louse'). This might seems like self-consciousness but it is also, in the traditional way, self-discovery.

As I write, the album of the week on B.B.C. 6 Music is *Legacy* (2021), by the great Nigerian musician Fela Kuti's son and grandson, Feme Kuti and Made Kuti.

There is again the sense of wonder at the self, the family and hence the world which makes us ask, 'What is it that we are part of/ And what is it that we are?', with Robin Williamson of the Incredible String Band, in 'The

Half-Remarkable Question' (*Wee Tam and the Big Huge*, 1968). The simple, connective questioning is part of being traditional.

Just as we are strangers to ourselves at times and this can be helped by a traditional attitude, so strangers are embraced by tradition. In *The Odyssey*, a stranger must be welcomed by the laws of hospitality, anointed and fed before even being asked their name. Public Houses are so-called, partly because it was once law here to entertain strangers. Tradition is often interaction and the agreements of travel and hospitality are part of it. The stranger coming into the family is an old trope and the conflicts or blessings that bestows can be a source of good writing, especially if the depth and ambiguity is embraced.

The making of home involves all these elements and helps us explore what is in front of our noses; helps us see the wood from the family trees. This deepening of the relationship to yourself is part of the writer's job, in order to reflect on the depths of the world. As Dorothea Brande says, in Chapter 2 of *Becoming A Writer* (1934), a writer must always try to find ways of keeping 'the ready sensitiveness of a child'. Our families are our roots, as are the family of hours, days and times that make a life.

Author's creative and traditional examples:

Spencer The Rover (version collected in Essex)

These words were composed by Spencer the Rover
Who had travelled great parts of both England and Wales
He being reducéd caused great confusion
And that was the reason he set off on trails

In Yorkshire near Rotherham he had been on his rambles
Being weary of travelling he sat down to rest
At the foot of yonder mountain there runs a clear fountain
With bread and cold water he himself did refresh.

It tasted more sweeter than the gold he had wasted
More sweeter than honey and gave more content
But the thoughts of his babies lamenting their father
Brought tears to his eyes which made him to lament.

The night fast approaching to the woods he resorted
With woodbine and ivy his bed for to make
There he dreamt about sighing lamenting and crying
Go home to your family and rambling forsake.

On the fifth of November I've a reason to remember

When first he come home to his children and wife
They stood so surprisèd when first he arrivèd
To behold such a stranger once more in their sight.

His children come around him with their prittle-prattling stories
With their prittle-prattling stories to drive care away
Now they are united like birds of one feather
Like bees in one hive contented they'll stay.

So now he is a-living in his cottage contented
With woodbine and roses growing all around the door
He's as happy as those that's got thousands of riches
Contented he'll stay and go rambling no more

SONS AND FATHERS

Sons of chauvinistic swine
Sons of fascists, we were thine
Sons of bleak authority
Sons of violence, emotion free

Sons of men who couldn't speak
Sons of strong disguising weak
Sons of intellectual scorn
Sons not asking to be born

I miss my father, even when he was still there
I miss my father, pretending that he didn't care
Sons and fathers stumble towards each other in the dark
Saying who the hell are you

Sons of monsters you repressed
Sons of secretly depressed
Sons of moral hypocrites
Sons of poison acid wits

Sons of job security
Sons of the soul's penury
Sons of leave the rich to rob
Sons of only doing my job

Sons of racist homophobes
Sons of sons who stole the globe
Sons of torturers and worse
Sons of sins of fathers' curse

Sons of bullies, bullied too
Sons of men we never knew
Sons of being right and safe
Sons of cannon-fodder's graves

Sons betrayed without a kiss
Sons sold out to industries
Sons of the polluted river
Sons of nuclear end forever

Sons who feel they've failed their mother
Sons who cannot help each other
Sons of sell the national health
Sons of don't have kids yourself

O my father, listen to my prayer
O my father, sometimes you're still here
All the good in you I saw, are all the things the world ignores
Daddy so I hardly knew
Sons and fathers stumble towards each other by and by
Asking who the hell am I

THE BOHEMIAN SWERVE

My Dad was a semi-recluse
down a long lane lived he
The lane was straight until it swerved
around an old oak tree

My Dad was hard to get around
firm and fast as oak
and people tell me I'm the same
and I can take a joke

My Dad was a poet, a singer
like his Dad before and me

That's the way we have to swerve
to see things differently

Now I'm grown up and my Dad has gone
and the oak tree's long gone now
though the same long lane still swerves
around it anyhow

It's my bohemian inheritance
to stand half-distantly
to sing and swerve around these things
like an old oak tree

And I am both the oak and swerve
paradoxically
I move and am moved like a dance
a bit mysteriously

No nearer or straighter will I go -
Tradition you can't see
is individuality
for my Dad, his Dad and me

The past is written through us
I take it seriously
Related, recalled, known, unknown
the deep world walks with me

Down the long lane with my song
I swerve mysteriously
in roots and strength and new green leaves
around the invisible tree

Writing Suggestions:

Write about gap between us; between self and others, and how to bridge it (see 'Trust' by D.H. Lawrence, Pansies, 1929).

Interview the oldest member of your family and record it, allowing them to get used to the process gradually, so they relax, as in Guy Garvey's 'Recording Dad' (B.B.C. Radio 4, 2018). Use this as a source for writing.

Write about an object from your childhood, which is a talisman; a powerful symbol beyond any intrinsic value, but which means something (not valuable but priceless) to you: a photo, a toy, an old book, a box, a ring, a piece of clothing, etc.

Write to inner child, your childhood self, in a message from your reassuring adult self. Or write to a family member, who is no longer alive. Listen to Richard Thompson's dark song, 'The End of the Rainbow' (album *I Want To See The Bright Lights Tonight*, 1974).

Use Dylan Thomas as a guide (*Collected Poems*, 1952), write in intense detail and language about a child, a parent or your own childhood.

Explore your Saints/days with a birthday Saint or a namesake Saint, or via books of days.

Using Hardy ('Heredity', 1976) as a text, write about a family trait reasserting itself and ambiguity of feeling that engenders.

Write about being blest by the strangeness of a stranger. Or yourself as stranger.

Write a story of a family event that goes wrong or is awful, but something useful and necessary is revealed to you or realised afterwards.

Think of works, such as novels about families, which you know (e.g. *Sons and Lovers, Fathers and Sons*, John Mortimer's film *A Voyage Round My Father* (1982)) and see if their approach offers something for you to use in your writing.

Use the structure of someone leaving home, achieving clarity and then returning, as in the traditional folksong 'Spenser the Rover'.

READING, WATCHING, LISTENING

Burns, Robert. 1896. *The Poetry of Robert Burns*. To A Louse, 152. London: Caxton.
Butler's *Lives of the Saints* 1756–9 sacred-texts.com. Accessed 8 May 2020.
Chambers Book of Days. 1869. thebookofdays.com. Accessed 10 May 2020.
The Copper Family. 1971. *A Song for Every Season*. Topic Records.
Curtis, Adam. 2002. *The Century of the Self*. London: B.B.C. Television.
Garvey, Guy. 2018. *Recording Dad*. London: B.B.C. Radio 4.
Hardy, Thomas. 1976. Heredity, 434. *The Complete Poems*. London: Macmillan.
Kuti, Femi and Kuti, Made. 2021. *Legacy*. Partisan Records.
D.H. Lawrence, 'Trust', from *Pansies*, 1929; *Sons and Lovers*, 1913.
Parton, Dolly. 1971. *Coat of Many Colours*. R.C.A. Victor Records.
Mortimer, John. 1982. *A Voyage Round My Father*. London: Thames Television.
Thomas, Dylan. 1952. *Collected Poems*. London: Dent.
Thompson, Richard and Linda. 1974. The End of the Rainbow. On *I Want To See The Bright Lights Tonight*. Island Records.
Turgenev, Ivan. 1965. *Fathers and Sons*. Trans, Rosemary Edmunds. Harmondsworth: Penguin.
Watts, Alan. 1973. *The Taboo Against Knowing Who You Are*. London: Abacus.
Williamson, Robin. 1968. In The Incredible String Band. The Half-Remarkable Question. On *Wee Tam and the Big Huge*. Island Records.

CHAPTER 10

Nature and Tradition: An Essex Apple

(i) An Essex apple

'I'm truly sorry man's dominion/ Has broken Nature's social union' (Burns, 'To A Mouse').

The idea of our split from nature and the need to heal it is no new thing, but rather a traditional breach which always needs attention, healing and realigning. From Eden in Genesis via *The Epic of Gilgamesh* and *Sir Gawain and the Green Knight*, it is one of the old stories which enacts the ritual of the rebalancing of man with his animal side. We strive with Gods, but we are not Gods. In this way we again see tradition as not a passive standing by or accepting of a status quo, but rather an active means of rebalancing, remembering and reminding ourselves of balances within our culture and our world. We are continually leaving Eden and the Green Man, like Christ or Dionysus returns to remind us of our roots. Tradition is both the journey out and the journey back, a ritual of seasonal connection.

It is easy to entertain nature without really connecting with it. We tend to pay lip service to its fashionable manifestations but sometimes we can ignore it while being part of its cosy image. Meanwhile the young rise up against climate change and face the uncomfortable side of it for us.

The temptations of the fall, which is the Fall from Nature, are all around us, as people prefer free money to hard-grown crops but all of us have our encounters with nature, or our disconnection from it. If you come from an inner city where nature is just a change in the weather, you still have your day and night, your winter and spring, your window box of light and many of us have a history of encounters with the sea and the woods, with the river and the field, with the park and the garden. These are places and spaces which hold the split in humankind between nature and culture ready for us to explore in our writing. The reconnection is 'Nature's social union', as Burns says.

I am an Essex apple, for example.

The Discovery apple is bright, full red, with a background of greenish yellow, of medium size and related to the Worcester Pearmain. Often the crisp, white flesh has a pink tinge from the red skin and it smells and tastes strawberry sweet. It blooms in May and is ready to pick in mid-August.

My discovery, or self-discovery, or self-revelation here began a few years ago when I came to what I call the Abandoned Orchard. I drove past this road junction site many times on the way to and from Great Bromley Cross where friends live. I stopped beside the hedge and walked onto the footpath. It was late August. There were some abandoned outbuildings, including a half-buried shed. But immediately the path entered what was obviously an overgrown orchard site. Apples were red and bright on the ground and on the trees. I recognised them as Discovery apples and remembered from somewhere that they had been a relatively recent apple, seen as a possible rival for the imports from abroad. Although good and popular, they had not really taken over, though still available now. I put six or seven in my backpack, thinking that a week's supply was a fair scrump. They tasted fine.

This became a place I often walked in and took friends to show. This whole area, my local pal Dave Sibley told me, was all orchards once, but had gone into decline. This area has many little, straight roads that served the orchards and still hides remnants of the once flourishing industry. Friends reacted after their kind. One filled her bag up to the brim, so she could barely carry it. Suzanne loved the place and later went to an improvisatory art class and made a wild painting of the scene in vivid and wild green and red splodges, which I have on my wall and have grown to love. She also wrote a lovely poem about the whole day and me lifting her tall and slim frame up to pick choice scrumpage.

The Abandoned Orchard became both living wild place and a history lesson, a place of freedom out of order, a peculiar balance of hopes and provision with its own enchanted quality, its suburban energy and ambiguity speaking to me from a secret, like the known secrets of childhood exploration. There was something fruitful at the edge of the roads and houses, something growing fruitful in spite of us.

The thing about apples is that they are very close to humankind. They are cultivated, cherished, tended, grafted and wild in a sense but also not wild. The beginnings of apples are the natural fruit, the local crab apple, notable for its lovely blossom and tart, mouth-shrinking taste. It is the cultivated apple that we eat. The source of the eating apple comes from far away, it is immigrant and connected with an Eden of deliciousness. 'The homeland of our domestic apple lies in the fruit forests of Kazakhstan', as *The New Book of Apples* says. Jane Morgan and Alison Richards' 2002 book is the pick of comprehensive guides to the subject. They quote V. Vitkovitch's *Kirghizia Today* (1960).

10 NATURE AND TRADITION: AN ESSEX APPLE

A bit like us, each apple variety has to come from one tree, otherwise infinite variation would be the norm. When apples are pollinated in the wild, the mix will produce something original. To achieve consistency, they have to be grafted, joined together from an original, or 'mother' tree or from one of her daughters. New apples are discovered by growing from seed, to see what happens. The Discovery apple happened like this and happened in Essex.

I am an apple because I am the same age as the Discovery. According to the sources, in 1949, George Dummer, a fruit farm worker, grew some apples from seed in the back garden of his cottage in Langham, Essex, U.K. This is two or three miles north-west of my footpath. The story is that George had only one arm, so that when he decided to plant the best one in his front garden, he needed his wife to help him. She broke her ankle and they had to leave the seedling wrapped in a sack until she was better. But it survived and its heavy fruit and stability led to it being called at first Dummer's Delight.

I grew up, unlikely, myself, in a small Essex village at the same time and was an unexpectedly fruitful thing, as it has turned out. The Beatles were right and Apple was right, which is what most turns up on your computer search, to choose the apple as our potential. The Beatles' record company advertised for strange songwriters to contact them. They sought to innovate and to bring things to fruition.

Anyway a man called Jack Matthews from Thurston in Suffolk heard of Dummer's Delight and it was commercialised and became Discovery in 1962. I visited the mother tree recently, which is still there in Langham. The exact location of it is not commonly known but a bit of detective work revealed it to be in Moor Road and you can easily spot it, as an extension to the house has been built around it. Visiting it felt like a sacred quest.

I stopped opposite the tree and photographed it from the car, in case such worship was forbidden. Apple trees grow keenly, like people. They seem eager to grow. I have a bow-shaped eye of apple where a branch split around another tree's branch and then rejoined itself. When some trees were pruned at the old farm where I grew up, I rescued this eye-shaped, handle-shaped piece of tree and hung it on my wall, feeling it was somehow lucky. This remnant of my own old childhood orchard I have recently taken down and contemplated, photoed and pondered on. The mother tree, or should I say Mother Tree seemed energetic, even in its winter state.

Magically, a person appeared. Not the owner of the cottage but a gardener, builder and carpenter, who had made the impressive oak gates near the tree. Marcus, from Homescape, knew all the history of the tree and was positive about my own interest. He emphasised how fruitful the tree was and told me it seemed to heal itself of any problems. The tree gets visited every few years and the owners are advised about its conservation.

They used to hold a party under the tree every year, I've read. This kind of wassailing is quite common with apples. The closeness to humankind was always acknowledged. 'O apple tree, we worship thee', an old Wassail song begins and gives thanks for fruitfulness and yearly benefits of seasons and harvests. Just like the connection to myself made via the growth-eye, the grafting keenness, I remembered a tune I had half-written. There was a terrific series on BBC television called *Mud, Sweat and Tractors* and the Apple Wassail song caught my ear, when they played a snatch of it. I later turned it into a Morris-like tune and called it Apple Dance, only realising where I had got it from later, when they showed a repeat of the programme, as tunes can creep in unbidden. My tune came after a courting song, like a version of 'In the Shade of the Old Apple Tree', though not in tone or rhythm.

Apples have eyes and cheeks, they have tails and flesh. The apple industry tracks our connection to the Romans, to the wider world. They say the European Common Market ruined the orchards here, as we had no protection against so-called Golden, so-called Delicious. And that coincided with the seventies when everything went wrong. There's no space to go into that here, but we neglected our own apples and maybe we are still paying the price in misplaced xenophobia. Orchards did not pay and indeed were paid to grub up their trees.

Around the time of visiting the Mother Tree, I went again to the Abandoned Orchard. The tangled old Discovery trees are still there round the path, but the larger, mostly inaccessible area to the left, once full of old trees, has been cleared. Piles of apple logs lay on the grass. There's still enough around the path though and the strange buildings are there still at present, including the half-buried shed which would have been used as an apple-store to keep them cool in Summer.

I have an old family photo, showing my Mum and Dad and Brother at apple harvest time in the orchard of the rented farmhouse where I was born, in south Essex. Family friend Frank took it and he wrote 'Tea Time in Apple Picking Time at Bovinger Lodge 1954' on the card frame he sent us. I would have been four years old. I'm now the only one in the picture still alive. Frank, the outsider, could see the seasonal, the familial, better than us and I see my family and him through his eyes as I look at the full basket, the step-ladder and mugs of tea. He must have sent the card later in the year as it is signed 'with affectionate Christmas Greetings … from your old friend Frank'. There I am and here I am still, reminded of the seasonal limits of life. Still standing in the cultivation of Frank's vision. An Essex variety.

The East of England Apples and Orchards Project, applesandorchards.org.uk has varieties of Essex apples listed: 32 dessert apples; 7 culinary. Among the lovely names are George Cave, Seabrook's Red, Maldon Wonder, Edith Hopwood, Twining's Pippin (from pre 1872), Rosy Blenheim, Tun Apple and D'Arcy Spice. They date from 1800 to the most recent which is the Discovery (1949). If you want to buy some, probably best to go to Crepes Fruit Farm (crepes.wordpress.com) in Aldham, run by a third generation orchard family. Cressing Temple has an orchard of local apples: thefriendsofcressingtemplegardens.wordpress.com.

Around the time of researching all this, I found, or rediscovered an old poem by my journalist father John May, published in *The Best of Essex*, an anthology compiled by *Essex Countryside* editor E.V. Scott from 1988. 'The Christmas Apple Tree' tells of an owner thinking to fell 'a wreck of a tree' with sour fruit, but being visited by a 'spectral' voice from an 'ancient gardener', who says 'that be your Christmas apple tree'. He spares the tree and at Christmas the fruit is 'crisp and sweet'. This reminded me of Frank's card, also of all the differing fruiting times listed, Discovery is one of the earliest, in mid-August. More recently I found my dear friend Suzanne Pemberton's poem mentioned earlier, taking its immediacy from the old orchard path, where she talks of the 'snap!' of the fruit plucked from the tree, from 'time travel', then later 'home with our small discoveries' and 'sense of small bonanzas'. She captured our identification with this harvest, seemingly of ourselves too, with that apple.

Another apple epiphany was recalling that I had bought, for a couple of pounds and at a boot sale a couple of miles from the old orchard, a print of 'Iduma and the apples of youth', which says it is 'after a painting by J. Doyle Penrose'. It shows ancient knights kneeling before the golden Goddess, who holds the gifted apple. Apples are associated with youth, with longevity. Our ordinary immortality. Iduma is from Norse mythology and gives and preserves youth for the Gods: she is an orchard keeper. She appears in the fourteenth century *Edda* and Loki has interesting encounters with her. In my print, now framed on the wall, the apple is golden but in the original it is red, like the Discovery and she is in white, not gold. J. Doyle Penrose (1862–1932) is easily found and his painting is there on the internet. In Iduma, youth and autumn are one and fruition is all to this kind of Diana, or Earth Goddess.

Apples are now high on the list of things celebrated as good and in danger of being lost. The organisation Common Ground started apple day on October 21st and much is celebrated, although orchards are disappearing fast. Another nice coincidence is that my band Face Furniture were supporting songwriter Steve Ashley at Colchester Arts Centre on 27th June 2019, and Steve wrote a song for apple day called 'Say Goodbye', easily found on the internet.

The ordinariness of the apple is evidence of its closeness to us, in both its fruitfulness and its changing seasons, its history and the history of how we value ourselves and our local cultivation of nature. G.K. Chesterton was an observer of the unexamined positives of life and Chapter ten of his *Autobiography* (1936) contains this lovely passage about fruition.

> [Some] believe in evolution exactly as the old Imperialists believed in expansion. They believe in a great growing and groping thing like a tree; but I believe in the flower and the fruit; and the flower if often small. The fruit is final and in that sense finite; it has a form and therefore a limit. There has been stamped upon it an image, which is the crown and consummation of an aim; and the medieval mystics used the same metaphor and called it Fruition. And as applied to man, it means this; that man has been made more sacred ... that his very limitations have become holy and like a home ...

We are fruit—the end product. Not the root or the branch but the seasonal cherished result of our nature and our cultivation. We do not need nature to be pure, but maybe to contain our ambivalence and our limits, if we need it to be our metaphor, if we want the earth to matter. We are our own abandoned discovery, our own nature, our own seasonal keenness to grow. Our apple is our potential, our mystical self. Cut an apple in half, the wrong way, horizontally and you will reveal the pentagram, the figure of a human with its five limbs, arms, legs and head. We are inside the apple and the apple is inside us. Like us, the Discovery apple was a great Essex hope and, like us, it still survives and fruits, if it gets the chance.

I am near the same age as the Discovery and my fruition, my cultivation was and is in the old paths and orchards of rural Essex. I'm waiting for August and the fruit to ripen. As I said, I am an Essex apple.

(ii) Iduna, Pomona and the symbolism of apples

The ordinary apple carries a weight of symbolism. In the world of myth, it is the epitome of fleshy fullness and bounty, the world and all its gifts. Its fullness and roundness are material boons. Its seasonal fruiting is the world on a plate. The apple stands for *plenty* and fulfilment of life. There is temptation and denial here and a wanting to own that power, that symbolic richness. There are two sides to this richness, then. One is what I would call traditional and the other is more the subject of mythical warnings about greed, beauty and the dangers of trying to grasp at immortality.

The Apple of Macintosh then seems like the one that seeks to grasp the power of nature for its own ends. Perhaps the Beatles' home grown recording label and arts laboratory, Apple Corps, was the more traditional side. There seems a great divide between a kind of colonial grasping and a local nourishment, but, finally, it was in an initially forbidding myth that I eventually found a kind of balance between nature as something to control or worship and nature that we might be in harmony with.

In Greek myth Helen was the victim of the gods' beauty contest, the prize of which was an apple of immortality from the Hesperides and worldly beauty is here seen as a kind of curse, even if it came from the orchard of the gods. These apples seem anything but golden, more like 'golden delicious', a mixed blessing at best, or more like a poisoned apple in Snow White. If it was an apple in Eden, it was also the knowledge of good and evil. Mythological apples are not to be trusted. So where can we find my sense of the homely, the ordinary apple as a symbol of community and closeness to nature?

Iduna, whose poster found me at the boot sale, has a story of a similar orchard to the Hesperides, the fruit of which keeps the gods young. Loki, the trickster, was persuaded to lure Iduna away from her orchard, by a storm-eagle monster god who wanted her for himself. How did he lure her? By the promise of some unusual apples somewhere far away. She goes and the storm-eagle carries her away. This is the temptation in the myth.

Loki is persuaded by the gods to try to get her back, as they are growing old without her blessing. We already have an image of the need for her fruitful balance, her nourishing presence and her quality of maintaining their world. Loki is disguised as a hawk and flies off to find her. He turns Iduna into a nut and carries her away, chased by the storm-eagle. They make it back to the orchard and the gods set fire to the storm-eagle's wings as he swoops after.

This is the story of an Eden returned to, a story of ordinary cultivation and interaction between nature and the world restored. Immortality is in its domestic place and all the tricky and evil worldliness not triumphant, for once. So Iduna looks at once a very high goddess, of stability and nature and at the same time more in control of the essences, more essential and harmonious. Experience happens, but as in Blake's songs, innocence can be restored, when in balance. She is the victim of others' stupidity and worldliness but is the keeper of nourishment, the goddess of keeping things right and good and the unacknowledged power behind all.

In the harsh world of Norse myth, she presents a subtle, positive message. The nut is the essence, the fruit is the fulfilment. She transcends immortality and mortal curses of knowledge or beauty, she is reconciliation and atonement and is married to the god of poetry.

In another source, the story of Iduna's marriage is told. Her husband is the god of poetry, Bragi. In another testing, Iduna falls into hell (or Hel in Norse myth) one day, but is rescued by Bragi, who wraps her in a wolf skin and nurses her through her hellish experience and stays with her when she recovers. This second testing seems one of the inner world and even the domestic world of love and care being overcome, not by tricksters, but by love. So Iduna has overcome both the outer world, with its lusts and thirsts for unearned immortality and the inner world of hells and despairs. Again, both sides of the apple.

Bragi the poet seems like the one to help them restore real balance. He reminds me of Merlin singing to the apple trees his songs of prophecy, as the wassailers, showing a proper attitude to nature's plenty, acknowledging the mystery of renewal. Iduna carries both the cultivation and the fulfilment. She has the blessings and is tested by the curses in her capture by the giant and the falling into hell. She is returned to her goddess role from outer and inner temptations, the world and the loss of world, and becomes the goddess of natural balances.

Ovid tells the tale of Pomona, which for me has close parallels with the Iduna myths, especially in the marriage motif. These seem to be old nature myths with sources lost. This seems true despite Pomona being Roman, therefore recent compared to Greek myths. Pomona is the goddess of apples and orchards and has similar problems with suitors, eventually marrying a god of the seasons, whose name means 'change', Vertumnus. He appears to her as an old woman and tells her a tale within the tale of love thwarted, before revealing his true self and the eventual happy union with Pomona. This is an unusual, gender-fluid metamorphosis, as usually it is female beauty which hides in the hag figure. Strikingly, as with Iduna, we have these soft, new men, Bragi and Vertumnus, creating harmony and fertility and seasonal good in partnership with the powerful, tested and testing goddess. There are statues of Pomona, with flowers and fruit and often with an apple in one hand and a bough in the other. Her place still exists and there are notable statues of her in Florence. These nature myths seem to have the traditional quality of being both old and new, like the seasonal renewal they rule over.

'For in her heart she loved/ Not woods, nor rivers, but a plot of ground/ And boughs of smiling apples all around' (Ovid, *Metamorphoses*, XIV, 629–31, translated by A.D. Melville). The 'smiling apples' emphasize the human connection.

Another image of renewal can be seen in the 1761 poem 'Jesus Christ the Apple Tree' by Richard Hutchins (1761). The sacredness of trees and the sacrifice in trees goes all the way back to Dionysus and other agricultural gods; gods of plenty. This poem has often been set to music:

> The tree of life my soul has seen.
> Laden with fruit and always green ...
> The trees of nature fruitless be.
> Compared with Christ the apple tree ...

This beginning seems to want to steal the apple from nature, as the mythic often does, while the traditional sees the connection. Both show the fruitfulness of the metaphor.

Getting these two sides of the human in balance is a problem but for me, the stories of Iduna and Pomona have a balance of positive creation myth and a local, domestic resonance, nursed by poetry. This seems reflected in Chapter 2, verse three of the Song of Solomon in the Old Testament: 'As the apple tree among the trees of the wood, so is my beloved ... I sat down under his shadow with great delight, and his fruit was sweet to my taste'. As H.R. Ellis Davidson says in her *Gods and Myths of Northern Europe* (1962), Iduna is 'an old symbol: that of the guardian goddess of the life-giving fruit of the other world', which I feel is the place where life and myth meet.

The mythic often then suggests the fruitful completion of the apple as the world, a wholeness, fulfilment and therefore a temptation to own the immortal, to be as gods and have the world in our hand. The apple tempts, the apple poisons; its beauty has two sides, sweet and rotten. The traditional side to the apple is in 'Nature's social union', so easily broken, but present in the wassailers' seasonal imprecations and in the apple's closeness to the human. The image of the apple is hidden inside it and its shape is human.

Author's Creative Example:

APPLE TREE SONG

> The wassailers sing to the apple tree
> *O apple tree we worship thee*

Where Merlin and Bragi sang prophecy
So close to woman and man

Helen was damned for her beauty
O apple tree we worship thee
Not that apple of immortality

That will curse us if it can
But the one so close to the human
So close to woman and man

See Iduna the goddess of orchards flee
O apple tree we worship thee
From her ordeal in a far country
But she returned triumphantly

To the orchard as quick as she can
So close to all that's human
So close to woman and man

When Iduna was tested again then she
O apple tree we worship thee
Married a poet of prophecy
Her rescuer, nurse and lover Bragi
Restored the world's balance and sanity

Our seasons and our span
So close to all that's human
So close to woman and man

Did Eve plant an orchard eventually
O apple tree we worship thee
When out from the Garden of Eden went free
Where knowledge is balanced harmoniously
No poisoned apple, no poisoned tree
But harmony, fertility
And fruitful domesticity
All in the ordinary apple tree

Our seasons and our span
So close to all that's human

So close to woman and man

Apples have eyes, apples have tails
Apples have cheeks and skin to hide
Apples have flesh; the human shape
The five-pointed star sign inside

Some say even Jesus was an apple tree
O apple tree we worship thee
And we worship Pomona, the mother tree

So close to all that's human
So close to woman and man

Writing Exercises:

The above song is cumulative, in that it grows bigger as the stanzas go along: write something that echoes the growth of a tree or fruit.

Part (i) of this chapter is itself a work of creative non-fiction about the author's identification with its subject. Find a fruit, or food, or product that is associated with your own area, or an area or place you know and write a piece which identifies you with it, in your own way. This need not be as it is done here, but could be something like the fact that the village of Stilton in the U.K. is not permitted to make Stilton cheese, for example.

Find an apple local to you and try to trace its mother tree and write about your journey. Eating the apple can open or close what you write.

Find an aspect of nature near you, a stream, a tree, a park, and write about its history and interaction with humankind.

Write about the two sides of the apple, as seen in Part (ii).

Eve's Orchard: did Eve create an orchard, as in 'Apple Tree Song' above? Write the story or/and a song based on traditional wassail songs, as is 'Apple Tree Song'.

Cut an apple horizontally and you show the five-pointed star of the human shape. Who is the person inside the apple?

Research one of the myths in Part (ii) and rewrite.

Rewrite Snow White as an apple myth.

Fictionalise or dramatise the story of George Dummer (Part (i)) and the annual party under the tree.

READING, LISTENING, WATCHING:

Ashley, Steve. 2006. Say Goodbye (Song for Apple Day). On *Live In Concert*. Dusk Fire Records.
King James Bible.
Burns, Robert. 1896. To A Mouse, 115. *The Poetry of Robert Burns*. London: Caxton.
Chesterton, G.K. 1936. *Autobiography*. London: Hutchinson.
Ellis Davidson, H.R. 1962. *Gods and Myths of Northern Europe*. Harmondsworth: Penguin.
Gaiman, Neil. 2017. *Norse Mythology*. London: Bloomsbury.
Grimm Brothers. 1987. *Grimm's Tales*. Trans. Jack Zipes. New York: Bantum.
Rendell Harris, J. 1919. *Origin and Meaning of Apple Cults*. London: Longmans Green.
Hutchins, Richard. 2019. Jesus Christ The Apple Tree. In *Divine Hymns*, 4. Complied Joshua Smith. London: Forgotten Books.
Morgan, Jane, and Alison Richards. 2002. *The New Book of Apples*. London: Ebury.
Ovid. 1986. *Metamorphoses*. Trans. A.D. Melville. Oxford: Oxford University Press.
Makenzie, Donald A. 1912. *Teutonic Myths and Legends*. London: Gresham.
Scott, V. *The Best of Essex*, 1988. Baldock, Herts: Egon.
Vitkovitch, Victor. 1960. *Kirghizia Today*. Moscow: Foreign Languages Publishing.
'Wassail Song', 'O Apple Tree …' English traditional. Roud Index 209.

PART IV

Tradition and Community

CHAPTER 11

Work, Craft and Creativity: Tradition—It's Better Than Working

There might be no clearer case for tradition than the model of the craftsperson versus the wage-slave. Everyone knows this but we are sometimes unable to believe it. The semi-conscious argument might go: progress has taken us so far with its medical and technological benefits that we are unable to get off its inexorable proliferation. We cannot feed the world with organic food. Some of this may well be true, but 'too late to stop' is the clichéd thinking of the addict.

Civilisation has always contained critiques of its own purpose. Even the Bible has someone like Ecclesiastes telling the pious that 'all is vanity'. Recent books addressing the craft question include Richard Sennett's *The Craftsman* (2008) and *The Individual and Tradition*, edited by Cashman, Mould and Shukla (2011). Both these books are about the benefits and contexts of craftspeople, especially the latter, where the focus is on specific practitioners. Sennett's book is more philosophical.

Like the current discussions of climate change, the gap for us is one of credibility. Work is sacred in the sense of being a place of sacrifice of self to a greater good. Is there a better model? Many secular gods have replaced religion and tradition. Understanding the traditional exchange, the model it offers in non-material wealth might be a key to a credible alternative. There is a balance of gift and craft somewhere here.

Some of these traditions are already in place. When I was a young man, jobs were plentiful and I learned quickly that in a working-class view of work there was a tradition of healthy scepticism about the gung-ho views of one's better-paid superiors. This was a palliative against the slave tendencies of 'Working Life Out To Keep Life In', as the English traditional song has it. The cynical humour of the underclass was a powerful reminder of humanity's ability to create a positive from a negative.

Jack, the bricklayer, told me, as his labourer, that he would teach me how to make a chair from two bricks. This was my first day as his 'mate', meaning his general helper or labourer. We got into the empty house where we were working and I watched him place one brick on its end, with the narrow side against the wall. He then placed another brick on top of the first, horizontally with the bigger surface (the face) on top, balanced like a T shape. I copied him and then we both sat on these seemingly improvised mini-stools for a rest and a chat, before going to the café for 'breakfast', after which we would start work again. The chair was a joke obviously, a delight, an attitude, a way of life and a philosophy lesson. It was also an effective and comfortable perch. As a purchase on life it was invaluable.

I did not ask him if someone had taught him this, when he had been a labourer or apprentice. He might well have invented it but my feeling was that the whole attitude it represented had been passed on, and had been passed on from previous generations of working men. They did their work but they had their dignity and witty culture and they did not kill themselves with work. They had their grace and their self-respect. Jack, among several other craftsmen, or tradesmen, in the Building and Works Department actually wore the soft felt hats and occasionally the similarly Victorian-looking 'stock', or scarf-cravat, tucked into a collarless shirt. This was the 1970s, but they looked and acted like they were from another era. I was keenly aware that they were my teachers of a traditional attitude to work, which has lasted with me, as it seemed sustainable and sane. My gratitude to their casual grace grows with the years. Their message was not about money but about living.

Recently students I taught at university have had classes on 'Employability'. When, with my Creative Non-Fiction group, I taught a class on alternative views of work, it felt like I was challenging a grim orthodoxy and I found the students were excited by this. One student, who had been on benefits previously, said that their 'Employability' classes were the same as the ones he was forced to take, in order not to lose his benefit payments from the government. Something different from this grim and materialistic training seemed to address a hunger for something meaningful.

Sennett's book *The Craftsman* goes back to the Marxist concept of 'alienation', as did the feelings of my students. Alienation has become a widely used term with varieties of applications, but one of its original meanings, pre-Marx, was progressive insanity. Now it is used as a word for feelings of estrangement and powerlessness in relation to the world, especially the world of work and of large organisations. My feeling is that, as psychoanalyst James Hillman has pointed out, there is a link between common mental illnesses and the problems of the wider world. Has the world, in relation to work, become increasingly insane? The largest increase in diagnosis of mental illness is in the area of bipolarity. The manic money-worship of the 1980s seems not to have been decreased by the financial crisis of 2007–2008. If anything the religious mania for money was increased by this existential threat to its cause. It became even more fundamentalist in nature. It was around this time Sennett's book emerged.

On the first page of his 'Prologue', he makes the point in relation to the creation of the atom bomb that 'people who make things don't usually understand what they are doing'. He is indicating a major dissociation in humankind. The nuclear threat to the world seems to me now underplayed. For example when historic 'secret' bunkers are shown, it is as if they were only a thing of the past. An internet search easily reveals that new command nuclear bunkers for the government still exist. This is never mentioned.

Turning to mythology, Sennett says that Pandora's lesson from her gifts to humankind was that 'culture founded on man-made things risks continual self-harm' and that this has not changed or is increased with civilisation. In other words we need to attend to what we make and our relationship with making. This is a wide thought, not merely relating to work: 'parenting improves when it is practised as a skilled craft, as does citizenship'. We need 'hand and head', which reminds me of artist David Hockney quoting the Chinese saying that art needs 'eye, hand and heart' for its making. Practise of craft plus imagination sounds to me like tradition in action. If the useful ritual is repeated, then the meaning will emerge and life will flourish.

These are serious matters and not just praise for the humble, or unworldly. 'Practical activity has been demeaned', Sennett says, and 'removed from the imagination', when 'pride in one's work is treated as a luxury'. Again he brings on the myths, talking, in Chapter one, of Hephaestus from the *Homeric Hymns*. He is the civilising craftsman. He also quotes Plato saying that '"Craftsman are all poets ... [though] they have other names"'. The 'moral imperative' which work needs is easily lost between the 'command' of dictatorship and the 'competition' of capitalism.

Writing is a craft, but Sennett is aware of the problem of relying solely on sudden inspiration, which is usually 'a narcissist's fantasy'. Art of all kinds returns to skill as a context for its inspiration. Poet W.H. Auden said that when inspiration or the Muse arrives, it is best for the writer to be at work. This is the combination of craft and inspiration Dylan Thomas spoke of in the poem 'In My Craft or Sullen Art'. Writing involves the process or exchange between craft and illumination.

One myth Sennett does not cover is that of Sisyphus. This was the vainglorious King cursed to push the boulder up the hill, see it fall down, then push it up again forever. In Albert Camus' version, his triumph is one of accepting the absurdity of existence, making a kind of good out of an undeserved hell, which is a type of Existentialism. My story of the chair from two bricks comes to mind here. The humour used against the meaninglessness of the world seems to me both a craft and a tradition. I used to teach my Creative Writing students to put the back of their hands against their foreheads, look distressed and cry, 'I'll never write again!' in a melodramatic voice. This comic spell seemed to overcome the very thing it dramatised. An image springs to mind of my grandfather putting a pair of leather sandals in a bucket of water, in order to rot them for the compost heap in his garden. I feel sure he knew this was absurd but he was a natural, even traditional absurdist.

Songs from the depression like the American 'Hallelujah I'm a Bum' and the one that goes 'You ask me why I'm a hobo/ and why I sleep in a ditch/ It's not because I'm lazy, no/ I just don't want to be rich' offer a practical existentialist view of work and the imaginative tradition of making the best of the bad. Skills need to be worked at with imaginative resistance, as Sennett says elsewhere, which is what Gus Elen, the English music hall comic singer, meant when he said, 'Put your head back on your piller ... and wait till the work comes round'. Work always needs questioning and redefining and that is part of the tradition of a healthy attitude.

The creative response to problems seems at the heart of it and this is what prevents craft from becoming labour. The literary tradition has questioned the value of work continually. 'And why take ye thought of raiment? Consider the lilies of the field, how they grow; they toil not, neither do they spin ... even Solomon in all his glory was not arrayed like one of these' (Matthew 6: 28–29) reminds me of a drinker father of a friend of mine whose dictum was, 'Don't waste money on food or clothing'. Work tempts men to vanity, as further back in the Old Testament's book of Ecclesiastes: 'For what hath man of all his labour, and of the vexation of his heart ...?' (2: 22) and the answer, like a bell repeating its clang through the whole book, is 'vanity'.

Tennyson's expansion of the briefly told story of 'The Lotus Eaters' challenges the gung-ho hero of Homer's *Odyssey*. 'Surely, surely, slumber is more sweet than toil, the shore/ Than labour ...' is like a sea-based lullaby of 'S' sounds to persuade you onto the drug. Certain lotus flowers do have a narcotic effect and you can buy them still, though I am not sure it is legal. 'We have had enough of action', the Lotus Eaters say and swear to live 'careless of mankind'. Alternative lifestyles are always available. The thought-experiment of throwing off the 'mind-forged manacles', as Blake had it in 'London' is a necessary ritual of testing disconnection. The point should be to be able to regain some kind of perspective on work which is the kind we tend to lose in our myopic tendency to slavery.

'There's no point in work/ unless it absorbs you/ like an absorbing game', D.H. Lawrence wrote in his poem 'Work' (from *Pansies*, 1929). He says work should be an organic putting forth, 'as a snail its shell, as a bird that leans/ its breast against the nest, to make it round ...'. In another poem from the same book, he calls for 'A Sane Revolution', beginning, 'If you make a revolution, make it for fun' insisting that 'Work can be fun'. Mott the Hoople's 1973 LP *Mott* had this poem printed on the sleeve, so Lawrence fed the alternative world in the 60s and 70s.

Two more recent literary interrogations of work occur in Larkin's 'Toads' (1954) and Morrissey's lyric for 'Heaven Knows I'm Miserable Now' (1984), both of which show a guilty, mordant humour in the face of work and of work culture. Both recognise the slavish nature of the self and so present a complex picture of our self-alienation, verging on dissociation.

What they seem to offer in their writing is a kind of playful questioning of the human condition. Noel Coward said somewhere that 'Work is more fun than fun' and that was certainly true of his own version of playful questioning. Pat Kane has written about play and creativity in his book *The Play Ethic* (2005), where he quotes James Carse's phrase 'He who must play, cannot play' (from *Finite and Infinite Games*, 1986). This comes close to both the ambivalence of the world's work in Larkin and Morrissey and to the need to be free enough to make creativity part of your life. The dualistic writer, both child and adult, both wild creative and editor, both craftsperson and receiver of the wild message, enacts the process, the tradition of ritual creativity. These great questioners are close to the Trickster archetype, creating culture by mocking it into reality.

Credo Mutwa, in *My People: Writings of a Zulu Witch-Doctor* (1969), though now a controversial figure, is much aware of the ambiguities and difficulties of the whole of Africa, not least in attitude to work and office. There is irony in his book, especially in the chapter called 'The Softest Job in Africa', in fact often about the most arduous of lowly work.

In two discussions of creative writing, novelist Rachel Cusk defends the playful freedom of questioning, in discussing writing being taught at universities. 'If creative writing culture represents only that – freedom – it is justification enough', she concludes her essay 'How to get there', from her collection *Coventry* (2019). An earlier piece in the 'Author, Author' *Guardian* series (30.1.2010) defends creative writing teaching as a kind of relearning to use the fresh language of a child. The balance of making work a balanced thing is an aspect of being human we all need to attend to, if work is to be life and life is to be worth living.

Work is of significance not just to the personal, possibly alienated self, but to the tenor of the wider world. Our work defines us. How we are at work is how we are in the world. It is all too easy to be tied into work with a kind of culture of inevitability. We become slaves imperceptibly, to a micro-culture which reflects our whole community and world. Work creates the world as well as the culture and we should take it more seriously than we are encouraged to do. Work should be a calling, a passion, a means to grow and flourish. So should writing. How can we make our work, our writing, address its own problems? Nothing is 'just the day job', it is what we do and what we do is passed on, for good or ill. Is it bad addiction or good tradition?

Addressing this problem within ourselves, our work, our place, is key to any real change in the world. The phrase 'the dignity of labour' seems a folkloric or traditional one which demands an answer from us. The creative person must feel part of this demand. W.H. Auden, in 'The Poet and the City' (1962) tells us that artists are seen as useless or as having lost their usefulness but we must find a way back to the traditional role of the artist as collective being, as reminder of the dignity of all human work and life.

Returning to the tale of Jack the Bricklayer and the chair of two bricks, what he was really doing for me was a kind of initiation. It was an ironic, or paradoxical test of my ability to accept the absurdities of work and of pacing yourself. We did the work too and well, but the respect for ourselves in our role was a key to sustaining a workable environment. Initiation involves a separation from the normal world, the strange encounter which changes you and then the return to the world. It is a primary mythic and traditional cycle or three steps to enter a new life. There must be business courses that address this kind of thing but its prime function is religious or ritual in nature. Slowing down enough to pay attention to what you are doing is at its heart. Apprenticeship too has its mythic or traditional passing on of knowledge, personified in the mentor figure, which derives from Mentes in *The Odyssey*.

Robert Bly, in *Iron John* (1990), uses the titular Grimm's tale as a story of initiation into the world of men. He starts with the idea that our models for growing and gender have gone wrong. The whole book is about initiation and what that means. By implication, we feel that we need some deeper sense of how we grow to maturity. Fairytales are often about maturation. They are not for children, nor for adults, but for all to learn of how to be initiates of life. Work should be no less serious.

The lyric and poem below describe, first, working with people like Jack the Brickie and, secondly, the great change in agriculture in the history of the U.K., when the land began to be fenced and much common land was lost. This fall from rustic innocence has a great resonance in the world, where the start of industrialism and our current views of work started to arise. Are we enslaving ourselves or making ourselves free? Are we taking our lives seriously? Beyond the much discussed benefits of work, are we earning our sense of a positive life of benefit to all?

Author's Creative Examples:

MAINTENANCE

When I was young I had a job with the council
As a carpenter's mate
We'd ease your windows, mend your fence
Re-hang your garden gate
I never thought of the department's name
But helping people made sense
And now I think it's significant
To be in Building and Maintenance

Maintenance; keeping things mended, keeping things tended
That made sense; not faking or escaping and not world-shaking
Just maintenance, old mate; not false caring but just repairing
All around the estate

The old craftsmen that I worked with there
Had a curious grace
They were in tune with a public good
Outside the normal rat-race
I wore a scarf like a workman's stock
And a bib and brace
We pushed materials in an old hand cart
And with a slow and steady pace

It seemed a small or an old-fashioned thing
Part of something gone by
But for me those noble old men
Passed on an attitude I
Cherish and practice to this day
And one word comes to my lips
In my home and increasingly my health
In jobs and relationships

When you see some old or new friends
When you share in a song
When you just put the rubbish out
Doing small things that can't be wrong
Worth loads more than the latest bore
Of motivational theory
Like when you phone me to check I'm ok
And say you love me, it's really

Just maintenance old mate
It's man's and woman's estate
Mending or making emends
So I can say without ironic constraint
Good evening friends

THE ENCLOSURES

We used to have things in common
We used to have things to share
More than just the right to say
Put a wall just there

A plain enough case of class robbery
Who steals the common from the goose
Seems to be a thing that all men share

A demon that we can let loose

It's just before the enclosures
And life may never be the same again
Just before the enclosures
A way that humans go insane

Boundaries can be useful
Walls keep out the cold
But consider when you're safe at home
All the freedoms of old

Before you build the enclosures
Before you fence me in
You can keep out one small evil
But let a greater one come in

Before you build the enclosures
Make sure you understand
You will need some gates and gaps
And gates shouldn't be too grand

It's always just before the enclosures
Just before they close you down
But there is a balance to be struck
Between the country and the town

And just before the enclosures
Think what they are for
Just before the enclosures
Just before the war

And it's just before the enclosures
Things may never be the same for you –
But could just before the enclosures
Be just before freedom too?

Writing Exercises:

Imagine a future where you would avoid work: would it be viable, could you do it and what would be the advantages or problems of not working?

Explore the 'gig economy' of work. Interview someone who does this kind of work and create a piece of writing which tells their story and its implications.

Go to meet a craftsperson and write from their point of view about the world and the world of work.

Write a prose or poetic meditation on 'Leisure', after reading the poem of that name by W.H. Davies, which begins, 'What is life if, full of care/ We have no time to stand and stare?' ('Leisure', from *Songs of Joy and Others* [1911]).

Describe a day in your own working life or a portrait of someone you work with.

Read 'Toads' by Philip Larkin. Can you think of another metaphor for work?

Invent a modern equivalent of 'The Lotus Eaters' (1832) by Tennyson or 'The lilies of the Field' (Matthew 6: 28–29) from the Bible.

Does Marx's theory of alienation fit the technological world? Dramatise this, after researching the concept.

Are drug addicts all as desperate as depicted in the media? Are there positive or useful drug experiences? Turn into drama or verse.

Investigate non-profit working and community-based working and write in favour of these alternatives.

Write an anonymous letter to your boss.

Write about a mentor who initiates you into a role in the world. Perhaps find a fairy tale as an analogue.

How does your work relate to your parents' or ancestors' work experience?

Reading, Listening, Watching:

Auden, W.H. 1962. The Poet and the City, 72–89. In *The Dyer's Hand*. London: Faber and Faber.
King James Bible.
Bly, Robert. 1990. *Iron John*. Reading, MA: Addison-Wesley.
Camus, Albert. 1990. The Myth of Sisyphus. Trans. Justin O'Brien. London: Penguin.
Cashman, Mould and Shukla. 2011. *The Individual and Tradition*. Indiana: Indiana University Press.
Cusk, Rachel. 2019. How to get there, 177–189. In *Coventry*. London: Faber and Faber.
Davies, W.H. 1911. *Songs of Joy and Others*. London: Fifield.
Kane, Pat. 2005. *The Play Ethic*. London: Macmillan.
Larkin, Philip. 1954. Toads, 21. In *The Less Deceived*. Hull: Marvell Press.
Lawrence, D.H. 1929. *Pansies*. London: Martin Secker.
Morrissey. 1984. *Heaven Knows I'm Miserable Now*. Rough Trade Records.
Mutwa, Credo (Credo Vuzamuzulu Mutwa). 1969. *My People: Writings of a Zulu Witch-Doctor*. Harmondsworth: Penguin.
Sennett, Richard. 2008. *The Craftsman*. London: Allen Lane.
Tennyson, Alfred. 1969. *Tennyson: A. Selected*. Harlow: Longman.

CHAPTER 12

Church Going? Religion and Community

There is a natural movement for anyone interested in tradition towards thinking about religion and this might also be true of writers. W.H. Auden, in 'Christianity and art' (*The Dyer's Hand*, 1963) says that to the imagination such things as the sacred and the heroic are natural. To a traditionalist it begins to seem obvious that the communal, shared experience of religion has suffered at the hands of individuality and the individual relation to God. The secular religion of self-belief has taken us from our shared experiences. Recent events, such as the current viral pandemic, have reminded us, in the restrictions imposed on socialising, how important community is to us. Our aloneness has been exaggerated by a world become strange and we are driven back on the importance of family and community, which are traditional concerns. While it would be unhelpful to blame our sins for the pandemic, there is nonetheless an odd rightness about a disease that drives us further away from each other and seemingly further away from the truth of our being, which is in relation to others. At times it feels that a revelation is near, as W.B. Yeats indicated in 'The Second Coming' (1920).

As well as sociologist Durkheim's work on religion, for example in *The Elementary Forms of Religious Life* (1912), who pointed out that early religions were not overly concerned at all with belief, recent writers and thinkers call our attention to a more collective feeling about the self. Philosopher Charles Taylor writes about our time in *A Secular Age* (2007) and Michael Sandell in *The Tyranny of Merit* (2020) cites Christian socialist R.H. Tawney, author of *Religion and the Rise of Capitalism* (1926). That being said, most religious books concentrate on belief, as do most churches, it seems, in their attempts to engage the consumer towards religion. My own experience has been one of being drawn towards religion by my concerns with writing and tradition, but of being repelled by the evangelical and individualistic aspects of religion as it manifests in the world.

You only need to ask a few people their views of religion to get the picture. The anti-religious are evangelical in their materialism and alleged rationalism. The religious are defiant in their rules and narrowness. Like Tweedledum and Tweedledee, those traditionally crossed figures of nonsense, they stand opposed in absurdity, almost in banality, in a kind of fruitless opposition. Their self-belief is massive.

G.K. Chesterton's book *Orthodoxy* (1908) is a bracing read for anyone interested in religion as tradition and not as a source of pointless argument. That said, he does turn argument on its head and points out the absurdity of much of the thinking of his and our times. He is infinitely quotable and refreshing to read.

Chesterton found that religion answered questions he was seeking for elsewhere: 'How can we continue to be at once astonished at the world and yet at home in it?' he asks, in Chapter 1. 'We need a life of practical romance; the combination of something that is strange and something that is secure', which involves both, 'wonder and welcome'. The book describes the same process that anyone interested in creativity and a creative relationship with the world, via for example, myth and tradition and what they might find. It describes 'how I found at last in an anarchist club or Babylonian temple what I might have found in the nearest parish church'. His second chapter tackles the key concept of self-belief, the one we seem still obsessed by, sometimes to our detriment and which Ecclesiastes nailed in his opening line 'All is vanity', as we have seen.

Perhaps the most memorable incident in the book is Chesterton's sudden revelation about self-belief. He describes a publisher who says that someone will 'get on' in the world, as he believes in himself. At this point, at the start of Chapter 2, Chesterton sees a bus which states the destination on the front, which is 'Hanwell', then the site of a major mental hospital. It dawns on him that these places are full of people who have massive self-belief. Later in the chapter he says that 'materialism has a sort of insane simplicity', as it covers 'everything', but also leaves 'everything out' and he suggests that embracing human frailty, weakness and folly are not bad places to start to find an alternative. Only 'materialists and madmen never have any doubts'. We will return to Chesterton's book in relation to humility and to direct defence of tradition.

The 'nearest parish church' brings me back home, in the traditional manner and to poet Philip Larkin's great poem 'Church Going' (1954), with its visiting activity sense as well as its verb of disappearance, which might ask for a question mark. Are churches going away? Giving room for locality, as in Chapter 8, made me think of Larkin's poem and of our strange relationship in the U.K. with the huge amount of buildings for worship which remain, despite every diminishment of gathering in them and every retreat into the self. There are many chapels too, of all kinds of protestant groups, spiritualists and so on. It is hard to find an old street without a place of worship. My feeling has long been that their preservation is significant and that, even in their ruin, they stand for something. Many are beautiful and have extraordinary and old features inside. Anyone with a sense of this visits, like Larkin, with mixed feelings but with a kind of compulsion. My own default feeling is always: this is a place that was dedicated to the good, and that is not a bad thing.

I was inspired by churches and it was not just history and not just wonder but some 'old time religion' somehow. Thinking about this, I was suddenly intent on going to a strange chapel just a mile or so from where I live. As Larkin's poem, famously and sometimes cited dismissively, goes by bike, I did the same. Taking my camera, I weaved across town to this small, ornate building, made of tin and painted a kind of powder blue. Although not in use, it was still owned by the Congregational church, the grass around it cut. I took some pictures and copied down the phone number on the notice board. I couldn't really see inside but the whole vibe of the place was touching and a reminder of some lost good intent. The internet revealed some of its history. These 'tin tabernacles' were ordered in kit form in the latter half of the nineteenth century and this one had a local preservation order. I tried to organise a visit to see the interior, but the person who used to run services there and whose number I had called did not call me back. The chapel is now for sale.

It stands in a troubled area of town near a notorious street, resplendent in its incongruity. Like religion itself in a secular U.K., it speaks a different language from us, reminding us of how divorced we are from our past, just as we are from our present. I email a fellow writing teacher and suggest we buy it and call it The Church of Creativity, knowing he will understand my ambivalent care for the place. Creativity is imaginative, a kind of fluid belief and many creative people have sympathy with religion. I bought a book about *Tin Tabernacles* (Ian Smith 2004), mainly of photographs. I feel a kind of unfinished feeling about the place, as if I need to go in and say a prayer.

When I got back, I looked at the Larkin poem again and it seemed to me even better than I thought. It was the main focus of an attack by critic Al Alvarez, in the introduction to his 1962 anthology *The New Poetry* (revised 1966) of recent U.S. and U.K. poetry. Here he attacks English poetry for its 'gentility' and cites Larkin's poem as its prime example. Like many, I feel he misses the humour of Larkin and also the importance of the poem, even with its reference to cycle clips. I had no need of them myself as modern trousers are no so wide-legged, but I do have some somewhere. Perhaps people like Alvarez and me feel that religion is also too genteel. Here I must doubt the truth of this. I remember Alvarez seeming to say that poetry should be aggressive and up to date. I disagree. It seems to me that the critic's view has dated much more than Larkin's. It is a long poem and a serious one. It opens with the visitor checking that nothing is happening, a small detail which informs the whole poem, in its poignant emptiness, which is hardly genteel.

If you are visiting a church and not going to a service, the image of nothing happening seems to me a profound one. The circumstances of your visit are so opposite of those attending services, as to be post-religious and tinged with regret. This kind of subtlety might be gentle but it has depth and resonance easily missed by the posturing of poetry in the late twentieth century. In the poem, he cannot resist mounting the lectern and speaking a mock phrase in archaic language about endings. The comedy again draws attention to its tragedy somehow, the funnier it gets. He has gone there to feel the loss, to wonder about how all these faiths and lack of faiths fail, but finally acknowledging the seriousness of the building, of the place. Like Shelley's statue in 'Ozymandias', there is impressiveness and a sense of loss that attempt with doubts embraced to see something beyond. The church has made him think bigger and wider and even more sympathetically about the world.

Is this the reason why these lovely old buildings remain? The wisdom Larkin alludes to might still be there somehow, however out of reach. This rich poem does not deserve its mockery and has lasted better than the toughness of poetry, as shown in *The New Poetry*, which still seems to me damaging to the genre. Larkin found a way to take humanity seriously, to mix comedy and tragedy, which says the old poetry was altogether richer. In the middle of the penultimate stanza, Larkin acknowledges that churches now seem to be used for things that separate us, rather than bind us together: death, birth, marriage. Churches were places that held us together. I quite often visit a big, medieval church close to my home and a volunteer, who was opening it for visitors told me that it was better to fill people with God rather than to fill churches with people. I smiled and we carried on chatting, but I thought 'more separation' and of Chesterton's bus.

However empty, churches offer mystery rather than certainty and questioning, rather than self-possession. Looking for positives amid the negative is what tradition in action amounts to. Back to Chesterton again: towards the end of Chapter 4 he does the mental exercise of imagining what you would save from a shipwreck, which seems relevant to the old churches. 'All good [is] a remnant to be held sacred' seems to be another defining use of religious tradition. The communal acknowledgement of mystery seems to me profound.

If we replaced 'gentility' with 'humility', we might find another use in religion, which again points us towards community. It hardly needs pointing out how humility is not seen as a virtue in the commercial self-centred world and yet has always been an aspect of religion. Accepting limits and being content in the ordinary goodnesses of life sell no units. Yet we strive not to strive and be 'in the moment' as the saying goes. Like Chesterton, we might at last realise that some of these qualities and qualities of life are available much more nearby than we imagine. Feeling at home in the world is something to be aspired to in a humble way.

Prayer seems another thing we might feel worth accepting. Prayer can be aimed at the level of having good hopes for ourselves and the world. Prayer seems an urge which people have when in distress and could then be seen as a kind of natural meditation. The New York sister band The Roches had a album *Zero Church* (2002), by Suzzie and Maggie of prayers collected, in the folkloric way, from many sources, which they set to music. Prayers are a good traditional form for use by writers.

The idea of sacrifice is useful, partly because of its strangeness to us now. Its literal meaning is 'making sacred' and has something to do with returning things from the world of man to the wider world of nature and towards something bigger. Giving something up sounds like offering a gift and we have a need to do that, escaping our limits and our desires in an attempt to find unity or even oneness with the world. It is a whole subject to explore, from the Ancient Greeks and elsewhere. One of the poems below, in the author's examples, has a take on the subject. Having to give something up is a direction, as well as a direction towards a better goal.

Linked to sacrifice is the religious idea of wilderness. The wilderness is a place of purification, a place not ruled by the human cosmos, but by the chaos of undifferentiated creation. In the Bible it is the place of prophesy, temptation and testing of the self. The isolation of the self for remaking is a religious tradition, or a ritual of self-definition or of transformation. It is like the dark wood in European folklore. It is the place where, as in Mark 8:35, 'whosoever will save his life shall lose it ... whosoever shall lose his life ... shall save it'. The resonance of these symbols is powerful in writing. For one example, I was moved to hear that London Stansted Airport was built on a piece of land once known as The Wilderness.

The motifs of otherness, transformation and encounter with what is outside the human realm bring us close to inspiration. When Jesus left the wilderness, he began preaching, having found his voice and the blessing of the wild in John the Baptist, 'crying in the wilderness' (Matthew 3:3). Another creative example below, 'What You Shall Sing' is inspired by Matthew 10:19–22, where Jesus instructs his disciples in preaching, ending here with a song about inspiration. I heard these verses partially quoted in the old British film *Lease of Life* (dir. Charles Frend, 1954), where a minister talks from the heart, changing his planned sermon by reference to Matthew: 'take no thought how or what ye shall speak: for it shall be given in the same hour what ye shall speak'. This can be seen, if you like, as the unconscious knowing better than the conscious mind, or about trusting the inspired motive, but which ever way, it is liberating.

The obvious place to find the traditional and inspirational are in the ceremonial, or the ritual aspects of life which religion attends to. These days, in the secular west, we tend only to know Christmas and yet there are many and various movements through the seasons and the year which religion is good at. My number one book of inspiration is *Chambers Book of Days* (1869 and now found easily online), which I have mentioned before, but there are many books, full of good material, such as Jean Harrowven's *Origins of Festivals and Feasts* (1980). Older religious stories are good sources too, such as *The Lost Gods of England*, by Brian Branston (1957). The ritual aspect of religion is one that even the non-religious tend to use, to mark transitions such as marriage and death. Rituals are everywhere in life and serve a function of marking the time and punctuating experience. Even making a cup of coffee, as we know, has its ceremony.

This chapter then has an obvious link back to the literary tradition of Chapter 2 and it is worth repeating that religious books are great sources of literary knowledge and inspiration and, as we have seen, some are even directly about tradition and inspiration. Religious sections of secondhand bookshops are not often crowded, but they are worth browsing, to find the odd scholarly or inspired volume. The King James Bible, again as Chapter 2 indicates, is a constant source of inspiration for me. I am amazed by the contemporary feeling of the 'poetic books' of the Old Testament and the Book of Job, where the whole idea of God is challenged and questioned, is no exception and the whole question of what true riches are is raised, among many questionings.

Much of the book is taken up with dialogues of Job, the rich man brought low, with his friends, who offer him speeches with little comfort, hence the expression 'Job's comforter', as someone who really offers further discomfort. The whole story is said to be folkloric and has tragedy but a positive ending and much self-examination and despair. C.G. Jung write a whole book about the doubts it raises, *Answer to Job* (1954) and the position it puts humans and their limits in. One of Job's friends speaks in a list, likely to be of known proverbs from the time, which, however uncomfortable, seems like a lesson on tradition. This is Bildad, from Job 8:7–15:

> 7 Though thy beginning was small, yet thy latter end should greatly increase.
> 8 For inquire, I pray thee, of the former age, and prepare thyself to the search of their fathers:
> 9 (For we *are but of* yesterday, and know nothing, because our days upon earth *are* a shadow:)
> 10 Shall not they teach thee, *and* tell thee, and utter words out of their heart?
>
> 11 Can the rush grow up without mire? can the flag grow without water?
> 12 Whilst it *is* yet in his greenness, *and* not cut down, it withereth before any *other* herb.
>
> 13 So *are* the paths of all that forget God; and the hypocrite's hope shall perish:
> 14 Whose hope shall be cut off, and whose trust *shall be* a spider's web.
> 15 He shall lean upon his house, but it shall not stand: he shall hold it fast, but it shall not endure.

The first four verses seem a direct plea for the use of tradition. The idea of life growing is one we still try to find. To call on Jung again, life seeks some kind of fulfilment of the person and should arrive at its end with a fuller maturation. This remains a challenging thought, especially for an older person in their folly and wisdom. The second verse (8) instructs us to go further back than we normally might, to seek connection. Our need for the largeness of tradition, in the bracketed verse 9 is typical of the kind of lyrical line thrown up in the 'poetic books'. If we have a tender feeling towards our past, we too can have a bigger 'heart' in our words (10).

The stanza I have separated (11 and 12) presents an image of quick growth which does not last, but withers early. This comments on Job as someone tested by being cut down in his early success.

My final stanza seems to me to imply that the tradition outlined above is in fact 'God' himself. In my notes I called these verses, 'God is Trad. by Bildad'. Make your own connections to the frailty of the 'web' and all who lean on such shaky ground. Could you create a piece of writing from this partial reading and interpretation? If not, browse and find something that jumps out at you.

The shape of initiation seems key here again. The last section is a separation, while the first is a renewal of integration via the image of life as a moment of revelation. Even if Job cannot hear the ancient sages, he will come to hear from God directly in his own book's initiation.

Other sacred books offer similar messages of losing the self and becoming bigger, or wider in relation to the world and to life. The *Tao Te Ching* by Lao Tzu has a similar lowness of self to that of Job, in the twentieth section or poem of the text:

The multitude of men look satisfied and pleased, as if enjoying a full banquet, as if mounted on a tower in spring.

I alone seem listless and still ... I am like a child that has not yet smiled.

This is from a translation by J. Legge (1891) and again the self is in the wilderness, preparing itself for a transformation. This self-ness seems to me to speak to our time and a whole religion, called 'Taoism' is based in part on this wonderfully modern text. There are recent versions by Ursula Le Guin, among many others. One of my favourites is a translation by R.B. Blakney from 1955, subtitled 'The Way of Life'. The next stanza talks of starting again and going back to the new Way, which is the old Way, as in Bildad's recitation of proverbial wisdom.

Local religion has been an inspiration to me, where rebel ministers have challenged the orthodoxies of the secular world with their bigger vision. These include the figure of the Peasants' Revolt, John Ball, who seems to be from my home town. Also a man who write a book about Ball and also one about Skiffle Music from 1950s Britain, Brian Bird. The musical duo I share created a whole show of skiffle with a gospel tinge around Bird and Ball. This included a song against the banalities of how religion is often discussed, which I long ago heard describes as 'Christianity' and the unconvincing evangelism which puts so many off, as well as a poem which began, 'If only religion were boring again ...' Looking up Larkin's 'Church Going' might be a good place to start and remembering its invisible question. And maybe visiting a local church to you and seeing what you might say about it which is subtle, wide and with an awareness of tradition, as well as of rebellion.

The first, some claim, English poet Caedmon and the preacher Ecclesiastes have both inspired me to be honest and brave in my writing and not to be above embracing the wider, more serious issues of life. I helped edit a book in 2011, the year that the King James Version of The Bible was 400 years old, called *KJV: Old Text—New Poetry* (edited by Joan Norlev Taylor, Adrian May and Pam Job). Recent virus thoughts have turned me back to Dante's *Purgatorio*, after it fell, seemingly of its own volition, from a bookcase in my bedroom. Visiting the great Last Judgement painting at Wenhaston, Suffolk, U.K., called a Doom, resulted in a story called 'The Medieval Blues'.

Our transformation in our wilderness then seems to be this traditional move. We must stop thinking of religion in terms merely of the self. This goes for belief too, as that too often involves transferred doubt towards God figures. Likewise the afterlife is a transferred anxiety and the rules and conventions of religion are humans' own prisons. There are many religious thoughts which are these mirror questions, as in D.H. Lawrence's poem where questions about love are directed back to the asker by the handing of a mirror ('Intimates', from *More Pansies*, 1932, published posthumously).

It is better we avoid the selfhood, that religion seems to be often manifested as, and think of the comfort of a congregation, so recently unavailable, even if we went to find one, unless for a funeral at last. If we think of the mysteries of death, love and life itself and of nature and wildness compared to ourselves, of prayer and 'making sacred', of the seasonal and of human frailty, we are thinking both religiously and traditionally. Here are the places of writing and of inspiration.

The Trinity of parent, child and holy mystery echoes the transformation of self where the child is separated by selfhood, then through embracing the mysteries, reunifies with the parent too, in a ritual of traditional transformation and integration.

Author's Creative Examples:

WHAT YOU SHALL SING

Take no care what you shall sing
What you shall sing
For it shall be given in the same hour
What you shall sing

For it is not you that shall sing
But your father who sings in you
And it is not you that shall sing
But your mother who sings in you

Though brother shall turn against brother
And father shall turn against son
And children rise up against their parents
But still good things shall be sung

Though you may be hated of men

And despised of your generation
Yet you will be blest when you sing
Though nation shall rise against nation

And it is the Muse and the Holy Ghost
The god-like genius, the fool
And you shall know the truth in your voice
And that vanity is all

MAKE YOURSELF SACRED

Make yourself sacred
Make yourself scarce
Commune with nature
Or hide under the stairs
Just go missing
Go for a wild swim
Or a wild hotdog
One with everything

If you're asking for change
You're asking for change
Change comes from within
Or without – it is strange
Go back to the old truth
See if it's still true
Strangely familiar
Ancient but new

Now it is stale
Once it was fresh
Now it's just words
But word was made flesh
We went to the pub, or
We went to the sea
We made ourselves sacred
How sweet to agree

I make my confession
I am the worst
I find myself housebound
I find myself cursed
The past seems to crush me
I can't rise above
How can I be sacred
When fear ruins love?

But I might just go drinking

Or go to church
I'll make myself sacred
Or do something worse
I might act my age
Or like I'm not alone
I'll wrench myself sacred
Like I've never done

Rend yourself scared
Sleep on a bench
Or in a palace
Give it a wrench
A drought or a drench
With love or with hatred
Forcing your rhubarb
Make yourself sacred

SPACESHIP STEEPLES

All those beautiful old churches
Only seen through nostalgia as worth noticing
Overlooked, taken for granted as invisible past, can stand for England

All these I keep trying to see as present, like Larkin's 'serious' places
And keep thinking I'll even attend, though I rarely do -
Though once in trying to see, I had a vision, some God rewarded me

Approaching Stoke-by-Nayland, where the lofty rocket-like church aspires
Shy-bold dominating the landscape around, lit up at night
This daft and over-tall story came to me, right-wrong appropriately

> A vision of all the steeples of England
> Rising like spaceships
> But silently

> Manned by a
> Peter Sellers, or female
> Vicar, perched on a misericord

> First elevated in the air
> Twenty cubits up
> Then taking off

> Quiet towards the sky
> And disappeared into heaven all
> Spaceship steeples away!

As if sick of our trying to remember ourselves
As if God was taking the rise, showing the shame, ruinous glory
As if unworldly aspiration of universal love still counted in England

Writing Exercises

Write about a shared experience of community which has an element of mystery about it.

Write a prayer to an unknown god/goddess.

Visit a local church, the more strange the better and use as a prompt to respond to Larkin's 'Church Going' (1954). Or, investigate a local religious figure who inspires.

Browse the King James Bible, or another old, sacred text and find something that connects with you, then research its context and write something in response.

Turn the verses above, quoted from Job, into a piece of writing.

Read the *Tao Te Ching* (Lao Tzu, *Tao Te Ching*, trans. J. Legge, 1891) and find a section/poem which chimes with you. Then seek other versions and write your own 'translation'.

G.K. Chesterton says that 'Tradition means giving votes to the most obscure of all classes, our ancestors' (*Orthodoxy*, 1908, Chapter 4). How could that be done and what would they say?

'If a [person] would make [their] world large [they] must be always making [them]self small' (as above, Chapter 3). Write about humility.

Write a new wilderness tale, where a transformation takes place.

Investigate the time of year of writing in terms of ceremonies and rituals and make that a source for writing.

Investigate the Saint John Coltrane (1926–1967) African Orthodox Church in San Francisco (founded 1971) and/or the religious ideas of Sun Ra (1914–1993) and write about jazz and religion.

Create a faith of creativity and describe its rituals, or list its non-rules and initiations.

Reading, Watching, Hearing

Alvarez, Al. 1966. *The New Poetry*. Harmondsworth: Penguin.
Auden, W.H. 1963. Christianity and Art, 456–461. In *The Dyer's Hand*. London: Faber and Faber.
Branston, Brian. 1957. *The Lost Gods of England*. London: Thames and Hudson.
The Bible.
Chambers Book of Days. 1869. London: Chambers.
Chesterton, G.K. 1908. *Orthodoxy*. London: The Bodley Head.
Coltrane, John. 1965. *A Love Supreme*. Impulse! Records.
Cupitt, Don. 1984. *The Sea of Faith*. London: B.B.C. Publications.
Durkheim, Emile. 1912. *The Elementary Forms of Religious Life*. Trans. Joseph Swain. London: Allen and Unwin.
Frend, Charles.1954.*Lease of Life*. Ealing Studios.
Harrowven, Jean. 1980. *Origins of Festivals and Feasts*. London: Kaye and Ward.
Jung, C.G. 1954. *Answer to Job*. Trans. R.F.C. Hull. London: Routledge and Kegan Paul.

Lao Tzu. *Tao Te Ching*. 1891. Trans. J. Legge. sacred-texts.com. Accessed 12 July 2020.
Lao Tzu. *Tao Te Ching*. 1955. Trans. R.B. Blakney. New York: Mentor.
Larkin, Philip. 1954. *The Whitsun Weddings*. London: Faber and Faber.
Lawrence, D.H. 1932. *More Pansies*. London: Martin Secker.
Roche, Suzzy and Maggie. 2002. *Zero Church*. Red House Records.
Sandell, Michael. 2020. *The Tyranny of Merit*. London: Allen Lane.
Smith, Ian. 2004. *Tin Tabernacles*. Pembroke: Camrose Media.
Taylor, Joan Norlev; May, Adrian; Job, Pam. Eds. 2011. *KJV—Old Text—New Poetry*. Wivenhoe, Essex: Wivenbooks Press.
Tawney, R.H. 1926. *Religion and the Rise of Capitalism*. Harmondsworth: Pelican.
Taylor, Charles. 2007. *A Secular Age*. Harvard: Harvard University Press.
Yeats, W.B. 1950. The Second Coming, 210. In *Collected Poems*. London: Macmillan.

CHAPTER 13

The Radical Tradition Today

In Zadie Smith's *On Beauty* (2005), charismatic poet and teacher Claire Malcolm takes her class out to a spoken word club, in Part II, Chapter 7. Here we get a description of one of her ideas about poetry and about writing. She uses the quoted word 'fittingness', as matching the desire to express with the capacity to do so, making a symmetry between writer and text which amounts to a feeling of rightness, of creative fulfilment. There is something both natural and transcendent here which reflects in the title of the novel itself. In this place where the classroom meets the untutored rap poet Carl, tuned to the moment, we are given Claire's rationale for her massively popular class. For me, this indicates the kind of integration of truth in the writer and attention to creative aliveness which tradition also offers. In her way, the poet in Smith's inspiring and funny novel is an old-fashioned teacher, who believes in the power of art to transform and to fulfil. She seems both radical and old-fashioned in a useful way, a communal way and an inspiring way.

For me this is nothing new. As I indicated in Chapter 1, the introduction to this book, my luck has been to be inspired by the radical tradition, by those, like the fictional Claire Malcolm, who turn life into beauty by their brave connecting of knowledge and inspiration to the here and now. A bit later in the novel, in Chapter 10 of Part II, we get another description of her teaching method, where she reads well-known poets' work and treats it the same as her students' own, in sensitive attention and appreciation. Here the students not only feel present but also part of a continuum of writers; another definition of being a traditional writer. This happens to the rapper Carl, who joins her class unofficially, and who ends by writing a sonnet, much to his own surprise. What she has created is a culture of creativity and a community of poets. At best, classes can do that for you and so can communities. We need to be part of something bigger, something which is beyond commercial success or making a living. Something that really is being alive. This is radical, even thinking that this is possible today.

The instinctive, protesting rapper feels at odds initially, but he does turn up. The radical tradition offers a counterbalance to the false and lazy idea that tradition is essentially anti-progress. Recent popular movements like Extinction Rebellion, #MeToo, LGBTQ+ issues, Black Lives Matter and anti-racism can be seen in this grass-roots tradition of world changing. As we saw in Chapter 7, protest and world changing are not unfamiliar in the true, deep world of tradition, as opposed to any idea of tradition as trivial, backward-looking or resistant to change. Tradition, it can be said, is tuned in to change, but in a way that has more in common with seasonal truths coming around to shake us from our complacency. Claire's privileged poets come to the street to learn and the exchange is of true wealth, as reflected in the title of *On Beauty*.

To prove this more conclusively, we need to go back to some of the literary traditions of Chapter 2, as well as the protest of Chapter 7. The story of Dionysus, mentioned in Chapter 2, is the old god of change and his tales can show us much hidden radical energy. The world-turned-upside-down energy represented by a medieval, historical figure like the gender-fluid Lord of Misrule offers a ritual of reshaping the world. The blind prophet of Greek epic and tragedy Tiresias has such powerful insight into the world of power and gender, that he is still controversial and complex today. Speaking the uncomfortable truth outside of human vanity is a function of the radical tradition. From these we can move to modern thinkers and notions of reconnection and creativity, useful to writers.

The figure of Dionysus is a stranger. He is Bacchus to the Romans and Dionysus to the Greeks, though even the spelling of the Greek name is disputed. Saying 'he' I am not sure is even correct, as the God is gender fluid, just as he is of many names. In *Lempriere's Classical Dictionary* (1864), he lists these: 'Libor, Bromius, Lyeus, Evan, Thyoneus, Bicornis, Brisaeus, Iacchus, Dithyrambus, Messateus, Lampter, Aegobolus, Nyetelius, Polites, Melanegis', etc. This is in addition to Ceres and various spellings of Dionysus. He/she is a slippery God. I will refer to him as 'he', as that is the literary convention, but keep in mind his fluidity. The best way to get to know him is through the Greek tragedy *The Bacchae*, meaning the female followers of Bacchus/Dionysus, by Euripides.

Why is Dionysus so important? He represents otherness more than any other figure in literature. Dionysus and the play represent all that we tend to suppress and how civilisations go wrong. As the prophet Tiresias says of King Pentheus, who tries to suppress the God, human life is not ruled by force but by forces within us. He represents a reminder which the tradition of literature teaches about the tendency of corruption in human civilisation and of the need to acknowledge otherness and nature. He is essentially a God of nature and of agriculture, of growth and decay. He is fertility and change, newness which is old as the primal Gods of life. *The Bacchae* is a story of the need for reminding ourselves of our need to be part of a bigger picture of the world. He is the God of returning, of returning Spring, who reminds us of what we tend to forget. Against all forms of stasis, he is the traditional God.

He is also important because he is all about identity. This is the God of self and other, self-consciousness and nature, the animal versus the rational, the needs of the unconscious striving towards liberation and the God of wine and drunkenness. This God is part of what we cannot control, what is beyond our attempts to rationalise. He is outside of us and challenges our need to control others. Gilbert Murray's translation (1902) ends with lines that include this: 'A path is there that no man thought'. This is about change, about seasons and cycles, but also about transgressions, and, in the play, about orgies, drunkenness, dismemberment and death. Recent writing looks pale beside it and the figure of Dionysus has baffled and frightened many, including those in the play. The moral of the play might be that we must accept what we cannot control, with all the wild or moral implications of that. These things are hard to understand.

In *The Bacchae* the God arrives with his female followers, who begin their wild rituals on the hills above the 'civilised' city of Thebes. The women of the town join him in his rites, much to the scandal of the King, Pentheus and the powerful men below. Pentheus captures Dionysus, but Dionysus seduces the King into going to watch the women performing their rites. He persuades Pentheus to dress as a woman so as to spy unobserved. Pentheus is then sacrificed in a ritual killing. We somehow sense here that he has become Dionysus in his death, as if the death is a ritual of the scattering of seed to provide new growth. The death of Pentheus is thus Christ-like and symbolic of some rebalancing of human vanity with the unknown power of the God.

While the play is a tragedy, it has many elements of comedy. It has comic reversals, costume changes: if the hero is the God, he and his followers of the title survive. It is a story of rebirth and renewal, however dark and violent. When I used to lecture on it, I would suggest setting it in the nineteen-sixties, with Jim Morrison of The Doors, who knew they play, as the sexually ambiguous God and the repressed leader of the C.I.A. J. Edgar Hoover, as Pentheus. Hoover did, apparently, like to dress as a woman in secret, despite being excessively repressive to others. All authority is challenged.

Near the beginning of the play, we see the prophet Tiresias and the figure of Cadmus, two old men, deciding to go to the ceremony of Dionysus, in all humility. This too is a comic scene, a paradox which throws into doubt, even into condemnation the conventional behaviour expected. He tells Pentheus (beginning at line 266) that his eloquence is foolish, in the face of the God. Pentheus is a man convinced of his masculine certainties against the stranger God. The new God is the old God, of age and youth, and the places of change, and contains more wisdom than the certainty of power. The power of the earth and the power of wine come from the Gods. 'Prophecy/ Cleaves to all frenzy, but beyond all else/ To frenzy of prayer. Then in us verily dwells/ The God himself, and speaks the thing to be'. This description of the connection of religion to the wild, shaman-like trance of seeing what is other than the self is lost on Pentheus, but we can sense a wider truth being uncovered, a ridding of the self and vanity that is offered, which is a morality based on something fundamental and something changing and cyclic. The ritual is necessary to embrace this.

Many have said that the play and the figure of Dionysus represent a return to primitive violence, to unthinkingness, but Tiresias tells us otherwise, if we listen closely. The message is traditional, in that it balances old and new, thought and frenzy and tells us we need to do this. The unbalance is not in the God but in us and we need to do the ritual to remind ourselves of this truth. Tiresias specialises in telling truths that people miss easily, that is his blind insight, which is a hard lesson. Through the prophet and the God, we see ourselves in our limited vision, in our inability to change. This is the true radical message of Dionysus, to give place to the other, the stranger, the changing, the unexpected and the rebalancing that humility offers. 'Dream not force is wisdom', says Tiresias, the blind seer, the prophet.

The play was challenging in its day, in its new revival of old, earthy truths and it stays controversial. Many think it immoral but looked at as a traditional ritual of renewal it is highly and subtly moral, as well as being deeply serious.

There is an element of the Trickster archetype in Dionysus, seen in a folkloric figure like The Lord of Misrule and other figures who turn the world upside-down. *Chambers Book of Days* is again a good place to find The Lord of Misrule, while Lewis Hyde's book *Trickster Makes This World* (1998) is a good guide to this figure who mocks human vanity. The rituals of meeting these figures turn the world round and have a process involved which rebalances the world.

Konrad Lorenz has a chapter on 'The Break with Tradition' in his book *Civilised Man's Eight Deadly Sins* (1974), where he outlined a process of rejection of tradition, followed by negative effects of 'neophilia' which, if the world is flexible enough, is followed by a new kind of acceptance of tradition, which acknowledges its non-material value. This process might be found in *The Bacchae* and seems therefore to be part of tradition itself. Lorenz notes how growth is important and that this is about culture and people rather than science and therefore our culture needs leading towards positive tradition, rather than it becoming part of division. The process of individuation in the young is natural, but then finding, or re-finding the old truths and freedoms tradition can offer key to a healthy culture. As we have seen, tradition is on the side of good rebellion.

Despite genuine fears about our digital future, one thing the internet has been useful for is the inspiring of genuine popular movements towards rebalancing the world towards the good. Recently, Extinction Rebellion, #MeToo, LGBTQ issues, Black Lives Matter and anti-racism have benefited from the internet actually doing what its positive side was built to do, reconnecting us to ourselves, rather than the opposite of dividing to rule or to sell. Is this a new kind of cultural ecology, where bigger issues are brought to our attention by a focus beyond the personal? I believe it is and we can gain from a traditional understanding of its moral rite and role.

If the personal has suffered from the modern world and its 'neophilia' and everywhere people are suffering from 'impostor syndrome', the radical traditionalist can ask, what would 'authenticity syndrome' look like? It might be the new God that speaks to the less powerful, like the women and old men, or the Lord of Misrule who turns the world upside-down, so the rich are poor and the poor are rich in heart. If we picture a dynamic opposite of the youthful God and the ancient prophet, turning the world and usefully renewing it, we might be getting close to this idea of authenticity which respects the world. If we know who we are, we can be open to the stranger who comes to town with an old/new message of growth and truth.

For someone interested and protesting about Climate Change and concerned with Extinction Rebellion, the traditional and ancient confrontations of nature with culture can provide strong parallels and sources of inspiration. From Odysseus' suspect encounter with the Cyclops, to Gilgamesh and the above tragedy of *The Bacchae*, the balance of nature has long been a theme of art and of radical art. Achieving a balance between, for instance, the over-civilised Gilgamesh, who has become corrupt and The Gods in their Green Man style messenger Enkidu is a archetypal motif in literature. *Sir Gawain and the Green Knight* has the same theme of death and rebirth, of nature in balance and in its cyclic form of self-renewal, of fertility. Fertility is our own image of inspired cultural as well as natural ecology.

While the recent pandemic has taken over as a headline concern, what was noticed when the world seemed to shut down to avoid the virus was a slowing down of the endless traffic of man, a revival of interest in nature and in the local awareness of nature. This strange climate reminds of how the climate is strange for writers, faced with the climate crisis. How can writers respond?

The climate is doubly strange for writers, when they ask themselves, how do you write about an accretion? How do you dramatise an accumulation? How can you wake up the world? Are writers to retreat into their usual self-absorption? Does all other writing seem superfluous at best and at worst ignorant to the point of self-deception in the face of climate change?

It is inspiring the way the young are risen up and involved actively in what is the most pressing and some would say the only issue worth being involved in. This extends to their writing, as I found out while asking my Creative Non-Fiction undergraduates to choose a topic for a group project. There was no hesitation in their choice, as one had lately attended Extinction Rebellion events in London. Their engagement and detail impressed me greatly and they got a very high mark for their collective efforts. But the thought still nagged me that many writers over, say, 30, might not have the answer to the question of how to respond well and effectively.

Part of the problem is the slowness of what has happened. When Martin Amis wrote about 9/11 (in *The Second Plane*, 2008), it was the singular nature of the subject, fixed in time and memory, which defined his response. There is no single event in climate change. We do not even know where it starts. The Industrial Revolution? Victorian industry? We can be sent back to Ruskin, to 'Dover Beach' by Matthew Arnold? When did anthrocentrism begin? Ecclesiastes says 'All is vanity'; so where do you start?

The apocalyptic is a mythical problem and science and the current news has emphatically entered the eschatology business. Do we need a religious solution? How do we focus on such a big thing?

Perhaps we must make a whole literature. Just as New Nature writing has been on the rise, we must rise to the challenge on a huge scale and call on all our traditional sources to help. The literature of protest, of nature, of revolution even but, above all, of reminding people of what they choose to forget must be refocused somehow and reapplied to the task. We might stumble but we have to try, even if guilt is our subject.

Protest, however, is a traditional subject and therefore the oldest and the newest in its topicality, its newsworthiness. 'Honesty's all out of fashion/There are the rigs of the times', as the old English folk song says. Courage and honesty, and addressing what we might prefer to ignore are the voice of prophecy. Surely we must seek a new religious urgency, even if our God is Pan, or Ghia.

Our cultural ecology must find its 'world in a grain of sand' with William Blake. The small must illustrate the large. The small shock of a pollution issue in a river near you is going to be as effective as a generalised statement. We need to turn our back on mere propaganda and focus our energies like 'sixties radical traditionalists such as songwriter Malvina Reynolds. Her song 'Little Boxes' (1967) paints a picture of conformity by making the world seem small. Her other great song 'What Have They Done to the Rain?' (1967) also takes a wide view of a small event, simple rain with nuclear fallout. Gil Scott-Heron's 'Whitey on the Moon' (1970) still makes a relevant comment on space and poverty. Rachel Carson's *Silent Spring* (1965) is still such a resonant title for books about chemical pollution.

Philosopher Simone Weil's *The Need for Roots* (1949, trans. 1952) was written in London, in exile from her native France and, as well as emphasising what was lost to France, she talks of the need for it to become a place of inspiration again through a new rootedness. Another philosopher, Hannah Arendt, in *Between Past and Future* (1961) discusses the crisis in the West, after the world wars and seeks, through acknowledging the ending of tradition as a central aspect of thought, to regain an essence of tradition which will renew, as it is meant to do when alive. John Dewey's *Art As Experience* (1934) argues for art to be in process of the balancing of life and experience, not as a commodity or something worshipped from afar, not to be divorced from recognisable living. Some aspects of modern art, engaged with real people, such as Jeremy Deller's real men dressed as First World War soldiers appearing like ghosts in the world attest to the kind of thing Dewey was talking about.

Dewey ends *Art as Experience* with a quotation from Shelley's *A Defence of Poetry* (1950) and insists that art balances experience of the world in the imagination for the benefit of all. The most radical of all artists do tend to be those most interested in the powerful, almost primal strength, the seriousness of older art forms. The traditional has the power to go beyond mere materialism and mere propaganda, beyond the veils of fashionable theories and band-wagon trends and cut to the quick of such things as freedom, justice, fairness, goodness and love. Tradition takes art out of its shiny package, out of its museum and back onto the raw streets where change and unity and rebalancing are possible.

Tradition sees writing as morally powerful, even as essentially concerned with defining the human qualities in a world that seems intent on self-destruction. It likewise addresses our cultural self-destruction. Radical writing, inspired by connective tradition is potentially life-changing, world changing and community building.

The first author's creative example below shows an engagement with the past and its relevance to now, via the way Brian Bird wrote about John Ball, the 'hedge-priest' figure in the 1381 Peasants' Revolt. The second one looks with humour towards the future more directly and celebrates the natural change that nature demands.

Author's Creative Examples:

THE PIECES OF JOHN BALL

In Coventry and Chester, in York and Canterbury
Are the pieces of John Ball

He trusted the King to be above
He trusted his men in the God of love
Remember that we come not as robbers and thieves
We come seeking justice to mend our griefs
      He refused to beg their pardon
      For leading the rebellion
      They executed, quartered him
      In four places displayed him

O the pieces of John Ball are still disunited
In four corners of England, common to all
Part of this seems good but we need to put together
The heart and the head, the passion and the blood
Of the pieces of John Ball, the pieces of John Ball

Things will not go well in England until

We can realise that now is the time
Now pride reigns supreme in every place
And greed's not shy to show its uncaring face
    Only in the evening
    Can you say the day went well
    Until he's whole you just can't tell
    When John Ball sings and rings your bell

Six hundred years later, surely things were better
But it's still the 80s, the rich are getting richer
A Bird told us why, even back then
Multi-nationals, monopolies are all out for gain
    Their manipulations have us
    More ruthless and more callous
    Than Kings in days gone by
    How subtly they control us

We haven't got the heart, cause love's a private matter
We haven't got the head; the government know better
We haven't got the passion, except for games and dross
Nor the blood of unity, cause no one gives a toss
    His facts are still fought over
    By the cool and clever
    Yet that broken hope of unity
    Still lives in him forever

In Coventry and Chester, in York and Canterbury
Are the pieces of John Ball

RECYCLE MY POEMS

Recycle my poems
That's all they're worth
Let my late style be
Right down to earth

Recycle my poems
It's all that I've got
The end is the same
Written to rot

If poets compete

I'd like to show 'em
Recycled words
Make a much better poem

Words, poems recycled
Tradition's my boast
Heap up my old verbiage
And call it compost

Recycle my words
Words earthy, words pure
Words only make sense
When they end as manure

Recycle my poems
Just watch them fade
I love to watch poetry
Biodegrade

Recycle my poems
And set them free
Recycle my poems
Then recycle me

Writing Exercises

Write about a fruitful meeting of the newest with the oldest, as in the class of Zadie Smith's poet Claire Malcolm, in *On Beauty*.

A woman reads 'The Wife of Bath's Tale' and liberates herself from an oppressive work relationship by writing an answer to Chaucer (*Canterbury Tales*, trans. Nevill Coghill, 1951).

A stranger, of an unknown colour, race, language and culture, comes to a city, but oddly speaks the city's language perfectly, and has the power to transform those of many who attack them, with a few soft words. Eventually, the stranger vanishes but writes a message to the city. Write the message.

Dionysus goes to work in the office of a huge internet company. The LGBTQ+ employees join the Goddess/God in a plan to liberate the internet from prejudice and money. How does the male boss react?

Write about the tradition of respecting a stranger, as seen in conflict in *The Bacchae* (Euripides, *The Bacchae*, trans. Gilbert Murray, 1902) and as seen in The Bible, where 'strange angels' are invited in, in Hebrews 13:2, 'Be not forgetful to entertain strangers: for thereby some have entertained angels unawares'.

Write about a King Pentheus figure: someone in power who is ruined by their own force and challenged by a new/old figure of change (Euripides, *The Bacchae*, trans. Gilbert Murray, 1902).

Research the story of Tiresias, especially as found in Ovid's *Metamorphoses* III (translated A.D. Melville, 1986), where he changes gender and give his/her new fluid view.

Write 'From Ovid to Covid', about apocalyptic scenarios, researching how Ovid deal with disaster in *Metamorphoses* (translated A.D. Melville, 1986).

Create a Green Woman/Man/Dionysus/Enkidu figure arriving now to warn us about the balance of nature. Perhaps use the Pied Piper tale as another parallel.

Research and write about John Eliot, a missionary from Essex, U.K. to the U.S., who wrote *A Primer to the Language of the Algonquian Indians* (1684).

Create a plan of how to be authentic, to counteract 'impostor syndrome'.

Create a ritual to achieve the aims of a cause you support, where the positive effect is shown in a memorable way.

Find an image of conformity or of nature's violation, as in Malvina Reynolds' songs and turn into a story or into verses.

READING, WATCHING, LISTENING

Amis, Martin. 2008 *The Second Plane*. London: Jonathan Cape.
Arendt, Hannah. 1961. *Between Past and Future*. London: Faber and Faber.
Bible, King James Version.
Bird, Brian. 1987. *Rebel Before His Time: A Study of John Ball*. Worthing: Churchman.
Carson, Rachel. 1965. *Silent Spring*. Harmondsworth: Penguin.
Chaucer, Geoffrey. 1964. The Wife of Bath's Tale, 182–239. In *The Canterbury Tales*. New York: Bantam.
Dewey, John. 1934. *Art as Experience*. New York: Minton, Balch.
Eliot, John. 1684. *A Primer to the Language of the Algonquian Indians*. Cambridge: Samuel Green.
The Epic of Gilgamesh. 1960. Trans. N.K. Sandars. Harmondsworth: Penguin.
Euripides. 1902. *The Bacchae*. Trans. Gilbert Murray. London: Allen and Unwin.
Homer. 1872. *The Odyssey*. Trans. Alexander Pope. London: Routledge.
Hyde, Lewis. 1998. *Trickster Makes This World*. Edinburgh: Canongate.
Lembriere, J. 1864. *Lempriere's Classical Dictionary*. Halifax: Milner and Sowerby.
Lorenz, Konrad. 1974. The Break with Tradition, 46–57. In *Civilised Man's Eight Deadly Sins*. Trans. Marjorie Latzke. London: Methuen.
Ovid. 1986. *Metamorphoses*. Trans. A.D. Melville. Oxford: Oxford University Press.
Reynolds, Malvina. 1967. Little Boxes; What Have They Done to the Rain? On *Malvina Reynolds Sings the Truth*. Columbia Records.
Scott-Heron, Gil. 1970. Whitey on the Moon. On *Small Talk at 125th and Lennox*. Flying Dutchman/R.C.A. Records.
Shelley, Percy. 1950. *A Defence of Poetry*, 102–138. In *English Critical Essays (Nineteenth Century)*. Ed. Edmund D. Jones. Oxford: Oxford University Press.

Sir Gawain and the Green Knight. 2009. Trans. Simon Armitage. London: Faber and Faber.
Smith, Zadie. 2005. *On Beauty*. London: Hamish Hamilton.
Simone Weil. 1952. *The Need for Roots*. Trans. Arthur Wills. London: Routledge.

CHAPTER 14

Conclusions and Occlusions

For anyone who has read this book up to here, I hope I have convinced them that the idea of tradition is one useful to writers in all kinds of ways. Reclaiming tradition as a central part of our lives might be a bigger or more difficult task to achieve in a short book for writers, but its potential is there and I believe, here, sufficiently should anyone choose to go along in that direction. My own experience is that taking this stuff seriously does connect you with a liveliness beyond the worldly grasp of most ways of approaching art and life.

The old saying goes that you have to know where you are from to know where you are going. There is something in the receiving of the gratuitous and more importantly in passing on that which connects you to the future as well as to the past. Tradition must be held open, like a doorway, as the usage of the word tends to get narrowed down and diminished, which Raymond Williams noticed in *Keywords* (1976). The world at present seems full of people rediscovering their roots and identity in order to express and realise themselves into the new. The futurity of tradition makes new connections, new freedoms and new equalities in difference.

Finally I want to celebrate these positives, as tradition is nothing if not celebratory, toasting the past and the future. I also want to outline some of the enemies of tradition, which stop up the flow in reductive prejudices. Also I will outline some of my own experiences with promoting, or attempting to promote the kind of reclaiming I advocate, before accepting that not everyone will join my ceremony of rooted forward thinking and sing the old new song. Not everyone wants to live in Old Newton (which is actually a charming village in Suffolk, U.K., not far from where I live and where I once attended an event run by the East Anglian Traditional Music Trust).

Everyone wants to own tradition, but, luckily no one does. It is yours. You just have to pay attention and life is richer for free, as I indicated in Chapter 1, the introduction. Children are traditional, they cry the old cry and want the same story every night. This is only partly mere repetition: it is more entering a world of safe rhythms, more subtle than their adult selves will demand in novelty and 'no spoilers' youthful growth stages. And it is never really the same. The Old Queen wants the same story too, as she knows it is the entrance to a way of thinking about the world magically, as all connected. In the folkloric song, 'that old time religion is good enough for me' and the old time tradition is good enough for me. There is something eternal and nourishing here we know by instinct, if we are innocent or wise enough to see it.

To privilege the simple and primal, which is what tradition does at root, like children and the prophets, attracts all kinds of snobbery. There is even the snobbery of who is a real traditionalist and who is a mere revivalist. We have already noticed, in Chapter 5, Bob Dylan's early encounter with 'the folk police', when he did not know if he was being helped or condemned. This kind of purism is a kind of traditional fundamentalism which becomes a way of condemning others and can be deadly to the survival of the very thing promoted. It is snobbery out of knowledge, not out of ignorance, as seen in the song lyric 'Folk Police', in the creative example below. The irony is how untraditional this purism is. The old singers in the folk world, like the Carter family, took material from anywhere, not living by rules but by what was singable in their culture.

There are those also who love tradition but somehow put it in a box, in the way of not seeing it as part of their life, but as a cherished relic, not to be touched. The skill of the instrumentalist or the decorative singer can be taken as the art, which again keeps the tradition apart from life. This can be a reaction to the casual misuse of the word, in its narrowing tendency. There is real occlusion here, which we might claim as part of tradition. Holding the way open is something to pass on. If tradition is the lesser taken footpath, it needs to be clearly but plainly signposted and kept open to remain useful. In Kipling's poem 'The Way Through the Woods' (1910) is lost but somehow still there seems to be indirectly about this, as does Frost's poem 'The Road Not Taken' (1944) which also has the traditional woodland setting, where old paths lead to new views.

In my own career, the going has not always been easy. The fashion in the academic worlds has been to deny the existence of tradition entirely, not too helpful for my innocent revivalism, as you might imagine. A creative view of tradition was just confusing, or seen as outrageously dumb or dangerous. In 2007, a Tunisian friend invited me to a university in Tunis. Tolerant of my neo-primitivism, he smiled indulgently when I said what I would talk about and how I would not be 'reading' my 'paper' but just improvising from notes in a non-academic way. Being a Yeats scholar, he was tolerant, but I understood I was likely to be a minor part of the weekend of papers, where the big cheese would be Terry Eagleton. His reputation as a massively famous critic put mine as a minor junior writing tutor in the thoroughly occluded shade.

It was an odd time though, as there had been airline strikes and cancellations. But my flight was never cancelled and the nearly empty plane-ride was fun and got me talking to my fellow passengers. However, I was extremely surprised when my host, who was organising the whole conference, entitled *On mutual (mis)understanding*, met me off the plane. I assumed he would be busy with tending to the stars of the event, like the eminent Professor Eagleton, who was to be the keynote 'plenary' speaker, as the poster announced. It was great to see my pal, though my heart sank a bit when he explained his unexpected concern for me. I was the only non-Tunisian academic who would be present on the Saturday morning, when Eagleton was due to appear, and he was not coming. The air strikes had put him off and he had cancelled. As the only outsider, I would have to take his place.

What I did not realise at the time was that this time-slot of the conference was to be attended by professors from the home university and also by dignitaries from the Tunisian authorities. This was in the pre Arab-spring days. When I arose to address lines of the serious ranks of the important, I was faced with solemn moustached government faces and serious academics. It was the kind of audience I would usually avoid. However, I also noticed that many young Tunisians had come in to the back of the hall. These were the students who had been reading Eagleton's sonorous works and seemed aware that I was not what was promised at all.

I stuck to my notes and gave my passionate pitch about the universality of tradition and how the common culture of all places had everything in common and was the rich root of all culture. The students listened and seemed to like it. The serious ones at the front looked confused and suspicious. Who is this joker, this chancer, this non-substitute for substance, preaching peasantry? Nonetheless I felt I had gone down well.

A Tunisian professor identified himself and asked a question about Edmund Burke. I confessed I did not know the answer. There was a pause. The laughter swelled from the back of the room, to my bemusement. I might have answered another question sensibly, but by then I felt I had given what I had and was glad to quit the podium. I was mobbed, as I left the hall, by young students. These elegant Tunisians seemed amused by my outrageous admission that I could not answer a question. No Tunisian academic would ever admit this, especially not to an audience of the great and good. The students dug what I said, though, and they sensed their own power to be real in the face of their stern-faced 'betters'. They told me how poor they were and how hard it was to maintain being a student and they wanted to come to England with me. I was moved and felt I wanted to cry.

Later, a woman teacher from the university gave me a lift back to the hotel and told me an Arabic proverb: 'often you will find in the smallest stream what you cannot find in the greatest ocean'. This tied in with my theme of localism, linked to tradition. I felt then that I had been a success, even if a ludicrous one. The combination of brave humility in the face of grandeur is one which is not unfamiliar to me, with all the mockery, snobbery and strange acceptance thrown in. I was emphatically not Terry Eagleton, but I was someone, even if just an amusing distraction from the serious business of accumulative neophilia and status-gathering cultures of academia.

There was a traditional joke told about Terry Eagelton at the time, both mocking and serious. He had recently been appointed Professor at Manchester University. I knew a student who had signed to do an M.A., hoping to study with the high-status Professor. The joke went: What is the difference between Terry Eagleton and God? The answer: God is everywhere but Terry Eagleton is everywhere except Manchester University. We were both somehow part of that traditional mockery.

Another great Marxist I had to encounter was via a famous book. When I first saw the title of Eric Hobsbawm and Terence Ranger's *The Invention of Tradition* (1983), I thought, from my naive but positive knowledge of the English folk music scene, that it meant somehow the *inventiveness* of tradition. To put it kindly, it is about how the idea of tradition can be misused. From the opening pages of Hobsbawm's introduction, I think that he has, in the way I have indicated, also reduced and misused the word. His first sentence announces his target. The use of words here like 'ancient' and phrases like 'an immemorial past', and his naming of 'pageantry' and 'ceremonial' and 'the royal family' give us a strong hint of his agenda. Even if he is merely describing the misuse of tradition, he seems to be associating the whole of the word here with the pointless and the posh, the showy, the fake.

He describes 'Traditions' reductively, in quotations and with a capital 'T', as items which want to brainwash you with repetition. He dismisses by implication any chance that invention, in a positive sense, might have a link with what is passed over to us. He puts this repeating against the kind of neophilia we have already encountered. The attachment to change and progress no longer seems a good place to stand these days.

He eventually gets uneasy about his own narrow terms. By the fifth page he is expressing reservations. He even uses the word here positively, but perhaps he has forgotten that he meant 'customs', the word he chose to be the good side of tradition earlier. He seems to be inventing his uses as he goes along and to have been at least hinting at some positive side. Finally, by page eight, he is saying that 'genuine tradition' is not to be confused with the book's title, which amounts almost to an admission of the loaded nature of the project. By page eleven, he seems to half remember his use of the other term, when he refers to 'the decline of old tradition and custom'. My feeling at the time I encountered this book was that it was used to mock someone like me by those who had not actually read how inconsistent and loaded its message really was. The put-down of the title now seems to me more interesting than anything the book had to say.

What I learned from these encounters was a traditional message in fact. Mockery is something anyone interested in tradition has to learn to live with, just as prophets, fools, mythographers, magicians and writers who hold to some hidden truth must. Tradition has its secrets and practitioners need sometimes to keep their practices special. This goes for writers too. Everyone wants to be a writer but few writers write in public with a commentator, as in the Python sketch, featuring the unlikely or best choice shy writer Thomas Hardy. Hardy was the one who pointed out that revivalist folk dancers looked like they were enjoying themselves, while the real traditional ones did not, in *The Return of the Native* (1929), which we will explore below. Hobsbaum's title is just another jeer.

If we need evidence of this propensity to mockery, we can turn to Shakespeare for proof. Act IV, scene ii of *As You Like It* features the strange ritual of the wearing of stag horns for the hunter. In this play the exiled court are playing at being wood-dwellers, or else being revivalists of such a traditional life. The Lords/Forresters know an old traditional song and it is a song about mockery. 'Have you no song for this purpose?' Jaques asks. 'Sing it. 'Tis no matter how it be in tune, so it make noise enough', he says, ushering in, for me, the punk rockish version of 'Hal an Tow' by Oysterband (1994).

> What shall he have that killed the deer?
> His leather skin and horns to wear:
>> Then sing him home the rest to bear
>> This burden:
> Take thou no scorn to wear the horn,
> It was a crest ere thou were born,
> Thy father's father wore it,
> And thy father bore it.
> The horn, the horn, the lusty horn,
> Is not a thing to laugh to scorn.

We are told here that we must perform the old ceremony and put up with the scorn. We note that the old song has a dual meaning of burden, the weight of it and the chorus, for which 'burden' is another word, as well as meaning the message. There is irony here from Shakespeare's sophisticated traditionalism but the echoing of 'father's fathers' genuinely commands the archaic, raucous celebration of fertility. Horn dancers remain in England to this day.

In *King Henry V*, we have an even more blatant example of the traditional mockery of tradition. The mockery of the Welsh for wearing leeks is argued and fought over and Gower admonishes it: 'Go, go; you are a counterfeit cowardly knave. Will you mock at an ancient tradition, begun upon an honourable respect, and worn as a memorable trophy …?' (Act V:i; lines 71–75). Mockery and 'galling', which means jeering, comes with the traditional.

The special, almost taboo, which amounts to the same thing, aspect of traditional activity means that being traditional has a way of hiding. It hides both behind its own easy-to-mock nature, just as it keeps quiet about its old ceremonial rites, to keep them sacred. This means to keep them part of a bigger picture of life than the everyday can handle. I still believe that used subtly and confidently, the 'little stream' can contain the fluent and passed-on riches.

As mentioned above, Thomas Hardy's *Return of the Native* (1929) presents much of Hardy's own ambivalence about his roots. In book 2 Chapter 4, we find Eustacia, who is generally against the traditions of the heath where the novel is set, is confronted with one of the Mummers, who are to perform a traditional play, generally of death and rebirth. A peasant lad calls and is asked.

> 'What, are you one of the Egdon mummers for this year?
> 'Yes, miss. The cap'n used to let the old mummers practise here.'
> 'I know it. Yes, you may use the fuelhouse if you like,' said Eustacia languidly.
>
> The choice of Captain Vye's fuelhouse as the scene of rehearsal was dictated by the fact that his dwelling was nearly in the centre of the heath. The fuelhouse was as roomy as a barn, and was a most desirable place for such a purpose. The lads who formed the company of players lived at different scattered points around, and by meeting in this spot the distances to be traversed by all the comers would be about equally proportioned.
>
> For mummers and mumming Eustacia had the greatest contempt. The mummers themselves were not afflicted with any such feeling for their art, though at the same time they were not enthusiastic. *A traditional pastime is to be distinguished from a mere revival in no more striking feature than in this, that while in the revival all is excitement and fervour, the survival is carried on with a stolidity and absence of stir which sets one wondering why a thing that is done so perfunctorily should be kept up at all.* Like Balaam and other unwilling prophets, the agents seem moved by an inner compulsion to say and do their allotted parts whether they will or no. This unweeting manner of performance is the true ring by which, in this refurbishing age, a fossilized survival may be known from a spurious reproduction.
>
> The piece was the well-known play of Saint George, and all who were behind the scenes assisted in the preparations, including the women of each household. Without the co-operation of sisters and sweethearts the dresses were likely to be a failure; but on the other hand, this class of assistance was not without its drawbacks. The girls could never be brought to respect tradition in designing and decorating the armour; they insisted on attaching loops and bows of silk and velvet in any situation pleasing to their taste. Gorget, gusset, basinet, cuirass, gauntlet, sleeve, all alike in the view of these feminine eyes were practicable spaces whereon to sew scraps of fluttering colour. [Italics added.]

The 'feulhouse' at the 'centre of the heath' provides the 'spot' where they converge, like a dance. The 'fossilised' or 'spurious' choice belies, for me, this traditional approval. Even the girls lacking of 'respect' is part of it somehow. We feel here Hardy's relish at the ambiguity of the scene and the absurdity of the conventions of the tradition. In a way, it is the absurdity of the survival that both intrigues and is the vessel for scorn. Hardy himself was torn between the sophistication of his writerly life and the humble roots of his family and yet this is the source of much of his energy as a writer. Robert Gittings, in *Young*

Thomas Hardy (1975) highlights the Puddletown poor area where many of Hardy's relatives lived, by the river Piddle and how ambivalent he is about this rough home place. It was the kind of place that people these days might boast about: straight out of Puddletown.

The mockery is traditional and even the very play he describes is not without self-mockery. Tradition is rarely 'unweeting', or unwitting, but often full of wit. It is no coincidence that Morris sides in England very often have their own 'fool' figure. This is one who dresses strangely, talks to the crowd to encourage them to give money and generally makes the whole thing festive, while containing the mockery, as part of the tradition. English traditions have the same kind of feature as the tendency of the English to deny their own intellect, as a way of weeding out the pretentious. Playing cards also have jokers and in the case of tarot cards, the Fool is an archetype. The Beatles' Paul McCartney has 'The Fool On The Hill' (1967). Anyone entering traditional activity is subject to this mockery and it can be comforting to think that one's mockers are performing their role well and unwittingly participating in the ritual.

When I joined the group Potiphar's Apprentices to perform folksongs collected in Essex by Ralph Vaughan Williams, we named ourselves after the first singer he encountered, who seemed to have changed the composer's life. Charles Potiphar was our hero. We were well received by the folk music community, but the real reward and interest came from elsewhere. When we played some churches, village halls and historic and musical societies in our county, we reached ordinary people, without a folk music background and who were moved by learning about their own inheritance and hearing the songs plainly and directly. In the right setting, the tradition of passing the songs on, it seems to me, was performed and appreciated. Often, we seemed to reach the ears of those normally not predisposed towards folk, by its easily mockable images. Sadly, in England, we seem all too ready to mock too hard at our own traditions. This seeming guilt at our imperial past always strikes me as being a way of making things worse. To respect other cultures, you need to be aware of the life of your own traditions. Luckily, anyone who is in folk music in England has heard and appreciated all the jokes. We sometimes used to threaten to sing every single song, in one evening, Vaughan Williams collected in Essex; well over one hundred.

Another aspect of traditional hiding, as with the mockery, is the hiding from the self. Part of tradition is realising what is already inside you. This has become real to me as I have been writing this book. Sudden connections have been made from a lifelong interest in these kinds of things. There has been a kind of harvest of my previous attempts to bring these positives to the fore in a world not predisposed towards it. Tradition is in us or it is nowhere. Paying it respect, shielding it from the mockery while bearing that burden is one aspect, but knowing how and when to express it is what I feel a writer might do.

Most writing instructional books acknowledge the unconscious as playing a large role in creativity. The traditional use of conscious and unconscious is a more complicated process, I believe. If the material is somehow already within you, as well as hiding in plain sight all around, how does a writer bring it to their work? It is somehow like the recognising of someone as a kindred spirit. 'I felt like I've known you always', one might say to a new lover or new, old, in the sense of already familiar, friend.

So it is not so much bringing the unconscious to consciousness, as most psychological or psychoanalytical processes work. It is more bringing ordinary life to the unconscious, thence back into the conscious mind. It is a reminding, like a traditional ceremony itself. We find the mocked, the overlooked, the obvious, the undervalued and the rejected connections. We let them go deep, then we bring them back to the world. This is how traditions function when alive and good, absorbing the negatives and processing them into positives for the good of the whole. This is why it is, for me, so close to creativity itself.

Writing with a traditional awareness of movements in the world larger than the self have their roots, or their rediscovered roots in Romanticism, so they say. Shelley's *A Defence of Poetry* (1821) ends with this widening thought, perhaps a positive view of the 'unweeting' (unwitting) desire to maintain the open width which tradition offers. The mockery is protection against narrowness, as it is the openness of the attitude. I have often wondered what Yeats' meant by 'the ceremony of innocence', in his prophetic poem 'The Second Coming' (1920) and it might be that this kind of openness is a similar kind of deliberate unknowing which Keats called 'negative capability'. In the final film of Jean Cocteau's *Orphic Trilogy*, entitled *The Testament of Orpheus* (1960), the protagonist is accused of being 'guilty of innocence', in the appropriately mocking and serious way. The width, the resistance and the mockery are absorbed as part of the traditional process.

Here is part of Shelley's final paragraph, where writers.

> measure the circumference and sound the depths of human nature with a comprehensive and all-penetrating spirit, and they are themselves perhaps the most sincerely astonished at its manifestations; for it is less their spirit than the spirit of the age. Poets are the hierophants of an unapprehended inspiration; the mirrors of the gigantic shadows which futurity casts upon the present; the words which express what they understand not; the trumpets which sing to battle, and feel not what they inspire; the influence which is moved not, but moves. Poets are the unacknowledged legislators of the world.

The absurdity and grandeur of this position is still compelling and the unwitting and unrecognised elements have echoes of the traditional role of writers, as does the absurdity itself. If we just said 'Poets are the unacknowledged', we might get a hint in the full stop of the quietness of the traditionalist, who does not go round boasting that their dancing the summer in on May Day actually turns the world round. If they keep quiet about it, that is sometimes the best way to maintain it. Tradition is something you practice, not a publicity element in itself. Fashion is uneasy with tradition, just as the commercial world and academia are uneasy. Its off-grid charms, its magic is unavailable to those without a sense of what 'the ceremony of innocence' might be, except something which is gone.

In my view, current events such as the pandemic and climate change point us back towards finding these old positive connections and I do see it reflected in the activities of our time. Max Porter's recent novel *Lanny* (2019) is about an innocent, knowing boy and his mocking, mythical mentors, who triumph over suspicion and the narrowness of the world around and seems to be to have a traditional, environmental message. On the day of beginning writing this, there were two women, classicist Natalie Haynes and author Shadi Bartsch (*The Aeneid*, 2020) talking enthusiastically on radio about Greek and Roman Literature and how inspiring it was to them in their stand-up comedy and translation work. Later, a radio programme about sacred things, even the sacred object of a deceased mother's phone and still leaving her messages on it. A friend asks me about female Tricksters and we discuss the Arkan Anansi tradition.

The television is showing the 1956 film, *The Rainmaker* (dir. Joseph Anthony; written by N. Richard Nash from his own play). The titular conman, via Burt Lancaster, enlivens the intelligent but reluctant unmarried female lead, Katherine Hepburn to join the world, even though she chooses to stay when he moves on. His absurd, bigger view of the world seems to show the livening traditional role of the rainmaker in all his absurd mockery, both given and received. And he does make it rain and turn the seasons for all the characters. He is the trickster/traditionalist/mocking and mocked fool and her role is the quiet acknowledgement of his usefulness and his transfer of power to her.

Is the current awakening of the young to climate change and the issues mentioned in Chapter 13 a new move towards a harmonious relationship with the other as well as the earth? The way tradition takes into account the relation of the self to the wider whole and to the other has the most powerful implications. Tradition can be seen in cross-cultural respectfulness for time-honoured aspects of all arts, a kind of universal language of something bigger than the self, somehow necessarily at times partly occluded, rightly containing its own mocking and its own secrets. In a further paradox, these secrets are available to all. Tradition is within, as well as without.

Traditions need to be alive and non-static and the occlusions have their in-built guards against mere convention and stasis. The rainmaker makes rain despite the drought and in the face of human limits, in his absurd, defiant creativity. The world is rediscovered and recovered. Tradition provides the favour, the gift which requires the passing of it on to a stranger, as described in Lewis Hyde's *The Gift* (1983), I referred to in, Chapter 1, the introduction. As Gustav Mahler reputedly said, tradition is not the worship of ashes but the preservation of fire.

Mockery is absorbed in the lyric below, followed by the image of an open door framing the familiar and the strange, the welcoming and the welcomed.
Author's Creative Examples:

FOLK POLICE

I was happy singing frivolous words like these
Then I got a visit from the folk police
They're eager to point out your inferiorities
When you get a visit from the folk police
    Folk police, folk police
    When I sing I don't want to make peace
    Folk police, folk police
    I'm happy disapproved of by the folk police
All those people who look down on you
And if they don't condemn, they can patronise too
Looking for folk to be superior to
So from a great height they can piss on what you do

I used to write poems with breeze and trees
Till I got a visit from the poetry police
Egad I used archaism, thous and thees
Then I got a visit from the poetry police
    Poetry police, poetry police
    Soon you'll find you're doing time
    Poetry police, poetry police,
    You've committed the ultimate crime – rhyme!
All those people who look down on you ...

They fix their minds on purities
Then you get a visit from the pedantry police
Idealistic authenticities
Then you get a visit from the pedantry police
    Pedantry police, pedantry police
    The truth is far too dirty to seize
    Pedantry police, pedantry police
    Being a purist is a nasty disease
All those people who look down on you ...

The least self-consciousness are the most traditional
Till you get a visit from the trad police
So the most traditional are the most original
I just got a visit from the paradox police
  Folk police, poetry police
  Accuse you of robbery and of yobbery

Pedantry police, thought police
But I accuse them of elitism and snobbery
All those people who look down on you...

So I'm happy singing frivolous words like these
And away to folk - with the folk police

AN ENTRANCE TO TRADITION

I opened the door
It was strange and familiar
Hidden and open
Out in the somewhere
It could be a childhood
It could be a love
It could be connections
I hadn't thought of
All I could tell
Has been here before
All I could say
I opened the door

'Don't open that door –
Doors are old hat –
And hats are old hat
So stop wearing that
We must overthrow' –
But I'd done that once
I sought the old wisdom
They looked askance
I found the old secret
They said it was dross
I shrugged in my exile
Content in my loss
I got all these riches
Called nothing, or more
I told them to mock on
I opened the door

I opened the door
And there I was, old
New, past and present
Ancient and green
Self and other
Seen and unseen

Told and allowed
Lover and fool
My own and all yours
All potential
All forgiving
All dead, all living
And less and more
A clown in the wisdom
A mummer in store
Framing my welcome
I opened the door

WRITING EXERCISE:

Using an object, as in the exercise in Chapter 1, the Introduction, create a secret ceremony to help you with beginning your writing. The object is your connection to the past, another object might be something like a full pen or a blank or open new page. A third object should be something strange to you, and an accompanying chant might be something ironic like, 'Old, new, borrowed, true ... I don't suppose you don't know no-one who don't want to buy no poems/ plays/ stories/ novels/ songs?' Delete as appropriate to your work. Use the ritual when you write and pass it on only to a stranger who writes, with whom you feel sympathy.

READING, LISTENING, WATCHING:

Anthony, Joseph. 1956. *The Rainmaker*. Paramount Pictures.
Badoe, Adwoa. 2008. *The Pot of Wisdom: Ananse Stories*. Toronto: Groundwood.
The Beatles. 1967. Fool On The Hill. On *Magical Mystery Tour*. Apple Records.
Cocteau, Jean. 1960. *The Testament of Orpheus*. In *Orphic Trilogy*. Cinédis France.
Frost, Robert. 1944. The Road Not Taken, 128–129. In *Come In and Other Poems*. London: Jonathan Cape.
Gittings, Robert. 1975. *Young Thomas Hardy*. London: Heinemann.
Hardy, Thomas. 1929. *The Return of the Native*. London: Macmillan.
Hobsbawm, Eric and Ranger, Terence. 1983. *The Invention of Tradition*. Cambridge: Cambridge University Press.
Hyde, Lewis. 1983. *The Gift*. New York: Vintage.
Kipling, Rudyard. 1910. The Way Through the Woods, 87. In *Rewards and Fairies*. London: Macmillan.
Oysterband. 1994. Hal an Tow. On *Deserters*. Cooking Vinyl Records.
Porter, Max. 2019. *Lanny*. London: Faber and Faber.
Shakespeare, William. *As You Like It*. *Henry V*.
Shelley, Percy. 1950. *A Defence of Poetry*, 102–138. In *English Critical Essays (Nineteenth Century)*. Ed. Edmund D. Jones. Oxford: Oxford University Press.
Williams, Raymond. 1976. *Keywords*. London: Fontana.
Virgil. 2020. *The Aeneid*. Trans. Shadi Bartsch. London: Profile Books.
Yeats, W.B. 1950. The Second Coming, 210. In *Collected Poems*. London: Macmillan.

Index

A
Actaeon, 43
Adams, Douglas, 62
Addiction, 5
Adrian, Saint, 110
Alienation, 107, 132
Alvarez, Al, 143
Amis, Martin, 157
Anglo-Saxon, 33
Anthony, Joseph, 173
Anthrocentrism, 158
Apple Corps, 122
Apple of Macintosh, 122
Apuleius, 49
Arctic Monkeys, 73, 77
Arendt, Hannah, 158
Arkan Anansi, 173
Arne-Thompson, 48
Arnold, Mathew, 31, 100, 158
Artemis, 44
Ashley, Steve, 121
Atwood, Margaret, 4, 13
Auden, W.H., 5, 133, 135, 141
Authenticity syndrome, 157
Avianthropy, 45

B
Bacchae, The, 62, 154
Ball, John, 147, 159
Band, The, 66
Baring-Gould, Sabine, 35
Bartsch, Shadi, 173
Bate, Jonathan, 103
Beatles, The, 18, 119, 122, 171
Bechet, Sidney, 62
Bede, 16
Bellamy, Peter, 54, 74
Berger, John, 16, 23
Bible, 17, 19–21
Bike, 143
Bildad, 146
Billy Bragg, 64
Bipolarity, 132
Bird, Brian, 147, 159
Black-tailed godwit, 29
Blake, William, 62, 123, 134, 158
Blakney, R.B., 147
Bling, 33
Bloom, Harold, 3, 13
Bly, Robert, 136
Boccaccio, 45
Bonzo Dog Band, 74, 83
Book of Job, 146
Boyd, Joe, 72
Bradbury, Malcolm, 1
Bragi, 123
Brande, Dorothea, 1, 111
Branston, Brian, 145
Brautigan, Richard, 22
Brown Jr., Oscar, 85
Brunvard, Jan Harold, 42
Buchan, Peter, 46
Buddha, 42

Burch, Malcolm, 76
Burke, Edmund, 167
Burns, 61, 63, 117
Burns, Ken, 64
Burns Nights, 63
Burns, Robert, 7, 46, 59

C
Caedmon, 16–19, 147
Campbell, Joseph, 6, 18, 102
Camus, Albert, 133
Carse, James, 135
Carson, Rachel, 158
Carter, Angela, 40
Carter Family, 64, 166
Cashman, Ray, 131
Castle Hedingham, 36
Chambers Book of Days, 110, 145, 156
Chandler, Len, 65
Chaucer, Geoffrey, 161
Chesterton, G.K., 36, 142, 144
Child, Francis James, 45
Children, 166
Christ, 117
Clare, John, 19, 63
Clarke, John Cooper, 59
Climate change, 117, 131, 157, 173
Cocteau, Jean, 172
Coen Brothers, 15
Coleridge, Samuel Taylor, 23
Coltrane, John, 151
Comedy, 83
Comic, 83
Common Ground, 121
Contrafacta, 90
Copper Family, 61
Coward, Noel, 135
Craft, 131
Crawford, Robert, 62
Creativity, 131
Crepes Fruit Farm, 120
Cressing Temple, 120
Crowley, John, 40
Cubbin, Sue, 67, 77
Culture of creativity, 153
Cupid and Psyche, 48, 49
Curtis, Adam, 108
Cusk, Rachel, 135

Cyclops, 157

D
Dante, 148
d'Aulnoy, Madame, 48
Davidson, H.R. Ellis, 124
Davies, W.H., 139
Dawson, Richard, 77
Deller, Jeremy, 158
De Menezes, John Charles, 87
Depeche Mode, 77
Depression, 86
Dewey, John, 32, 104, 158
Diana, 121
Dionysus, 44, 62, 117, 124, 154, 155
Discovery apple, 118
Dissociation, 133
Dmitrijeva, Alisa, 89
Doors, The, 155
Doubt(s), 142
Dr Feelgood, 76
Drunkenness, 155
Dummer, George, 119, 126
Duncan, Laura, 87
Dunn, Ginnette, 100
Durkheim, Émile, 141
Dylan, Bob, 2, 47, 59, 63, 64, 67, 102, 103, 166

E
Eagleton, Terry, 167, 168
East of England Apples, 120
Ecclesiastes, 20, 131, 134, 142, 147
Edda, 121
Eden, 117, 123
Elbow, 108
Eldon, Jim, 77
Elen, Gus, 134
Eliot, John, 162
Eliot, T.S., 2, 4, 16, 22, 31, 103
Ellington, Duke, 60
Employability, 132
England, 59, 63
English Music Halls, 85
Epic of Gilgamesh, The, 16, 42, 117
Eschatology, 158
Essex University, 32, 39

Estuary, 29
Ethernan, Saint, 110
Euripides, 16, 44, 154
Eve's Orchard, 126
Existentialism, 133
Extinction Rebellion, 157

F
Face Furniture, 121
Fado, 90
Faking, 49
Fall from Nature, 117
Family, 107
Fitzgerald, Edward, 21
Folk, 2
Folk clubs, 75
Folklore, 39, 43
Folk police, The, 65, 166
Folksong, 48, 59
Forster, E.M., 39, 64
Frend, Charles, 145
Freud, Sigmund, 40, 108
Frost, Robert, 166
Futurity, 165

G
Garbutt, Vin, 76
Garvey, Guy, 108
Gaughan, Dick, 61
Gauguin, Paul, 27
Gay, Noel, 87
Genesis, 117
Genre, viii
Ghia, 158
Giddens, Anthony, 4
Gilgamesh, 157
Gittings, Robert, 170
Graves, Robert, 6, 44
Gray, Michael, 65
Great Bromley Cross, 118
Greek Tragedy, 15
Green Man, 117, 157
Grenfell, Joyce, 85
Grimm, 49, 136
Grose, Francis, 68
Guthrie, Woody, 63, 86

H
Haley, Alex, 7
Hamp, Johnny, 72
Harburg, Yip, 86
Hardy, Thomas, 103, 109, 169, 170
Harlow Folk Club, 71
Harper, Roy, 73
Harrowven, Jean, 145
Harvest, x
Haynes, Natalie, 173
Heaney, Seamus, 24
Helen, 122
Henderson, T.F., 62
Henley, W.E., 60, 62
Hepburn, Katherine, 173
Hephaestus, 133
Hereness, 29, 54, 96, 102
Hesperides, 122
Hillman, James, 132
Hilton, James, 24
Hirshberg, Charles, 64
Historians, 35
History, 29
Hobsbawm, Eric, 168
Hockney, David, 133
Holiday, Billie, 87
Holland, Maggie, 76
Home, 96, 101
Homer, 16, 97, 134
Hoover, J. Edgar, 155
Horace, 42
Hoskins, W.C., 36
Housman, A.E., 40
Hudd, Roy, 84
Hughes, Ted, 2, 98
Hui-neng, 18
Humility, 144
Hutchins, Richard, 124
Hyde, Lewis, 4, 103, 156, 173

I
Icarus, 47
Identity, 155
Identity politics, 109
Iduma, 121
Iduna, 122, 123
Impostor syndrome, 157
Incredible String Band, 110

Ingrave, 67
Initiation, 136, 147
Ireland, 59
Irony, 87
Isle of May, 110
Issac, Oscar, 15

J
Jacobs, Joseph, 45, 46
Jesus, 145
Joans, Ted, 85
Job, Pam, 148
Johnson, Robert, 17
Jokes, 15, 95
Joyce, James, 24
Joyce, Robert Dwyer, 8
Jung, Carl, 40
Jung, C.G., 42, 146

K
Kane, Pat, 135
Kavanagh, Patrick, 7
Kerényi, Károly, 44
Kerouac, Jack, 41, 104
King James Bible, The, 146
King James Version, 148
King, Martin Luther, 36, 65
Kipling, Rudyard, 13, 166
Koestler, Arthur, 85

L
Lancaster, Burt, 173
Larkin, Philip, 62, 101, 102, 134, 142–144, 147
Lawrence, D.H., 23, 24, 27, 104, 108, 114, 134, 148
Lee, Roger, 76
Lee, Spike, 36
Legge, J., 147
Le Guin, Ursula, 147
Lehrer, Tom, 86
Lempriere's Classical Dictionary, 101, 154
Lessing, Doris, 22
Levi, Primo, 7
Libraries, 32

Lindsay, Jack, 35
Lives of the Saints (Butler), 110
Locality, 95
Loki, 121, 122
London Stansted Airport, 36, 145
Lord, Albert Bates, 41
Lord of Misrule, 154, 157
Lorenz, Konrad, 156
Lucan, Arthur, 87

M
Macpherson, James, 60
Magic, 6, 39
Mahler, Gustav, 173
Malcolm X, 36
Manchester University, 168
Mantel, Hilary, 35
Manuva, Roots, 7
Mark, 145
Marr, 46
Marra, Michael, 60
Matthew, 134, 145
Matthews, Jack, 119
May Day, 172
May, John, 120
Mayo, Sam, 85
McCartney, Paul, 171
McCully, Chris, 20
McQueen, Steve, 36
Meeropol, Abel, 87, 91
Melville, A.D., 124
Mentes, 136
Merlin, 123
Mersea Island, 35
Morgan, Jane, 118
Morris, 171
Morrison, Jim, 155
Morrissey, 134
Mortimer, John, 115
Morton, Pete, 47, 77
Mother Tree, 119
Mott the Hoople, 134
Mould, Tom, 131
Muddy Waters, 84
Mud, Sweat and Tractors, 120
Muir, Edwin, 64
Mummers, 170
Murray, Gilbert, 155

Mutwa, Credo, 135
Myth, 6, 39, 43

N
Names, 110
Nash, N. Richard, 173
Neophilia, 156
Newman, Randy, 74
New Nature writing, 158

O
Odyssey, The, 14
Old Mother Reilly, 87
Old time religion, 166
Ong, Walter, 40
Oral history, 41
Oral tradition, 40
Orchards Project, 120
Ossian, 60
Ovid, 43, 123
Oysterband, 33, 169

P
Pan, 158
Pandemic, 141, 157
Pandora, 133
Parallelism, 21
Parton, Dolly, 107, 110
Paterson, Don, 60
Peake's Commentary, 20
Peasants' Revolt, 147, 159
Pedlar of Swaffam, The, 103
Pemberton, Suzanne, 121
Penelope, 15
Penrose, J. Doyle, 121
Perry, Jimmy, 84
Phemius, 14
Pied Piper, 162
Plato, 133
Plotlands, 100
Pomona, 122, 123
Pope, Alexander, 14, 22
Porter, Max, 173
Potiphar, Charles, 6, 19, 67, 171
Potiphar's Apprentices, 67, 77, 171
Prayer, 144

Prittlewell, 33
Propaganda, 86
Protest, 83, 158
Psycho-geography, 101
Puddletown, 171

R
Radical, 153
Randall, Bob, 104
Ranger, Terence, 168
Ray, Man, 23, 45
Reader, Eddi, 60
Reading, x
Rego, Paula, 27
Reynolds, Malvina, 158, 162
Rhetoric, 41
Richards, Alison, 118
Rilke, Rainer Maria, 76
Robertson, Robbie, 66
Roberts, Paddy, 75
Roches, The, 145
Romanticism, 97
Romantics, The, 63
Roth, Philip, 96
Rotolo, Suze, 65
Roud folksong index, 45
Ruskin, John, 158

S
Sacrifice, 145
Sandell, Michael, 141
Sandlin, Tim, 48
Sarony, Leslie, 75, 83, 84
Satire, 86
Schmidt, Michael, 16, 18
Schwenk, Norman, 23
Scotland, 59
Scott, E.V., 121
Scott-Heron, Gil, 158
Scott, Walter, 46
Seeger, Pete, 22, 63, 86
Self, 107
Sennett, Richard, 131–133
Shakespeare, William, 44, 59, 62, 63, 83, 85, 99, 169
Shelley, Percy, 144, 159, 172
Sherill, Billy, 90

Shevchenko, Taras, 63
Shibumi, 62
Shindell, Richard, 86
Shukla, Pravina, 131
Sibley, Dave, 118
Silko, Leslie Marmon, 40
Simplicity, 3
Singers, 2
Sir Gawain and the Green Knight, 117, 157
Sisyphus, 133
Skiffle, 147
Smith, Ian, 143
Smith, Phoebe, 77
Smith, Zadie, 153
Snow White, 126
Snyder, Gary, 104
Solomon, 134
Solomon Northup, 36
Song of Solomon, 124
Southend, 33
Spenser the Rover, 110
St Augustine, 35
Sterne, Laurence, 16
St George, 59
Stilton, 126
St Leonard, 110
Storytelling, 3, 39
St Thomas's Gospel, 49
Sun Ra, 151
Suzzie and Maggie, 145
Syd Barrett, 75

T
Tabor, June, 47
Taliesin, 48
Taoism, 147
Tao Te Ching, 147
Tawney, Cyril, 72
Tawney, R.H., 141
Taylor, Charles, 141
Taylor, Joan Norlev, 148
Teddy Foster Orchestra, 36
Tempest, Kate, 24, 77
Tennyson, Alfred, 31, 134
Terry, Philip, 20
Tharpe, Sister Rosetta, 72
Thomas, Dylan, 36, 109, 133

Thomas, Edward, 8, 19
Thompson, Flora, 36
Thompson, Richard, 115
Tin tabernacles, 143
Tiresias, 154, 155
Transactional analysis, 108
Trickster, 135, 156
Tricksters, 173
Tunis, 166
Turgenev, Ivan, 108
Turner, Alex, 77
Tweedledum and Tweedledee, 142
Tzu, Lao, 147

U
Unconscious, 171
Universality, 167
Universal language, 173
Urban myth, 42

V
Variety, 75, 84
Vertumnus, 123
Virtue signalling, 86
Virus, 29
Vitkovitch, V., 118

W
Walcott, Derek, 14
Wales, 59
Warner, Marina, 42
Wassailers, 124
Wassailing, 119
Waters, Muddy, 72
Watson, Roger, 49
Watts, Alan, 107
Weilm Simone, 158
Wenhaston, 148
Wesley, Jeff, 101
Weston, Jessie, 8
Whitby, 19
Wilco, 64
Wilderness, 145
Williamson, Robin, 110
Williams, Ralph Vaughan, 6, 61, 67, 77, 171

Williams, Raymond, 5, 7, 165
Williams, Vaughan, 19
Wodehouse, P.G., 86
Wolf, Robert, 41
Wood, Chris, 87, 91
Worcester Pearmain, 118
Wordsworth, William, 1, 23, 32, 97, 98, 102
Work, 131
Wynette, Tammy, 90

Y
Yeats, W.B., 2, 96, 141, 166, 172
Young Tradition, The, 73

Z
Zen, 108
Zwonitzer, Mark, 64

The manufacturer's authorised representative in the EU is Springer Nature Customer Service Centre GmbH, Europaplatz 3, 69115 Heidelberg, Germany. If you have any concerns regarding our products, please contact ProductSafety@springernature.com

Printed and bound by CPI Group (UK) Ltd, Croydon, CR0 4YY

23/03/2026

02076746-0003